Looking to Learn

Promoting Literacy for Students with Low Vision

Frances Mary D'Andrea
and Carol Farrenkopf, Editors

PRESS
New York

The publication of this work was funded in part by a generous grant from the Peacock Foundation, Inc., Miami, Florida.

Printed in the United States of America

Library of Congress Cataloging-in-Publication Data

Looking to learn : promoting literacy for students with low vision / Frances Mary D'Andrea and Carol Farrenkopf.
   p.   cm.
   Includes bibliographical references and index.
   ISBN 0-89128-346-3
   1. Visually handicapped—Education.   2. Teaching—Aids and devices—Evaluation.   I. D'Andrea, Frances Mary, 1960–   II. Farrenkopf, Carol.
HV1638.L57   2000
371.91'1—dc21
                                 00-044194

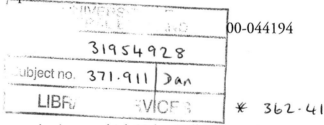

The American Foundation for the Blind—the organization to which Helen Keller devoted more than 40 years of her life—is a national nonprofit whose mission is to eliminate the inequities faced by the 10 million Americans who are blind or visually impaired.

It is the policy of the American Foundation for the Blind to use in the first printing of its books acid-free paper that meets the ANSI Z39.48 Standard. The infinity symbol that appears above indicates that the paper in this printing meets that standard.

To my mother, Margaret D'Andrea,
for fostering my love of reading.
—F.M.D.

To my husband, Duncan, for finding the right words.
—C.F.

Contents

Acknowledgments

The authors wish the thank the following individuals for their ideas, suggestions, and critiques of the material in this book. Thanks to Anne Corn, Ellen Goodman, Randy Jose, Elaine Kitchel, Alan Koenig, Nancy Levack, Amanda Hall Lueck, Toni Prahl, Ike Presley, Kevin Stewart, Mark Uslan, and Gale Watson. We would also like to thank those who contributed the photographs appearing in this book: Chrissy Cowan, Deborah J. Lapolice, Wendy Mons, Renae Shepler, and Mark Wilkinson. Special thanks to the students and their families who gave their permission to be pictured in these pages. Our editors, Natalie Hilzen, Ellen Bilofsky, and Sharon Shively at AFB Press, and Barbara Chernow, their production coordinator, deserve thanks for their many hours of assistance. We are also grateful to the Peacock Foundation, Inc., for their financial assistance in getting this book underway.

ABOUT THE EDITORS

Frances Mary D'Andrea, M.Ed., is Director of AFB Southeast, American Foundation for the Blind, in Atlanta, where she is also Director of the AFB National Literacy Center. Prior to joining AFB she was a teacher of students who are visually impaired in residential, itinerant, and other settings. She is co-editor of *Instructional Strategies for Braille Literacy,* author of several articles in the *Journal of Visual Impairment & Blindness,* and editor of *DOTS for Braille Literacy.* D'Andrea is chairperson of Division 16 (Itinerant Teaching) for the Association for Education and Rehabilitation of the Blind and Visually Impaired (AER), and is secretary of the Braille Authority of North America (BANA). She has traveled throughout the United States and Canada presenting on topics related to literacy for individuals who are blind or visually impaired.

Carol Farrenkopf, Ed.D., is a Special Education Consultant (Low Incidence) for the Toronto District School Board, and Instructor, Teacher Preparation Program (Visual Impairment), College of Education, at the University of Western Ontario in London, Ontario, Canada. She has been a teacher of students who are visually impaired, and has also taught students with behavioral disorders. She has published a number of articles on the education of children who are blind or visually impaired, and has presented numerous papers at regional, national, and international conferences.

ABOUT THE CONTRIBUTORS

Tanni L. Anthony, Ed.S., is Senior Consultant on Visual Disabilities and Project Director of the Colorado Services to Children with Deafblindness of the Colorado Department of Education in Denver. She has written articles, taught courses, and presented papers on working with infants and young children who are visually impaired and multiply disabled. Anthony is currently a doctoral candidate at the University of Denver.

Chrissy Cowan, M.A., is Educational Specialist with the Education Service Center, Region XIII, in Austin, Texas, serving as a consultant to programs for students with visual impairments and a teacher of visually impaired students. She was coauthor of *You Seem Like a Regular Kid to Me!* and has written about the education of young children with low vision devices.

Duncan McGregor, Ed.D., is a teacher of students with visual impairments and certified orientation and mobility specialist with the York Region District School Board in Ontario, and an instructor at the University of Western Ontario, training teachers of students who are visually impaired. He has written several articles for professional journals and presented papers at numerous regional, national, and international conferences.

Deborah J. Lapolice, M.S., is Vision Rehabilitation Coordinator at Duke University Eye Center and vision consultant and owner of VH Contract Services in Durham, North Carolina, as well as a lecturer at Duke University Medical Center. Lapolice is a certified teacher of students who are visually impaired and has written about the treatment of individuals with low vision.

Renae Shepler, M.Ed., is an itinerant teacher of students who are visually impaired with the Austin Independent School District in Austin, Texas. She has coauthored several articles in the *Journal of Visual Impairment & Blindness*.

Bonnie Simons, M.S., is a certified teacher of students who are visually impaired with the San Antonio Independent School District in San Antonio, Texas. She has written and presented about the teaching of braille.

Mark Wilkinson, O.D., is Assistant Professor of Clinical Ophthalmology, Department of Ophthalmology and Visual Sciences, University of Iowa Hospitals and Clinics and Director, Low Vision Services, University of Iowa Center for Macular Degeneration, both in Iowa City, Iowa; Consultant to the Low Vision Clinic of the Iowa Braille and Sight Saving School in Vinton; and Medical Director of the Vision Rehabilitation Institute of the Genesis Medical Center in Davenport. He has published articles and chapters on low vision services for children and adults. Wilkinson is Chairman of the Low Vision Section of the Iowa Optometric Association.

Introduction:
Paths to Literacy

FRANCES MARY D'ANDREA AND CAROL FARRENKOPF

IN NORTH AMERICA, as in much of the industrialized world, children are expected to learn to read and write in school, and the process of becoming literate is almost taken for granted. But what about a student like Javier, who cannot see the chalkboard from his seat? And what about Caroline, for whom the print in the third grade reader has become too small to be seen clearly? Students who are visually impaired also need to learn to read, and without extra help, they may struggle fruitlessly to keep up—or they may eventually give up. Neither of these alternatives is desirable or acceptable. As teachers of children who are visually impaired, we need to teach students who cannot use standard print how to read, write, and access information in ways that help them succeed.

Students like Javier and Caroline have *low vision*. That is, they have some vision so that, after correction and possibly with the use of low vision devices and visual skills training, they can use their sense of sight to plan and perform the tasks of daily living (Corn & Koenig, 1996). However, they need help in learning how to use and make the most of the vision they do have.

Many books have been written to assist teachers of students who are blind and read braille (Wormsley & D'Andrea, 1997; Lowenfeld, 1973; Olson, 1981; Rex, Koenig, Wormsley & Baker, 1994; Swenson, 1999). A great number of accommodations and modifications can be made to the school curriculum so that students who are blind may have access to the visual information around them. For example, reading materials can be transcribed into braille, diagrams can be created in a tactile format, and certain aspects of the curriculum can be modified to emphasize nonvisual information if the original activity is deemed to be "too visual." But many students who have low vision are able to work with regular print materials and diagrams if, for example, those materials have been enlarged on a photocopier or if a low vision device such as a magnifier has been used. The accommodation in these cases is minimal. Consequently, teachers sometimes assume that students who have low vision and can read print need less attention or direct instruction than students who read braille. After all, if a student can use standard or large-print books, what need is there for the specialized instruction provided by a teacher of students who are visually impaired?

However, such students often require intense instruction precisely because they are able to use print. They need to be taught how to maximize the use of the vision they do have to become more efficient in completing visual tasks. Students with low vision can learn techniques that will lead to the best use of their vision, and the techniques used may vary depending on the task. This instruction may involve teaching the student how to use specific low vision devices such as a closed-circuit television (CCTV) or a handheld magnifier. It may include teaching the student when and how to change lighting to complete a particular task. It may also include an instruction program that is designed to increase a specific set of visual skills that are described in the next section.

IMPORTANCE OF VISUAL SKILLS

A visual skills instruction program teaches students with low vision a specific set of skills that can be acquired through a systematic program of instruction (Corn & Koenig, 1996). According to Corn (1986), the goals of a visual skills instruction program are to teach students how to increase their *functional vision* (vision that can be used to plan and perform a task), how to use appropriate low vision devices, and how to make simple environmental modifications to maximize their ability to perceive information visually. According to Corn (1986), there are three approaches that may be used in a visual skills instruction program: visual stimulation, visual efficiency, and visual utilization.

Visual Stimulation

Visual stimulation reinforces visual functioning by providing a visually stimulating environment—that is, by presenting a variety of stimuli that encourage the individual's visual system to respond (Corn & Koenig, 1996). The visual stimulation approach emphasizes such basic visual skills as attending to a light source, attending to a single object, rudimentary tracking of a single object, shifting gaze from one object to another, and reaching for an object. This approach is primarily used with children who have severe visual impairments or young children who are just beginning to develop their visual skills.

Visual Efficiency

In a visual efficiency program, children with low vision learn how to use their vision more effectively. For example, specific activities are created to help the student learn how to discriminate fine details in pictures and designs, to differentiate between outlines and inner details, to discriminate patterns, to differentiate between light and dark intensity, and to transfer visual skills from concrete forms (three-dimensional objects such as a ball) to representational forms (a picture of a ball) to symbolic forms (the printed word *ball*) (Barraga, 1970).

Visual Utilization

In a visual utilization program, instruction focuses on teaching the student to modify the environment, and on teaching the student to use appropriate low vision devices that maximize the student's functional vision. For example, students can be taught to use task lighting and a handheld magnifier to locate a friend's telephone number in the phone book.

Visual-skills instruction, taught in an isolated, task-centered approach, has been challenged by some in the field of visual impairment (Ferrell & Muir, 1996). Specific visual skills can be taught most effectively within a meaningful context that is both important and relevant to a child. For example, lining up a series of pegs from shortest to tallest is in all likelihood far less meaningful to a child than lining up his or her friends from shortest to tallest and then playing a game based on the order. By tying skills to meaningful activities, the skills can be incorporated into the student's daily routines and can be more easily applied in new situations (Erin & Paul, 1996). If students with low vision have had thorough and meaningful training in locating a visual stimulus or a particular image in a complex visual array, they will be able to apply these skills in learning to use a monocular telescope or other low vision device. For example, because Javier knows how to scan a page systematically to locate Waldo in a *Where's Waldo* book, he can apply the same skill in trying to locate the price of today's special on the cafeteria wall menu using his monocular telescope.

Teachers of students with visual impairments therefore need to focus on teaching students how to use their vision more effectively. However, since most of what children are exposed to in school is print related, visual-skills instruction

---

Sidebar 0.1

Principles of Special Methods

Lowenfeld (1973) identified three basic principles necessary for teaching children who are blind or visually impaired:

• Providing opportunities for learning by doing.

• Providing concrete experiences.

• Providing unifying experiences.

According to these principles, students should be able to participate in hands-on activities that engage them fully with visual, tactile, and auditory input. They should be involved in a given activity from the very beginning, through the middle, to the end—and not just participate in pieces of it. For example, while cooking, the student should be involved in each step: reading the recipe; getting the ingredients out of the cabinets and refrigerator; mixing the ingredients while discussing their textures, odors, and appearance; putting the food in the oven (with assistance provided for young children); smelling the food while it cooks; taking it out when it has finished cooking and noting the change in its appearance. At the end of the process comes the reward—tasting the food. In this way, the student who is visually impaired is helped to integrate the information from all of his or her senses and to gain meaning from the experience. He or she is helped to develop a fully integrated concept that in turn helps the student understand his or her world.

---

programs also need to foster the ability to read and write. When children are taught how to use their vision better, they also need to be taught how to become literate in the process. Since children who have low vision are less able to learn incidentally through casual observation than sighted children, children with low vision need deliberate exposure to concepts. In order for students who are visually impaired to have meaningful literacy experiences, Lowenfeld's (1973) three principles of special methods need to guide instructional practices (Koenig, 1996). (See Sidebar 0.1.) Early literacy experiences are directly related to the acquisition of formal literacy skills, and they will directly influence comprehension of texts read later on in school.

To help students with low vision acquire literacy skills, teachers must first understand a student's literacy needs and then decide how these skills can be taught within the general education curriculum. Since the majority of students with low vision attend their neighborhood schools with the assistance of an itinerant or resource teacher of students who are visually impaired, the implementation of a visual skills program must be built into the school day even if it appears to take time away from other curricular areas. Visual efficiency skills are an essential component of the education program of students with low vision, and they are part of the expanded core curriculum. (See Sidebar 0.2.)

Sidebar 0.2

Expanded Core Curriculum

The expanded core curriculum is a set of skills that are intended to assist the student who is visually impaired in becoming an independent, confident, capable member of his or her community (Hatlen, 1996). It is a curriculum that goes beyond the regular core curriculum (such as reading, math, science, and other academic subjects) and focuses on skills that are disability-specific. The expanded core curriculum must be taught sequentially and systematically to students who are visually impaired in conjunction with the core curriculum for all students. The expanded core curriculum includes the following areas of learning:

• Visual efficiency skills.

• Compensatory or functional academic skills, including communication modes.

• Orientation and mobility.

• Social interaction skills.

• Independent living skills.

• Recreation and leisure skills.

• Career education.

• Technology.

• Techniques for teaching children with additional disabilities.

LEVELS OF LITERACY

Much has been written about the unique literacy needs of students who read braille; however, students who read large print or who use low vision devices also have unique literacy needs. Koenig (1992) outlined three levels of literacy—emergent literacy, academic literacy, and functional literacy—that may be applied to all learners, including those who have low vision. *Emergent literacy* refers to a young child's developing ability to bring meaning to reading and writing activities. *Academic literacy* refers to the type of reading and writing mastery skills that children learn during their school years. Finally, *functional literacy* refers to literacy activities that relate to the day-to-day completion of practical tasks, such as reading a street sign or a menu. Skills in all these areas are essential for students, and teachers play a critical role in helping their students develop these vital abilities.

Emergent Literacy

A young child with low vision must be directly exposed to literacy experiences early in life, such as looking at picture books, scribbling on paper, or observing a parent write a grocery list. Although the child may have enough vision to see what is happening in his or her environment, it cannot be assumed that enough visual information was gathered to make sense out of what was seen. That is, it cannot be assumed that the child was able to imbue what was seen with meaning. Consequently, the child may have missed out on a potential literacy experience. In order for an experience to contribute to a child's literacy development, its meaning may need to be made distinctly and unambiguously clear to the child.

Children with visual impairments, therefore, need to be exposed to and involved in everyday activities that involve literacy. Using Lowenfeld's (1973) principles of special methods—learning by doing, providing concrete experiences, and providing unifying experiences—the teacher may encourage the development of specific visual skills in a manner that also enhances emergent literacy skills. Examples of such activities might include looking for a favorite box of cereal, recognizing a common street sign, or noticing that dad reads the comics on Sunday mornings. The teacher of students with visual impairments can provide direct experiences related to these events by, for instance, visiting a supermarket with students to find the cereal in the cereal aisle, walking past a sign and discussing what it is about and why it is there, and bringing a newspaper to school and making a game out of finding the comics.

At the emergent literacy stage, a great deal of useful information about how a child uses his or her vision may be obtained by observing the young child in a variety of settings and lighting conditions. Even though formal literacy instruction has not yet begun, reading books with the child and observing how the child looks at pictures, starts to identify letters and words, scribbles and colors on paper, and plays with small toys may also provide useful information regarding the child's visual abilities and preferences. Consultation with the child's parents, caregivers, or other family members is important in order to learn about what activities the child enjoys at home and about how the child approaches visual tasks in a familiar environment.

Academic Literacy

The acquisition of basic academic literacy skills is of utmost importance during a child's school years (Koenig, 1996). To acquire competency, comfort, and flexibility in the area of literacy, students with low vision must learn how to use various low vision and technological devices, how to modify their surroundings (e.g., change the lighting conditions) to best enhance their visual abilities, and how to use their vision efficiently for near and distance tasks. These techniques must be taught by the teacher of students with visual impairments so the students can apply them successfully in the classroom and during personal recreation and leisure time. To further reinforce literacy development, the teacher of students who are visually impaired can teach the students' regular classroom teachers and parents how to implement the same skills, techniques, and environmental modifications.

It is also important to note that academic demands will change throughout a student's schooling. In the early grades, the student will most probably be using primary level materials with a larger type size and have a smaller workload. But as the child goes through school, the number of pages to be read for an assignment will increase, while the print size will generally decrease. These circumstances sometimes lead to visual fatigue and slower reading speeds for the student. The student will also have to learn to do complex tasks such as complete research reports; use reference materials; decipher complicated graphs, charts, and tables; and learn to use a computer. It is important that the student has a variety of techniques and strategies at hand to deal with academic tasks and to keep up with his or her peers. By starting to teach these skills in the early grades, the teacher of students with low vision will ensure that by the time the academic tasks increase, the student will be able to manage these increasing demands successfully.

Functional Literacy

Functional literacy does not necessarily mean reading and writing in the conventional sense, such as reading a textbook in school or reading a novel for pleasure; rather it involves reading and writing to complete a specific task, such as reading directions or signs and filling out forms. A variety of methods, such as optical devices (magnifiers, monoculars), nonoptical methods (changes in lighting, the use of a bold-line pen), synthesized speech, live readers, large-print or audiotaped materials, can be used at different times to access visual information in the environment just as they can be used for academic tasks (Koenig & Rex, 1996). For example, a person who is visually impaired may use a monocular telescope to locate the name of a particular restaurant while walking down the sidewalk; then he or she might use a lighted magnifier while seated inside the restaurant to read the menu; finally, he or she may go back to work and access his or her E-mail with a synthetic speech program installed on his or her computer.

Students who have low vision and additional disabilities may also use one or more of the methods noted above rather than conventional print tools to access visual information in daily life. The teacher of students with visual impairments can incorporate functional literacy activities into daily living skills, community access situations, and recreation and leisure activities while at the same time providing instruction in visual-skills acquisition.

THEORY AND PRACTICE

How can teachers of students who are visually impaired create practical and meaningful visual-skills instruction for students with low vision that will also enhance literacy skills? To assist the teacher with this task, the editors have attempted to bridge the gap between theory and practice by inviting several educators in the field of visual impairment to share their expertise and experiences with the reader. Our intention was to create a resource for teachers that is filled with ideas, suggestions, and ready-to-use forms and activities.

This book provides teachers with a framework for understanding the connection between visual-skills training and the acquisition of literacy. Teachers are taken through the steps involved in creating and implementing an exciting and appropriate visual-skills program for their students with low vision, one that also enhances their literacy skills. As described in Chapter 1, the first step is interpreting a student's eye report, typically the first glimpse the teacher has of the student. Chapter 2 describes how a functional vision assessment may be conducted, and it emphasizes the unique literacy needs of children with low vision. Chapter 3 outlines the role of the teacher when visiting a low vision clinic with a student—another essential component of creating an appropriate vision program for students with low vision. A detailed description of various low vision devices commonly used by students with low vision comprises Chapter 4. Since some teachers may not be familiar with the number and type of devices currently available, they will find this chapter a useful and informative one. Finally, Chapters 5, 6, and 7 contain detailed suggestions, games, and activities that can be used when teaching students how to use monocular telescopes, magnifiers, and CCTVs, respectively—low vision devices commonly used in school settings.

We hope that you enjoy using the materials in this book. There are many fun, creative, and meaningful activities and suggestions in each chapter that provide ideas on how to deal with challenging learning situations and on how to meet students' needs. We also hope that two important goals are accomplished through the use of this book: that the importance of literacy skills for students who have low vision is reinforced for readers and that resources to help teachers improve students' skills are made widely available.

REFERENCES

Barraga, N. C. (1970). *Teachers' guide for development of visual learning abilities and utilization of low vision.* Louisville, KY: American Printing House for the Blind.

Corn, A. (1986). Low vision and visual efficiency. In G. T. Scholl (Ed.), *Foundations of education for blind and visually handicapped children and youth* (pp. 99–117). New York: AFB Press.

Corn, A., & Koenig, A. J. (1996). *Foundations of low vision: Clinical and functional perspectives.* New York: AFB Press.

Erin, J. N., & Paul, B. (1996). Functional vision assessment and instruction of children and youths in academic programs. In A. L. Corn & A. J. Koenig (Eds.), *Foundations of low vision: Clinical and functional perspectives* (pp. 185–220). New York: AFB Press.

Ferrell, K. A., & Muir, D. W. (1996). A call to end vision stimulation training. *Journal of Visual Impairment & Blindness, 90,* 364–366.

Hatlen, P. (1996). The core curriculum for blind and visually impaired students, including those with additional disabilities. *RE:view, 28,* 25–32.

Koenig, A. J. (1992). A framework for understanding the literacy of individuals with visual impairments. *Journal of Visual Impairment & Blindness, 86,* 277–284.

Koenig, A. J. (1996). The literacy of individuals with low vision. In A. L. Corn & A. J. Koenig (Eds.), *Foundations of low vision: Clinical and functional perspectives* (pp. 53–66). New York: AFB Press.

Koenig, A. J., & Rex, E. J. (1996). Instruction of literacy skills to children and youths with low vision. In A. L. Corn & A. J. Koenig (Eds.), *Foundations of low vision: Clinical and functional perspectives* (pp. 280–305). New York: AFB Press.

Lowenfeld, B. (1973). Psychological considerations. In B. Lowenfeld (Ed.), *The visually handicapped child in school* (pp. 27–60). New York: John Day Company.

Olson, M. R. (1981). *Guidelines and games for teaching efficient braille reading.* New York: AFB Press.

Rex, E. J., Koenig, A. J., Wormsley, D. P., & Baker, R. L. (1994). *Foundations of braille literacy.* New York: AFB Press.

Scholl, G. T. (Ed.). (1986). *Foundations of education for blind and visually handicapped children and youth.* New York: AFB Press.

Swenson, A. M. (1999). *Beginning with braille: Firsthand experiences with a balanced approach to literacy.* New York: AFB Press.

Wormsley, D. P., & D'Andrea, F. M. (1997). *Instructional strategies for braille literacy.* New York: AFB Press.

Interpreting
an Eye Report

DUNCAN McGREGOR AND CAROL FARRENKOPF

WHEN DESIGNING A LITERACY PROGRAM for a student who has low vision, the teacher of students with visual impairments must draw upon the information gained from several different assessments, each performed with a different purpose in mind and each providing a different type of information. These assessments should include an ophthalmological or optometric eye examination, a functional vision assessment (FVA) (see Chapter 2), and a clinical low vision assessment (see Chapter 3). A learning media assessment should also be performed to determine the child's most appropriate literacy medium or media (that is, print, braille, or a combination of the two) (see Koenig & Holbrook, 1995).

One of the most important documents a teacher will need is the report from the ophthalmologist or optometrist, often referred to as the eye report. An eye report is completed by either an ophthalmologist or an optometrist who has examined the student's visual abilities in a controlled, clinical setting. An ophthalmologist, as a medical doctor, may also provide a diagnosis of the disease, anomaly, or injury that has resulted in the child's visual impairment. An example of an eye report form is contained in Appendix 1.A at the end of this chapter. The information contained in the eye report is a starting point from which the teacher of students with visual impairments can develop an appropriate initial assessment, one that should include interviews with parents, caregivers, or other family members; teachers and other professionals; as well as a formal functional vision assessment (see Chapter 2). Additionally, the eye report is often required by school districts for students to be eligible for vision services in their schools.

After the eye care professional has completed the examination, a parent may request that the eye report be sent either directly to the vision or special education department of the school district or directly to the child's school. The parent/guardian may also share the eye report directly with the school or vision/special education department. When the vision or special education department has received the eye report first, that department usually notifies the school that there is a student in the school who has a visual impairment. In some cases, the school district may be the first to suggest that parents take their children to the ophthalmologist or optometrist to have their eyes tested. Schools may also request a copy of the eye report. The referral of a student to a teacher of students who are visually impaired can be made by either the school or the vision or special education department. On occasion, a family may contact the school district's vision or special education department directly to initiate vision services.

OVERVIEW OF THE EYE REPORT

When a student who is visually impaired is new to a school district or when a sighted student suddenly loses his or her vision, the eye report is often the first glimpse the teacher has of the student. The eye report must be obtained and reviewed before the teacher of students who are visually impaired performs an FVA or begins working with the student.

For the student who already receives support from a teacher of students who are visually impaired, an updated, yearly ophthalmological report should be obtained. The teacher should review each updated eye report carefully and interpret the report with the same rigor and thoroughness as when reviewing the initial intake report. The results of previous eye reports should be compared with those of the most current eye report to identify any changes in the student's vision status. Sometimes, the updated eye report may be the first indication that a student's vision status has changed. If there has been a significant change in vision, the teacher should arrange to reassess the student's functional vision and compare the FVA results with the clinical findings in the eye report. When armed with the FVA and ophthalmological reports, the teacher of students who are visually impaired is able to make the appropriate modifications and accommodations to the student's educational program.

Confidentiality

An eye report is a confidential document. Written permission to release a report must be obtained from the student's parent(s) or guardian(s) before requesting a report from the ophthalmologist or optometrist. Sometimes, the parents may already have a copy of the report—and they are, of course, entitled to share it with the teacher of students with visual impairments if they choose to do so. However, keep in mind that it may be necessary to speak to the eye specialist for clarification of the report, in which case, parental permission will still be required.

Limitations of the Eye Report

The quality of information contained in the eye report may reflect the experience, areas of expertise, perspectives, and even biases of the doctor. Eye care professionals who have experience in working with children who have visual and multiple disabilities may provide a wealth of useful information, while someone who has little experience in assessing students with disabilities in addition to their visual impairment may describe them as "unable to be assessed." As a result, some children (on paper at least) may appear to have no usable vision, when in reality, they may have enough vision to allow them to complete basic visual tasks. The teacher of students who are visually impaired will want to avoid making assumptions about the absoluteness of the information contained in an eye report.

Even though the eye report contains useful information for developing an educational program for a student, the teacher cannot determine the student's educational needs solely on the basis of the eye report. The eye report does not tell anything about how the child performs visually in the real world of home and school. To supplement the medical information, the teacher of students with visual impairments must perform a functional vision assessment to determine how a student is using his or her vision in performing everyday activities, both in and out of school (see Chapter 2).

The testing situation in the eye doctor's office provides only one measure of the child's actual visual abilities. For example, measurement of visual acuity (the sharpness of vision, discussed later in this chapter) depends on contrast and lighting. That is, if the contrast between the print on the visual acuity chart and the background of the chart is decreased, the print cannot be seen as clearly. If lighting is too dim or too bright, clarity of vision may also decrease. Since contrast and lighting are optimal in a clinical setting, it is likely that the student's best possible vision will be elicited, and this result may lead to an overestimation of a child's visual ability. That is, the child may be reported as seeing better than he or she generally does in "real life." It is unlikely that the student will experience such perfect environmental circumstances during the school day or in other real-life situations. As a result, the student may not be able to function as well as the reported visual acuity results would imply.

Conversely, visual performance may also be affected negatively by the testing situation. The examination is typically performed in a doctor's office or by an eye specialist in a hospital—not a very comfortable setting for many children, especially for those who may have had a lifetime of medical conditions and complications. The child may experience stress that results from the fear of a strange place, the doctor, the examination procedure itself, or the eye drops or other medication that the doctor may use. Also, the child may be afraid of finding out that his or her vision has become worse or that other medical problems have developed.

In addition to the stress of the testing situation, less than optimal communication and a lack of rapport between the doctor and the child may result in poor cooperation and poor performance. As a result, an eye report may state that the child was "unable to be tested due to poor cooperation." Doctor–patient rapport, particularly involving children, takes time to develop. Many eye specialists may be unable to devote the time necessary to build a rapport with their young patients. The student may also not be amenable to participation for various reasons (for example, fear, discomfort, or behavioral problems). The teacher of students who are visually impaired may wish to accompany the student to the ophthalmological examination. Additionally, the teacher and/or doctor may suggest that the parent or parents be present during the examination rather than wait outside. The presence of the teacher and/or parent may make the student feel more at ease and comfortable with the testing situation. Better visual attention and cooperation may occur, thereby leading to results that reflect the student's actual visual abilities.

Finally, with many visual conditions, vision can fluctuate from day to day—or from one time of day to another. Optic atrophy and cortical visual impairment are two common visual conditions that involve fluctuating levels of visual ability. Also, if the student is tired or sick, visual performance may be affected negatively. Thus, the snapshot of a child's visual abilities at a particular time, one that is provided by a clinical examination, may not be an accurate picture.

The eye report is a vital tool for the teacher of students with visual impairments to use in designing a functional vision assessment—and ultimately, an educational program—for a student with low vision. With a careful interpretation of and with attention to each piece of information, the teacher should be able to address, in functional terms, most questions raised by the student, his or her teachers, or his or her parents about the student's visual condition and its implications.

CONTENTS OF THE EYE REPORT

The eye report may be written on a school district's standard form, on a eye specialist's standard form, or in a narrative format. Regardless of the format, a typical eye report contains all or some of the components listed in Sidebar 1.1. The teacher may find it helpful to use the list in Sidebar 1.1 to organize information that has been extracted from an eye report written in a narrative format. Sometimes, not all of the information about the student's eye condition will be included in the eye report. For example, the eye report may not indicate that eyeglasses have been prescribed, when, in fact, the student wears eyeglasses. Or the eye specialist may only include a distance visual acuity and not a near visual acuity. Just because the near visual acuity is not listed does not mean that the student's near vision is normal or that the acuity was unobtainable. The teacher must contact the eye specialist to obtain the missing information.

Identifying Information About the Student

It is important to have complete and accurate information about the student, including gender, date of birth, address, telephone number, and date of assessment. This information helps the teacher of students with visual impairments to determine what age-appropriate materials to bring for the first meeting

---

Sidebar 1.1

Contents of a Typical Eye Report

- Identifying information about the student.
- Ocular history.
- Etiology.
- Diagnosis.

- Visual acuity measures:
  – Distance acuity.
  – Near acuity.
- Contrast sensitivity.
- Visual field test.

- Color vision.
- Photophobia.
- Muscle function.
- Intraocular pressure reading.
- Pupillary reflex.

- Prescription for corrective lenses.
- Prognosis.
- Recommended treatment.
- Precautions and suggestions.

with the student. The teacher should cross-reference the information in the eye report with that in the student's school file to make sure that all of the contact information is accurate. In addition, if the date of the examination was not recent, the teacher may wish to contact the parents so that they can arrange to have an up-to-date visual assessment done.

Ocular History

The eye report will include details about what has happened to the student's vision in the past. The teacher can use this information to make a preliminary judgment of the student's present needs. The teacher should note whether the student's visual impairment is *congenital* (present from birth) or *adventitious* (developed later in life as a result of an accident or disease), as the age of onset may affect many aspects of the student's development and learning needs.

Etiology

The term *etiology* refers to what has caused the child's visual impairment. This is often included as part of the student's ocular history. In addition to noting whether the visual condition is congenital or adventitious, the teacher will want to know whether it is genetic—that is, whether it was inherited from one or both parents. If the condition is genetic, the teacher of students who are visually impaired may wish to suggest to the child's parents that they discuss with the ophthalmologist the implications of the eye condition for their other children (if they have any). Discussion of genetics with parents is better left to the ophthalmologist.

Diagnosis

Diagnosis refers to what the child's visual condition *is,* independent from what caused it, although the terms *diagnosis* and *etiology* are often used interchangeably. Knowing a student's visual condition is helpful in determining both what materials to bring to the functional vision assessment (FVA) and what to look for. For example, if a student has retinitis pigmentosa, possible effects to look for would include peripheral field loss and difficulties with depth perception, mobility (particularly at night), and functional vision in low light situations. The teacher should be cautious when reading the diagnosis because some ophthalmologists do not state the actual diagnosis; rather, they state a symptom of the larger problem (e.g., they may report that the student has nystagmus when, in fact, the nystagmus is merely a symptom of the student's optic atrophy). The *Manual of Ocular Diagnosis and Therapy* (Pavan-Langston, 1996) and the *Dictionary of Eye Terminology* (Cassin & Solomon, 1997) are two resources commonly used by teachers of students who are visually impaired when researching students' eye conditions.

Eye reports will frequently be written using many medical terms and abbreviations. Sidebar 1.2 explains the most common abbreviations found in eye reports. The Glossary at the end of this book explains many of these terms, as well as other vision-related terms used throughout the book, some of which are explained in other chapters.

Visual Acuity Measures

Visual acuity refers to how sharply a person can see an object at a specified distance. Visual acuity must be assessed both at a distance and at near point. Sometimes, an ophthalmologist or optometrist will only provide a distance acuity. Distance visual acuity is expressed as a ratio, such as 20/200 or the metric equivalent of 6/60. If a person has 20/200 acuity, he or she can see at a distance of 20 feet (approximately 6 meters) what a person with typical 20/20 (6/6) vision can see at a distance of 200 feet (approximately 60 meters). The top or first number in the ratio represents the distance at which the child was tested. The bottom or second number identifies the smallest sized symbol that the child being tested can identify. The symbol size is simply the distance at which a person with typical vision can identify that symbol.

In most school districts, the visual acuity score determines whether or not a child can be identified as visually impaired. Identification is necessary if the student is to receive support from a teacher of students who are visually impaired. Additionally, some state or provincial agencies require that a medical report indicate an acuity of 20/200 or worse before a child can access certain services provided by that agency. The teacher should take note of the visual acuity scores on the eye report because he or she may be the first person to inform parents that their child qualifies for additional services.

The teacher of students with visual impairments should also pay close attention to near-vision acuities (if reported) and to the testing of near vision during the FVA, insofar as the student's near vision is what he or she uses in reading textbooks and when working with computer monitors and most other materials used in school.

Visual acuity testing should be conducted with correction (*cc*) and without correction (*s̄c*). This means that the student should be evaluated with and without his or her prescription lenses (contact lenses or eyeglasses). In some cases, the two scores may not differ greatly. If the eyeglasses do not improve acuity, perhaps the prescription needs updating, or perhaps the student's eye condition is not one that can be improved by corrective lenses.

Sidebar **1.2**

Common Abbreviations Found on an Eye Report

ACL	anterior chamber lens	F + F	fix and follow vision	PKU	phenylketonuria
ACT	alternate cover test	FHx	family history	PLT	preferential looking test
ARMD, AMD	age-related macular degeneration	FPL	forced preferential-looking	PP	near point
B, bil	bilateral	FTO	full-time occlusion	PR	far point
BDR	background diabetic retinopathy	FTP	full-time patch	prn	as needed
b.i.d.	two times per day	f/u	follow-up	PROS	prosthesis
BFP	binocular fixation pattern	GL	eyeglasses	PRRE	pupils round, regular, and equal
BS	blind spot	gtts	eyedrops	Px	prognosis
c, c̄	with	h.	hour	q.	every
cc	with correction	HA	headache	q.d.	once per day
CC	chief complaint	HM	hand motion	q.h.	every hour
CE	cataract extraction	h.s.	at bedtime	q.i.d.	four times per day
CF	counts fingers or confrontation field	Hx	history	q.o.d.	every other day
CL	contact lens	IOL	intraocular lens	q.2h.	every two hours
CMV	cytomegalovirus	IOP	intraocular pressure	R	refraction or retinoscopy or right
conj	conjunctive, conjunctiva	LP	light perception	RD	retinal detachment
CSM	central, steady, and maintained fixation	LP + P	light perception and projection	REM	rapid eye movements
CSUM	central, steady, unmaintained fixation	MRI	magnetic resonance imaging	ROP	retinopathy of prematurity
CUSUM	central, unsteady, unmaintained fixation	MVA	motor vehicle accident	RP	retinitis pigmentosa
CV	color vision	N	near, near vision	Rx	prescription
CVF	central visual field	NKA	no known allergies	s̄c	without correction
CVO	central vein occlusion	NKDA	no known drug allergies	SEM	slow eye movements
d	day	NLP	no light perception	Sx	symptoms
D	diopter or distance or distance vision	NPC	near point convergence	TAC	Teller acuity cards
Dx, diag	diagnosis	OD	right eye (oculus dexter)	t.i.d.	three times per day
ENUC	enucleated	ON	optic nerve	tono	tonometry
ERG	electroretinogram	OS	left eye (oculus sinister)	Tp	toxoplasmosis
EW	extended wear contact lens	OU	both eyes (oculus uterque)	TRD	total retinal detachment
FC	finger counting	p.c.	after meal	Tx	treatment
FEM	fast eye movements	PD	prism diopter or pupillary distance	UTT	unable to test
		PDR	proliferative diabetic retinopathy	V, Va	visual acuity
		PERRLA	pupils equal, round and reactive to light and accommodation	VECP	visual evoked cortical potential
				VEP	visual evoked potential
				VER	visual evoked response
				VF	visual field

Distance Acuity

The Snellen chart is the most common test used in assessing distance visual acuity. This chart has a large letter at the top of the chart. Below this letter, there are lines of progressively smaller letters, with an increasing number of letters on each line. The "Illiterate E" chart is similar, but all of the letters on the chart are "E's" pointing either up, down, left, or right. This chart can be used with young children who do not know the alphabet. They respond by pointing in the direction of the arms of the "E." Other distance acuity charts include the Lighthouse Distance Visual Acuity Chart, and Lea Symbols. The latter are more likely to be used in a low vision assessment than in a medical eye examination. The Lighthouse charts have the same number of symbols (letters or numbers) on each line, regardless of the print size. The Lea Symbols are similar to the Lighthouse charts in design; however, they have pictures (apple, house, circle, square) that allow them to be used with small children and with students with multiple

Lighthouse Low Vision Products

Lighthouse near-vision acuity cards are among the assessment materials used to evaluate near acuity.

Table **1.1**

Approximate Equivalents of Near Visual Acuity Notations

Meters Equivalent (M size)	Snellen Equivalent	Jaeger Equivalent	Lowercase Type Point Size	Equivalent Size Print Materials
0.4	20/20 or 6/6		3	
0.5	20/25 or 6/8	J1–J2	4	
0.8	20/40 or 6/12	J4–J5	6	Telephone book
1.0	20/50 or 6/15	J6	8	Newspaper print
1.2	20/60 or 6/18	J8	10	Adult paperbacks
1.6	20/80 or 6/24	J9–J11	14	Children's books
2.0	20/100 or 6/30	J11–J12	18	Large-print materials
4.0	20/200 or 6/60	J17	36	Newspaper headlines
5.0	20/250 or 6/80	J18		
10.0	20/500 or 6/150	J19		
20.0	20/1000 or 6/300			

Source: Reprinted, with permission, from *Understanding Low Vision* (p. 148), edited by Randall T. Jose, 1983, New York: American Foundation for the Blind.

disabilities who may not know the alphabet or numbers. In cases in which children are preverbal or nonverbal, having them point to symbols that match those seen on the visual acuity charts can be used as a method of determining what they can see. However, children need to understand what "same" and "different" mean in order for this method to result in a reliable measurement.

Near Acuity

Near-point visual acuities are sometimes expressed as Snellen equivalents (e.g., 20/100 or 6/30), M-size equivalents (e.g., 2.00 M), or Jaeger equivalents or "J scores" (e.g., J 12). "M" units, or meter units, express the distance in meters at which lowercase letters subtend five degrees of arc. The M system is most compatible with the Snellen charts. The Jaeger system is a test of near vision using graded sizes of letters or numbers (Wilkinson, 1996). Testing is done at a standard distance of 16 inches (40 cm), unless otherwise noted on the eye report. Table 1.1 shows Snellen, M-size, and Jaeger equivalent acuities that indicate an ability to read various point sizes of print at 16 inches. Since the M and Jaeger notations only indicate the size of the letter, they are meaningless unless the distance at which the letters were identified is noted (e.g., J4 @ 4 inches, or M 1.0 @ 30 cm). If a student reads J4 (approximately 6 point) print at 4 inches, his or her visual acuity is not as good as a student who is able to read J4 print at the standard 16-inch distance. The Jaeger system has fallen from favor because of lack of standardization in print sizes from one chart to another, but it is still used by some doctors.

Contrast Sensitivity

Standard tests of visual functioning measure an individual's ability to see details in letters or other symbols with high contrast. Because most of what we are required to see in our daily activities is of lower contrast, contrast sensitivity testing can give a more accurate picture of one's visual functioning. A child with reduced contrast sensitivity may benefit from wearing tinted lenses or may require greater magnification of print materials (by using large print or a closed circuit television) than one might expect from his or her acuity scores (Wilkinson, 1996).

Contrast sensitivity cards usually contain letters, symbols, or simple line drawings of varying degrees of darkness. On some charts, there are a number of lines of symbols or print that start off dark on the first line and get progressively lighter as the student makes his or her way down the chart. Single image cards are also available, on which the first card in the series is the darkest and cards that follow it contain a single symbol that gets progressively lighter.

Visual Field Test

The *visual field* is the area that an individual can see without shifting his or her gaze (Ward, 1996). The typical visual field is approximately 160°. Visual field testing determines the outer limits of visual perception by the retina and the quality of vision within the retina (Pavan-Langston, 1996). *Peripheral* field loss—loss of vision at the side or perimeter of the visual field—is typically reported in degrees (e.g., 10 degrees in both eyes, indicating a small tunnel of vision). The results of visual field testing can provide important information that can be used in determining where a child should sit in the classroom and where materials should be placed when working with the child. A reduced visual field may also have an effect on the student's orientation and mobility and may cause difficulties in physical activities in class and on the playground, particularly in activities in which a ball or a player may come toward the student in a blind area of his or her field of vision.

In addition, a reduced visual field may be associated with other visual difficulties. The central part of the retina where the cones are concentrated, called the *macula,* is responsible for *central vision.* The cones are photoreceptor cells that provide clear visual acuity and color vision. Thus, someone with a central vision loss might also be expected to have reduced visual acuity and color perception. The outer part of the retina is responsible for peripheral vision. The rods,

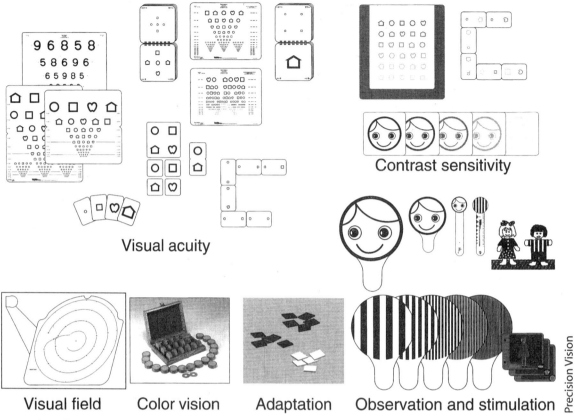

Contrast sensitivity

Visual acuity

Visual field   Color vision   Adaptation   Observation and stimulation

Precision Vision

Materials such as these are used to gather a variety of information during clinical assessments.

photoreceptor cells that provide perception of form and movement as well as night vision, are located primarily in this area. Many children with reduced peripheral fields also experience difficulties seeing at night or in low illumination.

Finally, if a peripheral, central, or scattered field loss is noted on the eye report, the teacher will likely observe that the student has eccentric viewing patterns. (A *scattered* field loss means there are random blind spots on the retina.) *Eccentric viewing* involves changing the position of the head or eyes so that the visual image is directed toward a portion of the retina that is functioning. If a field loss is noted, the teacher should also check where and how the student positions his or her head while viewing print materials up close and in the distance.

Color Vision

An eye report may indicate that a student has "abnormal" color vision. This may mean that the student is unable to distinguish any colors or that he or she has difficulty distinguishing only between certain hues (for example, he or she may have red/green color blindness). Unless information about the type of color vision loss is indicated in the report, the teacher of students who are visually impaired should be prepared to assess color vision in the FVA (see Chapter 2).

Photophobia

Students with photophobia, or light sensitivity, may have difficulty in bright light, and they may require a period of adjustment when moving between lighter and darker areas. They may have been prescribed sunglasses for use indoors as well as outdoors. If so, the teacher should check to see if the student has sunglasses with ultraviolet (UV) protection. Sunglasses that provide protection on the sides help to reduce the amount of light reaching the retina. In the classroom, a student who is sensitive to light should have his or her back to the light source.

Muscle Function

Testing for muscle function will indicate the presence of *strabismus,* the misalignment of one or both of the eyes. When the teacher conducts the FVA, he or she should take note of which way the eyes turn and whether the student displays a head tilt (eccentric viewing). The student may also have *nystagmus*—an involuntary rapid movement of the eyes—in either a horizontal, vertical, or circular direction. Most students with this condition are naturally able to locate their *null point* (the point at which the movement of the eyes is minimal) and may tilt their head in order to find the point of least movement. Teachers should not discourage students who display such a head tilt because it serves a purpose for the student. Nystagmus is generally not the primary cause of a student's visual impairment. Instead, it usually accompanies another visual condition. If another visual condition is not listed in the eye report of a student who has nystagmus, the teacher of students who are visually impaired should contact the treating eye doctor for further details about the student's eye condition.

Intraocular Pressure Reading

High pressure readings of the fluid in the eye—22 mm of mercury (Hg) or greater—may be indicative of glaucoma (Pavan-Langston, 1996). For a student who has glaucoma, increased intraocular pressure (IOP) can result in optic nerve damage. As a result, the IOP must be monitored carefully. Consistent pressure readings over time may indicate that the condition has stabilized. It is important that a student with glaucoma be diligent in taking his or her eye drops or medication.

Pupillary Response

A pupillary reflex is a response by the pupils to changes in light by expanding or contracting. This is an indication that the eye is sending a message, via the optic nerve, to the visual cortex of the brain. If the eye report indicates that there is no pupillary response to light or that the student has no light perception (*NLP*), the student may have very little functional vision. Even if a pupillary response is indicated in the eye report, the teacher should keep in mind that the response may be slower for some students than for others, especially for those students with Leber's congenital amaurosis or retinitis pigmentosa, or students who have visual and multiple disabilities. In either case, the teacher should make a note to him- or herself to check for the pupillary response during the FVA.

Prescription for Corrective Lenses

A prescription for a *plus lens* (e.g., +6.00) generally indicates a correction for *hyperopia,* or far-sightedness, while a *minus lens* (e.g., −4.50) is usually prescribed for *myopia* or near-sightedness (see Chapter 4 for an explanation of these terms). The number following the plus or minus sign indicates the number of *diopters* of correction required. The larger the number, the more powerful the lens. If a diagnosis is not given on the eye report but if the prescription is, the teacher should not assume that the student is either myopic or hyperopic. Clarification from the eye doctor is necessary.

The strength of the prescription is used by some government agencies in determining whether a student who has high myopia or high hyperopia is eligible for funding for corrective lenses. For example, in some states or provinces, a prescription of ± 6.00 is the minimum criterion for funding. If the eye report indicates that a prescription for corrective lenses has been issued, the teacher should expect to see the student wearing the eyeglasses or contact lenses according to the doctor's directions. For example, a student who has myopia and wears eyeglasses to see in the distance may not need to wear his or her glasses when reading material up close. Similarly, a doctor may recommend that a student with visual and multiple disabilities who is getting used to new glasses only wear them for short periods of time.

Prognosis

Knowing what is in store for a student, in terms of his or her visual condition, is important in designing an educational program that will prepare him or her for the future. Is the student's vision stable or progressive? Is the visual impairment the result of an injury that may recur if care is not taken (e.g., retinal detachment)? Is the condition permanent, or is it improving? Can it be improved through treatment or surgery? What low vision services will be available for this student should his or her vision worsen?

Recommended Treatment

Some treatments may occur at school and/or may affect the student's ability to perform at school. If eye drops have been recommended in the eye report, the teacher and other members of the educational team should know when the drops are supposed to be administered and how long it will take the student's eyes to adjust after taking the drops. Usually, children will have the drops put in their eyes before and after school; however, there are times when the drops will need to be administered during the school day. If the school has a nurse on the premises, he or she would be the best person to administer the drops. However, there are times when a teacher may be asked by the child's parents to do it. In this case, schools should request written acknowledgment by the parents that they have asked the teacher to administer the drops and that they are aware of the possible risks involved. If patching is recommended, a patching schedule should be obtained and shared with the educational team. Patching is a treatment often used to correct strabismus that requires covering the better eye. This forces the deviating eye to improve acuity (Bishop, 1996).

Precautions and Suggestions

Caution should be exercised when interpreting this section of an eye report. Some ophthalmologists will state that a student needs to read braille or large print. This is an educational recommendation, however, and should only be made by a qualified teacher of students who are visually impaired. This recommendation should be made only following a learning media assessment of the student. If there is a discrepancy between the teacher's and the ophthalmologist's recommendations, the teacher must be prepared to explain his or her decision to the student's parents.

The eye specialist may also make recommendations such as "no contact sports," "must wear lenses at all times," or "must wear UV sunglasses when outside." The teacher of students with visual impairments is responsible for discussing these recommendations with the appropriate people (for example, classroom teacher, physical education teacher, principal). There may be liability issues involved if a student is injured.

THE NEXT STEPS

Once the teacher of students who are visually impaired has read through a student's eye report, he or she will need to organize the information and take steps to get any additional information that is necessary. Then the teacher will be ready to get in touch with the parents and the student's school to make arrangements to conduct additional assessments of the student.

Make Notes

It will be helpful for the teacher of students who are visually impaired to make notes about important areas that are to be assessed in an FVA. The eye report may point toward an expected level of visual functioning and it should also help the teacher to determine which procedures, instruments, and other materials might be appropriate to use in the FVA (Bishop, 1988). Sidebar 1.3 provides some examples of questions the teacher of students with visual impairments might ask him- or herself after reading the student's eye report. These questions will help guide the teacher's thinking in the development of an appropriate FVA. The teacher of students who are visually impaired may wish to use the sample form provided in Appendix 1.B at the end of this chapter as an aid when organizing the information acquired from the eye report and from the student's school records.

The teacher of students with low vision may also consider any activities that may need to be modified or restricted for the student. For example, if color

---

Sidebar 1.3

Questions to Guide Interpretation of an Eye Report

- Does the eye report contain a diagnosis or a symptom?
- Is the student's visual condition stable or progressive?
- Does the student have any additional disabilities that will affect literacy?
- Will I need to focus on near or distant vision?
- What will be the student's preferred viewing distance for reading print?
- How close does the student need to get to see the chalkboard?
- How close will the student get to his or her work surface when printing or writing?

- Is the student likely to have difficulty with orientation and mobility?
- Does the student have a visual field restriction that may affect print literacy?
- Does the student's prescription make a difference to his or her ability to read print of various sizes?
- Is the student likely to have a problem with glare?
- Will the student have difficulty with changes in lighting?
- Will the student have difficulty discriminating between colors?
- What materials will I need to bring to the assessment?

loss is noted in the eye report, the teacher of students who are visually impaired should find out whether or not systems of learning based on color coding are used in the classroom (that is, red words indicate verbs, blue word indicate nouns). Also, if any restrictions on physical activities are noted in the eye report, the teacher should confer with the physical education instructor about activities during physical education class.

Research Visual Conditions

The teacher of students with visual impairments should consult ophthalmological and low vision resource books to obtain information on the condition(s) included in the doctor's diagnosis. Several such books are listed in the Resources section at the end of this book. A search on the Internet may also provide useful information. Teachers of students with low vision must be able to understand the functional implications of the student's visual impairment and to speak knowledgeably about the condition with other teachers, with parents, and with administrators.

Contact the Eye Care Professional

In some cases, information contained in the eye report may be incomplete, vague, or illegible. Consequently, before seeing the student, the teacher of students who are visually impaired will need to contact the ophthalmologist or optometrist (after parental permission has been obtained) to discuss the report and to fill in any missing information or to clarify something in the eye report. If the teacher has any questions related to the student's visual impairment that could not be found in any resource materials, he or she may wish to ask the doctor about the condition.

Contact the Parents

Once the teacher of students who are visually impaired has studied the eye report and clarified any vague statements with the ophthalmologist or optometrist, he or she should contact the student's parents to inform them of the process involved in identifying their child as eligible for vision services in the school. The teacher may also choose to discuss the nature of a functional vision assessment and the role of the teacher of students who are visually impaired. Any concerns the parents have regarding their child's visual functioning should be noted by the teacher and dealt with appropriately. For example, parents may have concerns regarding the amount of support their child will receive, how their child will cope in the regular classroom, or where they can go for additional information about their child's eye condition.

Contact the School

The teacher of students who are visually impaired should notify the school that he or she will be visiting the school to conduct an FVA. The teacher of students who are visually impaired should discuss with the school's administrator the procedure for identifying a student as eligible for vision services. Arrangements should also be made ahead of time to meet with the classroom teacher and to schedule a suitable time and location to conduct the FVA.

SUMMARY

It is important to remember that an eye report is only a clinical assessment of visual acuity and other medical information. It does not indicate how well a child will function visually in school. It is the first step in the process of identifying a student who needs the support of a teacher of students who are visually impaired. The contents of an eye report will guide the teacher and an educational team in their efforts to design an appropriate functional vision assessment, which will in turn, form the basis for any adaptations or modifications to the student's educational program. It is vital that the teacher of students who are visually impaired be able to interpret the acuity measures and other information in the eye report in a thorough and informed manner. The eye report is the teacher's first glimpse of the student who is visually impaired, and it will give the teacher an idea of what to expect when assessing the student.

REFERENCES

Bishop, V. E. (1988). Making choices in functional vision evaluations: "Noodles, needles, and haystacks." *Journal of Visual Impairment & Blindness, 82,* 94–98.

Bishop, V. E. (1996). Causes and functional implications of visual impairment. In A. L. Corn & A. J. Koenig (Eds.), *Foundations of low vision: Clinical and functional perspectives* (pp. 86–114). New York: AFB Press.

Cassin, B., & Solomon, S. A. B. (1997). *Dictionary of eye terminology* (3rd ed.). Gainsville, FL: Triad Publishing Company.

Koenig, A. J., & Holbrook, M. C. (1995). *Learning media assessment of students with visual impairments: A resource guide for teachers* (2nd ed.). Austin: Texas School for the Blind and Visually Impaired.

Pavan-Langston, D. (1996). *Manual of ocular diagnosis and therapy* (4th ed.). Boston: Little, Brown and Company.

Ward, M. E. (1996). Anatomy and physiology of the eye. In A. L. Corn & A. J. Koenig (Eds.), *Foundations of low vision: Clinical and functional perspectives* (pp. 69–85). New York: AFB Press.

Wilkinson, M. E. (1996). Clinical low vision services. In A. L. Corn & A. J. Koenig (Eds.), *Foundations of low vision: Clinical and functional perspectives* (pp. 143–175). New York: AFB Press.

Example of an Eye Report

STATE OF TEXAS
Interagency
Eye Examination Report

Patient's Name _____ Date of Birth _____ Social Security No. _____

Address _____ City _____ State _____ Zip _____

Attention Eye Care Specialist
Address **each** item below.
Your thoroughness in completing this report is essential
for this patient to receive appropriate services.

Ocular History (e.g., previous eye diseases, injuries, or operations)

Age of onset _____ History _____

_____

Visual Acuity

If the acuity **can** be measured, complete this box using Snellen acuities or Snellen equivalents or NLP, LP, HM, CF.

Without Glasses		With Best Correction	
Near	Distance	Near	Distance
R	R	R	R
L	L	L	L

Acuity with glare testing, if applicable: R _____ L _____

If the acuity **cannot** be measured, check the most appropriate estimation.

☐ Legally Blind
☐ Not Legally Blind

Muscle Function   ☐ Normal   ☐ Abnormal   Describe _____

Intraocular Pressure Reading   R _____   L _____

Visual Field Test

☐ There is no apparent visual field restriction.

☐ There **is** a field restriction.   Describe _____

☐ Yes   ☐ No   The visual field is restricted to 20 degrees or less.

Source: Reprinted, with permission, from *Low vision: A resource guide with adaptations for students with visual impairments* (pp. 203–204), by N. Levack, 1991, Austin, TX: Texas School for the Blind and Visually Impaired.

F. M. D'Andrea and C. Farrenkopf, Eds., *Looking to Learn,* New York: AFB Press, 2000. This form may be copied for educational use.

| Color Vision | ☐ Normal ☐ Abnormal | Photophobia | ☐ Yes ☐ No |

Diagnosis (Primary cause of visual loss)

_____

_____

Prognosis   ☐ Permanent   ☐ Recurrent   ☐ Improving

☐ Progressive   ☐ Communicable   ☐ Can Be Improved

Treatment Recommended

☐ Glasses

☐ Patches (Schedule):

    R _____

    L _____

☐ Medication _____

☐ Refer for other medical treatment/exam:

_____

☐ Low Vision Evaluation

☐ Other _____

☐ Surgery

☐ Hospitalization will be needed for approximately

_____ days

Name of hospital _____

_____

Name of anesthesiologist or group:

Precautions or Suggestions (e.g., lighting conditions, activities to be avoided, etc.)

_____

_____

Scheduling   Date of Next Appointment _____   Time _____

IMPORTANT   **Check the most appropriate statement.**

☐ This patient appears to have no vision.

☐ This patient **has a serious visual loss** after correction.

☐ This patient **does not have** a serious visual loss after correction.

_____
Print or Type Name of Licensed Ophthalmologist or Optometrist

_____
Address

_____
City   State   Zip

_____
Signature of Licensed Ophthalmologist or Optometrist

_____
Date of Examination

(   ) _____
Telephone Number

RETURN COMPLETED FORM TO:

_____
Name

_____
Agency

_____
Address

_____
City   State   Zip

This form should be used when an ophthalmological/optometric examination is needed for (the): Texas Commission for the Blind (TCB) • School Districts • Special Education Programs • Regional Education Service Centers (ESCs) • Early Childhood Programs (ECH) • Early Childhood Intervention Programs (ECI) • Texas School for the Blind and Visually Impaired (TSBVI) • Eye Screening Follow-Up Examinations • Texas Department of Health (TDH) • Texas Department of Mental Health/Mental Retardation (TDMHMR).

Student Information Summary

Name: _____ Age: _____ D.O.B. _____

School: _____ Address: _____

Phone: _____ FAX: _____ _____

Grade/Class: _____ Teacher: _____

Parent(s): _____ Address: _____

Phone: _____ _____

Diagnosis: _____

Age of Onset: _____ Eye Report on File: ☐ yes ☐ no Report Date: _____

Visual Acuity: Corrected   Uncorrected

	OD _____	OD _____
Near	OS _____	OS _____
	OU _____	OU _____
	OD _____	OD _____
Distance	OS _____	OS _____
	OU _____	OU _____

Prescription: _____

Medical/Ocular History:

Additional Disabilities: _____

Visual Field Restrictions: _____

Color Vision Loss? ☐ yes ☐ no ☐ unsure

Photophobia? ☐ yes ☐ no ☐ unsure

Prognosis: ☐ stable ☐ progressive ☐ recurrent ☐ improving

Notes:

Performing a Functional Low Vision Assessment

TANNI L. ANTHONY

A FUNCTIONAL VISION ASSESSMENT (FVA) is an evaluation of the day-to-day visual skills of an individual who is visually impaired. Unlike a clinical eye exam (see Chapter 1), the purpose of an FVA is not to diagnose a medical condition or to prescribe a therapeutic treatment such as patching (covering one eye with a patch to correct a lazy eye), surgery, or medication (Anthony, 1993a; Erin & Paul, 1996). The FVA should complement a clinical low vision examination (see Chapter 3). While an optometric or ophthalmological exam in an eye doctor's office can yield vital information about the student's eye condition, the results may not be readily transferable to other settings. Unless care is taken to observe the student's visual performance in real-life environments, where lighting and contrast cannot always be controlled, a true picture of a student's functional vision cannot be obtained. In fact, the results of the functional vision assessment will relate directly to the literacy needs of the student. For example, what lighting conditions are best for reading and writing? What is a typical reading and writing distance for the student? Will materials presented on an overhead be difficult for the student to read? Without a clear understanding of how the student uses his or her vision, it will be difficult to determine what the student who is visually impaired needs to function optimally in the classroom.

PURPOSE OF THE
FUNCTIONAL VISION ASSESSMENT

The purposes of a functional vision assessment are twofold: (a) to determine what a student sees and (b) to identify what helps or hinders the student's visual performance. The intent is to acquire an understanding of the student's functional vision in a variety of environments, throughout different time periods, and to determine what environmental conditions serve as "visual assists" that help the child to see or "visual obstacles" that interfere with seeing. This information is written in report form as a means to guide the teaching practices of persons in charge of the student's educational program.

The assessment may focus on different skills or abilities depending on how the results of the FVA are to be used. For example, an orientation and mobility (O&M) instructor may want to learn about the student's functional vision in indoor and outdoor settings, during movement tasks, and with prescribed telescopic devices for viewing at a distance. If the focus of the assessment is for academic purposes, some of the goals may be to determine the student's educational needs for specialized equipment, preferential seating, lighting, and literacy modes—that is, whether the student will use print, large print, and/or braille to read and write. For the student who has multiple disabilities or needs significant additional support to function at his or her best in the classroom, data should be gathered to build an optimal communication or literacy system and to learn more about how to engage the student visually. This chapter focuses on assessing students' functional vision as it affects their educational, communication, and literacy needs.

Completion of an FVA is typically the responsibility of a certified teacher of students with visual impairments and/or an O&M specialist. The FVA may be conducted by more than one person. One teacher of students who are visually impaired can administer the test, while another teacher observes the behavior of the student and makes notes. With a young child, a transdisciplinary style of assessment may be used wherein the child is evaluated by a number of professionals at one time (for example, a teacher of students who are visually impaired, an O&M instructor, a physical therapist, a speech and language pathologist). In this setting, an "arena" or circle assessment is utilized, in which one person interacts with the student while the rest of the professionals observe and take notes specific to their aspect of the evaluation. The teacher of students who are visually impaired may be the person interacting with the student, while one of the professionals completes an assessment protocol from the sidelines. If the latter is the case, it will be important for the person interacting with the student to have guidance on what tasks to present to the child. For example, when the assessor has the student's visual attention with a particular object, the teacher of students with low vision may quietly request that the object be moved slowly to monitor the child's visual tracking skills. (Tracking skills are discussed on pp. 52 and 53 in this chapter.)

OVERVIEW OF THE FUNCTIONAL VISION ASSESSMENT

Four primary strategies should be used to complete an FVA:

1. Review student records.

2. Observe the student.

3. Gather interview information.

4. Conduct the formal functional vision assessment.

Each of these steps plays a crucial role in building a comprehensive and accurate viewpoint of the student's functional vision (see Sidebar 2.1).

Review Student Records
Medical Records

Many school districts require a medical report as a means of determining whether a student is eligible for the services of a certified teacher of students with visual impairments, so there will be a medical report in the school files from an ophthalmologist or optometrist (see Chapter 1). There are, however, instances in which a functional vision assessment may precede a medical evaluation. In fact, the results of the functional vision exam may be the catalyst for a student to be evaluated by an eye care specialist for purposes of a diagnosis and possible treatment plan.

Sidebar **2.1**

Steps in a Functional Vision Assessment

1. Review the student's medical and educational records.

2. Observe the student in a variety of settings and across different times of the day.

3. Interview the student and also the people most familiar with the student.

4. Complete the functional vision assessment procedures.

If there is medical information on file, it can provide valuable insight into the student's general health and specific visual status. (Appendix 2.A at the end of this chapter provides information about the effects of factors such as visual and medical diagnoses on an individual's visual performance.) Information about any medical diagnoses such as diabetes, juvenile arthritis, cardiac complications, or seizure disorder should be carefully reviewed. For example, during one functional vision assessment, a new teacher of students who are visually impaired noticed that the student's lips were turning blue while he was navigating down the steps leading to his classroom hallway. The teacher of students with visual impairments had the wisdom to allow the student to stop for a few moments before encouraging him to continue. Later, when the classroom teacher was asked about this observation, she was informed that the student had a serious heart condition.

The student may also be taking medications for a health condition. As noted earlier, medications may significantly affect visual performance. Some medications may affect reading or other literacy related activities, whereas other medications may compromise balance or movement tasks. Medications may affect the student at different times of the day depending on when the medication was taken and when it starts to wear off.

Finally, the teacher should look for an audiological report on the student. It is critical that hearing be checked to ensure the student's optimal functioning. Many conditions which contribute to a vision loss can also affect a student's hearing. Even a history of ear infections can be significant to the language/communication development of a child who is young or has multiple disabilities. If there is no record of an audiological evaluation, it may be prudent to determine the school district's procedures for a hearing screening. Many states or provinces have regulations pertaining to an annual hearing screening of students with disabilities. If a student does have a hearing loss, it will be critical to consult with the audiologist and teacher certified to work with students who are deaf or hard of hearing. It will also be necessary to know whether the student uses any assistive hearing devices, such as hearing aids or an FM (frequency modulation) system.

Educational Records

There are pros and cons to gathering information about a student's developmental and educational status prior to the functional vision assessment. Many teachers like to "suspend judgment" by not knowing what other professionals have written about the student. There are certainly times when an educational or therapeutic report can bias the reader. At all costs, the teacher should retain an open mind about the student he or she is about to meet. This is especially true when completing a functional vision assessment on a student with multiple disabilities. With no other population of students does the results of the FVA depend so much on the sensitivity, observational ability, and assessment skills of the teacher of students with low vision (Anthony, 1993b). Teachers who have limited training, experience, or comfort with students who have multiple disabilities may not capture a true understanding of the student's capabilities. If the final assessment report is written in a manner that underestimates the student's skills or potential, it may perpetuate a history of low expectations of student performance.

On the other hand, knowing the general developmental level of the young student's cognitive skills will provide a wealth of information as to what types of materials to bring to and activities to plan for the FVA (Bishop, 1988; Levack, 1991). The person who completes an FVA will have richer assessment results, on the basis of his or her knowledge and experience, and he or she can sustain the student's interaction by presenting developmentally appropriate materials and activities. When materials are presented at an appropriate level, there is more opportunity for the student to engage visually at an optimal level.

Observe the Student

Students should be observed in their natural environments doing everyday tasks such as taking notes from the overhead projector, reading classroom materials, navigating through the busy halls of the school, running laps in the gym, or completing an errand in the community. If the student has multiple disabilities, it is especially critical to observe the student in a variety of settings, at various times throughout the day, and during different tasks.

These environments will afford several opportunities to see how the student operates in a variety of visual conditions (for example, lighting, contrast, familiarity of environment) and during a range of visual tasks. During this time, the strategies that the student uses on his or her own to perform visual tasks should be documented. For example, does the student bring objects up to face level for clearer viewing, bring an arm out to locate a wall in a poorly lit hallway, or position him- or herself by a light source when trying to read the small print in the science lab manual? These maneuvers will provide insight into what environmental conditions assist the student and, more important, whether the student is aware of what strategies help to increase visual efficiency.

Gather Interview Information

While a vast amount of information can be gathered from observation and formal assessment strategies, it is vital to take some time to talk to the student, the classroom teacher or teachers, related service providers, and parents, guardians, caregivers, or other family members. These conversations provide important insights into the FVA process. An FVA should not be considered complete unless it contains interview information from the student and the people involved in the student's life.

The student, family members, and service providers can be interviewed before or at the time of the assessment. Each service provider will have important contributions leading to insights into the student's educational progress and needs.

Student

It is critical for the teacher to talk to the student both to gather information and to validate assessment observations during the FVA process. A simple question—for example, "What can you do to see the print better?"—will offer helpful information about the student's awareness of his or her visual skills. This conversation also provides an opportunity for the student to learn about what and how he or she sees, and it can help set the stage for learning new strategies that the student may not have thought of, such as using task lighting (lighting used to enhance a particular working area), a handheld magnification device (see Chapter 6), or strategies involving other senses (for example, listening to taped materials, feeling tactile lines or braille).

Classroom Teachers

Classroom teachers can provide important insights into a student's daily work habits, preferences, and areas of difficulty, particularly with regard to reading and writing, that may not be immediately obvious to the teacher of students who are visually impaired. Sidebar 2.2 provides an example of some of the questions the teacher of students who are visually impaired may wish to ask the classroom teacher as part of the functional vision assessment.

Parents

Talking with parents can yield invaluable information. If a student is preschool age or has significant support needs, it is especially important to seek information from persons who know the child best. Sidebar 2.3 lists examples of some questions that the teacher of students who are visually impaired might use to obtain information from parents and other family members.

Parents can offer insights into how to interpret the student's behavior. For example, an individual with neurological-related challenges may appear not to be engaged in a visual activity until a family member points out a particular

---

Sidebar 2.2

Interview Questions for Classroom Teachers

1. Is the student reading at grade level?

2. Is the student's reading rate comparable to classroom peers?

3. Are the student's reading skills transferable across a variety of reading materials?

4. How have the student's reading and academic skills progressed over time?

5. Does the student demonstrate fatigue or inattention when using visual, auditory, and/or tactual materials for an extended period of time? Please describe.

6. Are assignments turned in on time?

7. Are there time considerations for the student to process and complete a literacy task?

8. How legible is the student's handwriting?

9. Does the student use any special devices to access print information (e.g., magnifiers, speech synthesizer, and so on)?

10. Are these devices available to the student after school hours?

11. Which of the devices are portable?

12. Are the devices promoting reading skills?

Source: Adapted with permission from "Literacy for Learners with Visual Impairment: Role of Classroom Teacher and/or the Reading Specialist," literacy fact sheet, Colorado Department of Education, Denver, 1997.

---

body response that is indicative of the child's interest. For example, during a team assessment, the mother of a preschool child with athetoid cerebral palsy (fluctuating postural tone resulting in involuntary body movements) showed the team how her son indicated "yes" with a slight downward movement of his hand every time the assessor asked him if he wanted to play with a particular toy. The motion went unnoticed by the team, including a teacher of students with low vision, because all eyes were on the child's face and head. Due to the frequency of his athetoid body movements, the team did not discern the very slight-but-consistent hand movement. Once the team understood this child's method of communication, it was used to confirm what he saw and understood.

Other Personnel

Other professionals, such as occupational therapists, physical therapists, speech therapists, and O&M instructors who are involved with the student who has low vision may be able to provide a great deal of insight into the student's behavior. For example, a young child's visual impairment may not be the only reason he or she is having difficulty with printing and with cutting and pasting

---

Sidebar **2.3**

Interview Questions for Parents

1. What activities does your child do for personal enjoyment?

2. Does your child watch television or listen to television?

3. Does your child have an awareness of environmental print (e.g., common food logos on cereal boxes, fast food restaurants)?

4. Does your child recognize a particular food or place by the way it looks?

5. Does your child identify pictures in books? If so, about what size picture can your child identify?

6. Does your child read print, braille, or both?

7. If your child reads print, what size print does he or she prefer?

8. Are there a variety of materials in this print size available to your child in your home?

9. How long is your child able to engage in sustained reading activities?

10. Does your child read for short periods of time (e.g., 10–15 minutes) and then stop for a break?

11. Does your child read "community print" items (e.g., menus, price tags, signs)?

12. Do you expect your child to read community print items independently?

13. Does your child wear prescriptive eyeglasses or use any low vision devices during specific home, school, or community tasks?

14. Does your child complain about glare in indoor and/or outdoor settings?

15. Does your child have difficulty adjusting to changes in lighting conditions (e.g., hesitates to go outside at night, slows down his or her pace when lighting in a room changes)?

---

activities. It may be that the child has fine motor problems that an occupational therapist has already discovered. The therapist may have a specific program in place that needs to be considered when making judgments about the student's ability to participate in fine motor activities.

Having completed interviews from all concerned parties helps confirm the accuracy of the other assessment findings. This is especially significant if the teacher has had limited opportunity to observe and assess the student. While it is ideal to observe a new student in a variety of situations and over a period of time, it is not always possible to do so. In this situation, it is critical that the teacher of students with low vision discusses the assessment findings with the people who work with the student on a daily basis.

Once the teacher has completed the other steps in the assessment process, if his or her findings are very different from the information obtained from interviews with people who know the student, the teacher needs to consider the possibility that the assessment procedures did not produce a complete picture

---

Sidebar **2.4**

How to Resolve Differences of Opinion

1. Find a common ground. A discussion about a difference of opinion should always begin with an attempt to find the common ground of each party. For example, wanting the best educational program for the student is something everyone can agree on. If each party agrees that this is the intended goal, getting everyone to work together on behalf of the student is a good way to encourage positive problem solving.

2. Create a positive environment. Honest and respectful communication is the key to resolving differences of opinion about a student's capabilities and needs. Remarks that do not contribute to the positive progress of the conversation should be avoided. Avoiding negative remarks is especially important if the student is present during the meeting.

3. Support opinions with objective data. Statements about a student should be accompanied by examples of student behavior. In many cases, differences of opinion may be supported by examples on either side. For example, a student may demonstrate different behavior at home and at school. Although both viewpoints may be entirely accurate, people may try to discount one viewpoint over the other. However, it is important to learn from the different points of view because each individual might just learn something new about the student.

4. Discuss timelines. If different strategies are recommended by different parties, it may be helpful to establish a time period during which one strategy is used at a time. Progress should be noted so that the strategy can then be evaluated for its effectiveness.

---

of the student. It is also possible that other people have a limited viewpoint of the student's skills because of their misconceptions about the student's capabilities or their biased expectations that are based on a medical diagnosis alone. While resolving such differences in opinion may be stressful for the parties involved, it also presents an opportunity to further discuss the needs of the student. Sidebar 2.4 provides some strategies to help resolve differences of opinion regarding the visual abilities and needs of a visually impaired student.

Conduct the Formal Functional Vision Assessment

An FVA also requires more formalized procedures for quantifying visual skills. Formal assessment procedures can be completed to help gain additional knowledge about a particular skill. For example, while visual field responses can be observed as the student interacts with a table filled with materials, it may be advisable to probe further for visual field capabilities and limitations. Or a teacher of students with low vision may deliberately want to experiment with different sizes of print to learn more about the student's reading preferences and abilities. Formalized or teacher-engineered activities/protocols will help to bring valuable detail to the functional vision assessment process.

Commercial Protocols

A variety of commercial functional vision assessment tools are available to help determine the student's literacy needs (see the Resources for sources of commercial literacy media assessments). Many teachers of students with low vision have a favorite tool(s) for completing an FVA. Some are familiar with a variety of protocols that can be used depending on the age and specific assessment needs of the student.

Teacher-Created Assessment Tools

Veteran teachers of students with low vision frequently formulate their own checklists, selecting items from a host of commercial tools as well as from their personal experiences of what assessment techniques have been successful with students. They also expand their assessment repertoire with supplemental materials. For example, a teacher-made binder containing examples of different sizes of print, various types of lined paper, everyday reading materials, color matching samples, and visual scanning patterns may be part of a teacher's functional vision assessment tools. Classroom materials can be gathered and used as a part of the assessment process (Sanford & Burnett, 1997). Assessment kits may include a host of materials that have been collected from the home, from school, and from local discount stores. Sidebar 2.5 gives examples of the types of useful materials that can be included in such a kit.

No matter what assessment tool is used, it is important that the teacher of students with low vision have an understanding of the skills being evaluated. The assessment content should not be restricted to the protocol's classic one or two examples of how a skill can be tested (Anthony, 1993a). For example, it is not enough to know that a pupillary response can be measured by shining a penlight in the student's eyes. The teacher of students with low vision should have a variety of assessment strategies for evaluating this reflex without the use of a penlight, such as observing the student's pupils when moving from a dark room to a bright room. Furthermore, the teacher should be able to explain why each testing activity is administered and what the associated functional skills are of each activity. If a student understands that tracking skills are needed to visually follow a moving ball during gym class or to keep an eye on the principal moving down the hallway, he or she may be more compliant during FVA tracking tasks. It is also helpful to parents and teachers to explain why a certain skill is being assessed or why a specific recommendation has been made.

Sidebar 2.5

Home-Made Kit for Conducting Functional Vision Assessments

Two types of homemade assessment kits can be made by the teacher of students who are visually impaired: one for a child who is already able to read, and one for children who do not read or are pre-readers. Assessment items in each kit should contain a variety of materials that are age-appropriate and grade-appropriate. Materials can be gathered from the home and classroom, while others can be purchased.

KIT FOR CHILDREN WHO ARE ABLE TO READ

1. Writing Tools:
   - Black markers/felt-tip pens of various thicknesses.
   - Ballpoint pens of various colors.
   - Colored markers, pencil crayons, crayons, paints, chalk.
   - Pencils of various thicknesses.
   - Black-lined paper/pads with varying degrees of white space between lines.
   - Regular blue-lined paper.
   - White sheets of paper (for drawing or coloring on).
   - A variety of colored paper (to check for contrast preferences).

2. Reading Tools:
   - Print materials of various font sizes, styles, and complexity.
   - Printed materials on a variety of colored sheets.
   - Examples of poor-quality photocopies, high-quality photocopies, and purple dittos.
   - Maps in large print and regular size print.
   - Math pages.
   - Dictionary pages (from primary-, junior-, and adult-level dictionaries).
   - Telephone directory pages.
   - Color filters (clear acetate sheets used for overheads or plastic paper protectors).

3. Miscellaneous Items:
   - Penlights and occluders (blindfolds, handkerchiefs, darkened glasses, small paper cups, or pieces of material that can be used to cover one or both eyes).
   - Objects related to the student's school environment (e.g., books, crayons, pencils, markers, scissors, glue, slate and stylus).
   - Games that can be used to assess various visual skills (e.g., Bingo, concentration games, a deck of playing cards).
   - Slant boards of various grades.
   - A tape measure.
   - A stopwatch.
   - Stickers that can be used as reinforcers for younger children.

KIT FOR CHILDREN WHO DO NOT READ OR WHO ARE PREREADERS

- Toys or objects that are shiny or that reflect light (e.g., a mirror, or sparkly paper).
- Toys or objects of different sizes (e.g., cake decoration pellets or two-inch objects).
- Toys or objects of different colors (e.g., pastel, primary, and neon colors).
- Toys or objects that have movement characteristics (e.g., Slinky or Bumble Ball®).
- Pairs or multiples of the same object.
- Age-appropriate real-life materials (e.g., cups, spoons, money, or clothing).
- A dark-colored and white towel, cloth, or large piece of paper for the backdrop of a visual display.
- A slant board to display materials at a student's eye level.

COMPONENTS OF THE FVA

This section describes the specific components of a functional vision assessment and discusses both formal methods and informal observational methods of assessing them. Sidebar 2.6 presents a menu of visual behaviors that can be assessed during an FVA. However, it is important to remember that an FVA may be short or extremely comprehensive depending on the purpose of the assessment. The initial assessment may include items that do not need to be reassessed each time the student is evaluated. For example, if a student has been tested for

---

Sidebar **2.6**

Components of a Functional Vision Assessment

- Appearance of eyes and presence of corrective lenses.
- Visual reflexes:
  - Pupillary response.
  - Defensive blink.
  - Doll's eye response (vestibular ocular reflex).
- Visual responsiveness and perception:
  - Light perception.
  - Light projection.
  - Shadow and form perception.
  - Detection of motion.
- Muscle balance.
- Eye preference.
- Oculomotor behaviors:
  - Fixation.
  - Convergence and divergence.
  - Tracing.
  - Tracking.
  - Shift of Gaze.
  - Scanning.
- Field of vision.
- Color vision.

- Depth perception.
- Figure-ground perception.
- Light sensitivity and light–dark adaptation.
- Contrast sensitivity.
- Visual acuity:
  - Preferred viewing distance.
  - Formal testing methods.
  - Near and distance acuity cards or charts.
  - Informal observation methods.
  - Functional acuity estimate.
- Current print functioning.
- Reading rate and comprehension.
- Visual motor coordination:
  - Visual fine motor coordination.
  - Visual gross motor coordination.
- Visual-cognitive skills:
  - Visual imitation of movement.
  - Identification, matching, sorting, and classification of objects and pictures.
  - Visual sequencing.
  - Visual perception skills.

color vision and no deficiencies have been observed, this may not be an area that would need to be reassessed each time the FVA is updated. This would be true unless a higher developmental level of matching or identification is being assessed at a later date or unless there is reason to worry about loss of color vision because of a degenerative cone dystrophy (progressive damage to photoreceptors in the central retina). Depending on the student's diagnosis, certain areas may be more diligently re-evaluated, such as light–dark adaptation for a student with retinitis pigmentosa.

Also, not *all* of the visual behaviors listed in Sidebar 2.6 will need to be assessed in *all* students who are visually impaired. For example, older students who are performing at or above grade level do not need to have an assessment of the "doll's eye" or defensive blink responses (discussed later in this section). It can be assumed that since these students are reading and writing at a level appropriate for their age, they are able to perform many—if not all—of the basic visual skills. On the other hand, students who are developmentally delayed may be unable to perform some higher level visual tasks, such as visual sequencing or fine visual motor tasks (e.g., writing), so the teacher would not need to assess these skills.

In addition, the assessment materials will vary from one student to the next. For example, reading passages in various font sizes, copying material from a chalkboard, scanning posters in the distance, and using a computer may make up part of the assessment for an academic high school student with low vision. Whereas, a younger student or one who is severely developmentally delayed may be involved with assessment tasks such as identifying pictures, matching familiar objects, or simple word recognition. Materials that are appropriate to a student's age and developmental level are essential in conducting an accurate FVA.

If the purpose of the FVA is to help to determine an appropriate literacy medium for the student—that is, whether it is most appropriate for the student to read and write primarily in print or braille—the teacher of students who are visually impaired will also need to conduct a separate learning media assessment (see Koenig & Holbrook, 1995, for details and procedures). A learning media assessment would involve the comprehensive evaluation of the student's primary and secondary sensory channels for learning; current literacy mode(s), reading rates, and reading comprehension; and a miscue analysis of the student's oral reading (that is, an analysis of the errors the student makes when reading aloud).

Finally, many factors other than an individual's visual ability can affect his or her performance on the visual tasks of a functional visual assessment. Many of these factors are noted in the discussion of the individual areas of the assessment, and Appendix 2.A at the end of this chapter gives an overview of these factors.

Appearance of Eyes and Presence of Corrective Lenses

The general appearance of the student's eyes and the area around the eyes should be noted. Any observed asymmetry such as a difference in the size or position of either eye (whether the eyes are turned in or out), should be documented because the student's ability to read may be affected. Other areas to observe include the clarity of the cornea, sclera, and pupil; evidence of excessively teary or matted eyes; the presence of styes (inflammation on eyelid), ptosis (drooping eyelid), or nystagmus (involuntary eye movements); and any deviation of eye gaze or position. If the student is wearing a conformer (a device that helps keep the shape of the eye) or a prosthesis (false eye), this should also be noted.

A student's eye movements should be observed for important information about the severity and type of visual loss (Jan, Farrell, Wong, & McCormick, 1986). That is, a distinction may be made between children with ocular and cortical visual impairment (see Appendix 2.A). Cortical or cerebral visual impairment (CVI) involves difficulty in interpreting visual information due to damage to the posterior visual pathways or visual cortex. Ocular visual impairment refers to vision loss due to damage to the structures of the eye. Slow roving eye movements that *accompany* short visual attention may be indicative of cortical vision impairment, whereas sensory nystagmus is always indicative of ocular impairment that has occurred during the first year of life. Slow roving eye movements without any periods of fixation may indicate a complete lack of vision in a child who is congenitally visually impaired (Good et al., 1989).

If the student has prescription eyeglasses, they should be reviewed for proper fit. The eyeglasses should fit symmetrically on the student's face and should not pinch the nose or the area around the student's ears. The lenses should also be checked for their clarity—scratched lenses may interfere with the child's ability to read. Furthermore, it should be noted whether the student wears the eyeglasses throughout the day or only for specific near-range or distance tasks. It is important to determine whether the student is able to clean properly, care for, and store the eyeglasses when they are not in use. Eyeglasses, contact lenses, or light absorptive lenses should be worn, as prescribed, throughout the FVA process. If the student does not wear the lenses that he or she has been prescribed during the assessment, the FVA cannot be considered complete.

Visual Reflexes

Visual reflexes are involuntary motor responses of the eye to specific types of sensory input. Certain reflexes are present at birth while others are completely developed during the first six months of life. Visual responses that should be tested in a functional vision assessment include the pupillary response, defensive blink, and doll's eye response or vestibular ocular reflex.

Pupillary Response

Under normal circumstances, the pupil responds to changes in immediate illumination by constricting with increased lighting and dilating with decreased lighting. The presence of a normal pupillary response does not rule out a problem with the visual system because a student with cortical visual impairment may respond with a brisk pupillary response to the presence or removal of light (Allen & Fraser, 1986).

A pupillary response to light is also not synonymous with actual visual awareness, but it does confirm pupillary pathway function (Nelson, Rubin, Wagner, & Breton, 1984). The absence of a pupillary response should be interpreted with caution insofar as certain medications and/or the presence of neurological dysfunction may inhibit this reflex.

A pupillary response may be noted when the student experiences a change in overhead lighting such as when traveling from the outdoors on a bright sunny day into a dimmer indoor setting. Both pupils should respond similarly; that is, if only one eye is stimulated by light, the other should respond as well. Thus, a hand or occluder can be placed over each of the student's eyes to determine whether there is a simultaneous pupillary response in the uncovered eye. This procedure can also be completed with a penlight that is alternated between each eye; as the light rays enter one eye, the teacher looks to see if there is also a constriction in the other eye. It should be noted whether the pupillary response is brisk and equal in both eyes, or slow and unequal.

If a penlight is used during the FVA process, care should be exercised. Some students may be light sensitive, while others may have an "after image" effect of seeing a light flash even after the light has been removed. The latter phenomena may compromise the next assessment activities because the student may need time to readjust. If it is necessary to use a penlight, this part of the assessment can be completed last. In fact, as a general rule, it is not necessary to shine the penlight directly into the student's eyes. Instead, the teacher of students with low vision can darken the environmental setting to accentuate the effects of shining a penlight beam on the student's forehead.

Defensive Blink

The defensive blink is a learned reflex: A child with normal vision will automatically blink as an object comes close to the child's eyes. By five months, an infant has a defensive blink in response to oncoming objects of various sizes in both the central and peripheral fields (Nelson et al., 1984). The presence of the defensive blink reflex can denote whether a student has gross light or object perception. A defensive blink can be elicited when a visual target is moved rapidly into the student's central visual field toward his or her eyes. Care should be taken to avoid creating a "wind effect" or draft as a result of the rapid approach of the oncoming object. Typically, a teacher of students who are visually impaired will splay his or her own fingers on one hand and move it quickly, without creating a draft, toward the student's eyes. Spontaneous blink responses to objects (such as a door edge, or branch) that appear unexpectedly in the student's field of vision throughout the course of the day should also be noted in the FVA. However, some students (such as students with CVI) may not demonstrate a blink reflex.

Doll's Eye Response

The doll's eye response is also called the vestibular ocular reflex (VOR)—an involuntary association of head and eye movement that is typically fully integrated by three months of age. While the reflex is present, the eyes appear to move in the direction opposite to the vertical or horizontal direction in which the head is turned (Erhardt, 1980). In actuality, the response to the head turning is delayed. That is, the eyes do not yet move as quickly as the head does; nor do they move independently of the head. As the infant matures, eye movements become fully independent of head movement, and the doll's eye reflex disappears. Students who have neurological complications, such as cerebral palsy, may not have full integration of this reflex. It will be important for the teacher to assess whether the student can separate eye movements from head movements. In other words, through observation of the student, the teacher can determine whether or not the student displays the doll's eye response. It is important to note the presence of the doll's eye response, especially for oculomotor tasks such as shift of gaze, tracking, visual tracing, and scanning. For example, reading a list from a closed circuit television and then copying it onto a sheet of paper requires a shift of gaze. If the student displays a doll's eye response, he or she may not be able to perform this task quickly or accurately. Similarly, visual tracking will be difficult for the student because he or she may not be able to read in a fluid, steady manner.

Reception and Perception of Visual Stimuli

Reception and perception of visual stimuli are made up of four levels of visual abilities: light perception, light projection, shadow and form perception, and detection of movement. Whereas *reception* of visual stimuli refers to the physiological potential of the visual system to take in the sensory information, *perception* of visual stimuli refers to the ability to react to the sensory information in a meaningful way. Information about these areas will provide a foundation on which to build the assessment. For example, if the student is able to orient him- or herself in the direction of a light source (light projection), the oculomotor portion of the assessment will have to be completed using a variety of different types of light sources as the testing items. However, if a student is visually aware of objects, it is not necessary to complete the visual responsiveness and perception section of the evaluation. That is, if the student responds visually to objects, there is no need to test the student's reception and perception of light, form, and movement because the student must already possess these skills in order to respond to objects. It can be assumed that the lower level visual skills have been mastered.

Light Perception

The first level of visual responsiveness is the ability to react to the presence of a direct light source. The teacher of students who are visually impaired can test for light perception by darkening a room, allowing the student time to adjust to the darkness, and then turning on a light source and noting any responses made by the student. Some typical responses to turning on a light source may include blinking, a head turn toward the light, squinting, closing the eyes, verbalizations, or prolonged attention with a direct gaze at the light source. These behaviors indicate that the student was able to perceive or notice that a light has been turned on. Most children respond best to a colored light source. Colored penlight caps or filters, cellophane paper, or transparent rubber "monster" pencil caps may be used to as a means to elicit a reaction to colored light with younger students.

Children whose eye reports indicate that they have "light perception only" will probably not be print readers. Instead, formats such as braille or tactile symbol systems may be necessary.

Light Projection

The ability to orient in the direction of a light source is called light projection. Once again, the teacher of students who are visually impaired may introduce a light source in a darkened room, a light source that appears within the student's field of view, and observe his or her behavioral responses. If a student has light projection, he or she will usually turn toward the source of the light. Lights in the natural environment (for example, a lamp or light in a hallway) or a deliberately introduced light source (a flashlight, lightbox, or flashing toy) may be used.

Shadow and Form Perception

The teacher of students who are visually impaired will need to spend some time observing the student to determine whether or not the student is able to perceive shadows and forms. The ability to discern both shadows and the general outline of a form may be demonstrated by the student's finger flicking (moving fingers in front of the eyes), light gazing (staring at lights), or moving an object back and forth in front of a light source (Jose, Smith, & Shane, 1980). The teacher may also pass large objects (for example, a large teddy bear, a large book) in front of the student so the light is blocked by that object. For example, the teacher can walk past the student slowly and make note of his or her response to the change in lighting. If the student has detected the teacher's presence, the student may display behaviors such as stopping what he or she is doing and attending to the teacher or turning his or her head toward the change in lighting. In order to see an outline of an object, the student must be able to discern that an object is blocking the light.

Detection of Motion

The ability to note visual movement involves the use of peripheral receptors in the retina. Suggested testing materials include items hanging from the ceiling or dangling from the assessor's hand, as well as objects with either internal or external movement. For example, a Slinky, balls that vibrate and jiggle on the floor and lava lamps can be used in the assessment. That is, the teacher of students who are visually impaired may purposely move these objects into the student's field of view to assess his or her ability to detect the motion of the object. An eye orientation or head turn in the direction of the moving object may indicate that the student detected the motion of an object. If testing a child's ability to detect motion visually, it is imperative that no sound accompany the movement because it would be difficult to state confidently whether it was the sound of the object or the sight of the moving object that prompted the head movement by the student. Simple observation of a child in class as people move around may yield interesting results.

Muscle Balance

Both eyes should be equally aligned in appearance by three to six months of age (Nelson et al., 1984). That is, both eyes should move in the same way, at the same time, and in the same direction if the eye muscles are balanced.

There are three common functional vision evaluation measures that assess the alignment of the eyes: the Hirshberg test/corneal reflection test, the cover-uncover test, and the cross-cover or alternate cover test. The first two tests address the possible presence of tropias or marked eye turns or deviations (e.g., esotropia, where the eye is continually turned inward). The third measure tests for phorias or a *tendency* for the eyes to deviate (e.g., exophoria, where the eye occasionally turns outward). The primary difference between a tropia and a phoria is that the latter can be controlled during fixation tasks (both eyes can be brought into alignment voluntarily), whereas a tropia cannot. In addition to turning in (*eso-*) and turning out (*exo-*), eyes can be deviated upward (*hyper-*) or downward (*hypo-*). These terms are used with both phorias and tropias. The actual diagnosis of a phoria or a tropia should be made by an eye care specialist.

The Hirshberg or corneal reflection test is used to determine what type of a tropia, if any, is present. To administer this test, the tester holds a light three feet away from the student's eyes. As the student looks at the light, the teacher of students with low vision observes whether the light is symmetrically reflected in each eye. A normal reflection should be located in the center of each cornea (Patterson, 1980). If the reflection is not centered or symmetrical in each eye, the condition may be indicative of a muscle imbalance. If a student has leukokoria (white pupil) or aniridia (total or partial absence of the iris), it may be difficult to see the reflection (Jose et al., 1980).

The cover-uncover test should be conducted with the student's prescriptive lenses on. Administration of this test involves establishing the student's fixation on a visual target (presented in a central position), then covering one eye and noticing (at the same time) whether there is any corrective movement of the uncovered eye. If there is no significant corrective movement when either eye is tested, the results are considered normal.

The cross-cover or alternate cover test may also be used to determine an ocular muscle imbalance. If the student has prescription lenses, they should be worn during this procedure. To administer this test, the assessor holds an object in front of the student. Once the student fixates on the object, the assessor covers one of the student's eyes with an occluder, then quickly passes the occluder across the bridge of the student's nose to cover the other eye, and then back; at the same time, the assessor watches for any obvious corrective eye movement in the newly uncovered eye as it resumes fixation on the object of visual interest.

Eye Preference

Information from the student's eye report may give information about a preference for using one eye over another. A student may have an obvious eye preference if there is a discrepancy of visual acuity between the two eyes (Levack, 1991). This condition, called *anisometropia,* can be determined through medical reports and visual acuity testing. If there is a discrepancy in acuity between both eyes, the student will likely prefer the eye with the better visual acuity. This condition may be demonstrated by the student's body and/or a head tilt position, or by the student's tendency to close one eye or cover an eye during tasks which require visual concentration.

An eye preference can also be assessed by asking the student to cover one eye and by noting which eye is automatically covered. Another strategy is to hand the student an object that requires one-eye viewing, such as a monocular telescope or a kaleidoscope, and observing which eye is used to look through it. Sometimes, a student will resist having a particular eye covered by the assessor because it is the preferred eye. The assessor should note the behavior of the student when an eye is covered. For example, does the nystagmus increase more dramatically in one of the eyes that is uncovered, or does the student move to work around the occluder?

Oculomotor Behaviors

Oculomotor behaviors, or the characteristics of how the eyes move, include the following six skills: fixation, convergence and divergence, tracing, tracking, shift of gaze, and scanning. In addition to factors that are particular to the specific skill, the size, color, contrast, and viewing distance of the visual target all contribute to the student's ability to perform these oculomotor skills. Other factors that may negatively affect oculomotor refinement include postural tone abnormalities that contribute to poor head stability, retention of the doll's eye reflex or other motor-based reflexes such as strabismus, and nystagmus. Retention of the doll's eye reflex is more common with children who have cerebral palsy or some other form of neurological involvement. Strabismus is a common problem for students who have Down syndrome, Fetal Alcohol syndrome, and cerebral palsy, as well as students who were born prematurely.

Fixation

The ability to establish and maintain one's gaze on a visual target is called *fixation.* It is a foundation skill for all oculomotor behaviors. For example, in order to track an object, the student must be able to fixate on it first. By the developmental age of six months, a child should be able to fixate with both eyes on a visual target.

Fixation can be readily observed during daily or school routines. For example, how a student looks at the objects involved in a specific task (e.g., looking at the eraser on the desk) can provide very useful information. Both near-range and distance fixation abilities should be evaluated. Factors to assess when evaluating a student's ability to fixate include the following:

◆ Eye widening or squinting.

◆ Eye, head, and/or body positioning.

◆ Eccentric viewing patterns.

◆ Demonstration of an eye preference.

If a student has a central field loss, *eccentric viewing* may be demonstrated during fixation tasks. The student may not appear to be looking directly at a particular visual target when, in reality, the student who has a blind spot in the center of his or her visual field is using peripheral vision to view the target (Levack, 1991). The child has learned how to look "around" the field loss—an adaptive response that should be acknowledged as a valuable visual skill.

Convergence and Divergence

The ability to maintain fixation on an oncoming object is called *convergence.* *Divergence* refers to holding fixation upon a retreating object. A factor to consider in assessing convergence and divergence is the ability of the eyes to work together (*binocularity*). Younger children may demonstrate better convergence than older children because their lenses are better able to change shape (*accommodative power*) when viewing objects at an extremely close range. As individuals age, they lose the ability to fully accommodate their lens; this condition, known as *presbyopia,* begins to occur at about 40 years of age.

Tracing

Tracing involves visually following a stationary line. It is used to locate and identify objects in the environment such as the shape of a roof as a landmark, the edge of a grass line leading to a driveway, or the line of a pole leading to a street sign. It is also used to follow the lines of a drawing (Smith & O'Donnell, 1992). To evaluate this skill, the teacher of students who are visually impaired may ask the student to visually follow three-dimensional vertical or horizontal lines in order to find an object at the end of the line (for example, follow the edge of a bulletin board to a drinking fountain). Or the teacher may draw a two-dimensional line on paper to note whether the student uses a finger to trace the line while following it visually.

Tracking

Tracking involves visually following a moving target. It is a different oculomotor skill than reading across a line of print. A child develops the ability to track a moving object in the following sequence: horizontal, vertical, circular, and diagonal. One way for the teacher to test whether the student can actively use all six extraocular muscles that are responsible for how the eyes move is to trace the letter *H* in the air. If the student can follow the hand movement of the assessor, all six extraocular muscles are being used.

Tracking skills can also be noted as the student follows moving objects in the environment, such as a person walking down the hall, a ball being thrown in the air, soap bubbles or a balloon moving with the air current, and so on. Full range *ocular motility* (range of eye movement) should also be assessed, as should the ease of crossing midline or the center of one's body.

Variables to consider in assessing tracking skills include the following:

- The student's head and body position.
- Eye teaming ability (the ability to use the eyes together, or binocular vision).
- Speed and movement pattern (direction and range) of the moving object being tracked.
- The quality of eye movements—whether they are fluid rather than segmented—and the presence of any accompanying head movements.
- Overall visual endurance.

Shift of Gaze

The ability of the eyes to release fixation on one target to look at another object is called *shift of gaze.* Shift of gaze can occur with targets at the same or differing viewing distances. An example of the latter is a student reading from the chalkboard and then from the book on his or her desk. It is also an important skill for students who use communication boards (e.g., picture or symbol displays) or those who communicate choices by directing their visual gaze, with or without accompanying head movement, to a picture or an object. The evaluator should be aware of the following characteristics:

- Spacing of the objects used.
- Presence or absence of visual clutter.
- Quality of the gaze release (with or without a blink).
- Presence of accompanying head movement during the gaze shift.

Scanning

Shifting gaze from one object to another in a visual search pattern is called *scanning.* Scanning involves using both head and eye movements to search for and find a target (Smith & Geruschat, 1996). The assessor can observe the student in natural scanning activities such as locating a wall clock, finding a familiar classmate in the classroom, or finding a particular item on a table that holds multiple items. The assessor can note the efficiency of the student's scanning skills. Systematic scanning (e.g., left-to-right, top-to-bottom) can be evaluated deliberately with teacher-made or commercial materials with patterns (Smith & O'Donnell, 1992).

Factors to note in assessing a student's scanning ability include the following:

- ◆ Visual field parameters of the search.

- ◆ Presence or absence of visual clutter.

- ◆ Body and object positioning.

- ◆ Visual coordination.

- ◆ Use of accompanying head movements.

- ◆ Overall visual endurance of the student.

It is important for the assessor to be aware of visual field problems that may be identified through scanning activities. For example, the student may consistently miss an item located in a specific area of the visual field.

Field of Vision

Field of vision is defined as the area an individual can see without shifting gaze or moving the head (Bishop, 1996). A normal field of vision is 160 to 180 degrees from one side to another and 120 degrees from top to bottom. A loss of vision may be noted in the center of an individual's vision (*central field loss*) or in any of the four quadrants defined by the directions *upper, lower, left,* and *right*.

Field testing is a critical aspect of a functional vision assessment insofar as many students with visual impairment have some type of a field loss. Examples of visual field loss and related eye conditions include the following:

- ◆ *Hemianopsia* (loss of half of the visual field in one or both eyes), which may be found with cerebral palsy or stroke-related *hemiparesis* (muscular weakness on one side of the body).

- ◆ Central *scotomas* (a gap or blindspot in the visual field) related to Stargardt's disease (a form of macular degeneration—degeneration of the central retina—that is characterized by rapid loss of central visual acuity; Bishop, 1996).

◆ Ring scotoma—a circular area of visual loss—and peripheral field loss associated with *retinitis pigmentosa* (a hereditary disease of the retina).

◆ Upper field loss associated with a *coloboma* (a congenital cleft or gap in some portion of the eye), corresponding with retinal damage in the six o'clock position of the retina.

◆ Areas of field loss found with certain retinal or neurological disorders.

There are several options for field testing. When possible, *monocular* (one eye only) testing should be completed during visual field testing to ensure accurate results. The most common type of field testing is *confrontation* field testing, in which visual targets are slowly moved into areas of the student's visual field while the student stares directly ahead. It is essential to have two people conduct confrontation field testing—one to present the object from behind the student and one to observe the student's eye movement. Typically, a child's eyes will move or flicker at the moment the object is seen. Some children may verbalize when the object is detected; others may simply move their eyes or head. The assessor should note whether there were any consistent delays or gaps in the student's response to the object in a specific area of his or her visual field. Care should be taken to eliminate any tactile, visual movement, or auditory clues that might reveal the location of the object during confrontation visual field testing. Also, the student must maintain his or her gaze directly ahead—the eyes should not move until the object has been seen.

Factors to consider in confrontation testing include the following:

◆ The precise location of the object in the visual field.

◆ Any irregular eye or head posturing.

◆ The presence of any accompanying head movements.

The teacher of students who are visually impaired may also test a student's visual field by using a technique known as *counting fingers*. The assessor sits directly in front of the student and asks him or her to look at the assessor's face. The teacher then holds up various numbers of fingers in the various quadrants of the visual field and asks the student to count them. The student should not move his or her eyes to do the counting—eyes should remain focused directly on the assessor's face. Sometimes, the assessor may put some kind of visual target on his or her own face so that the student has something other than a nose to look at (for example, a red clown nose, a sticker placed on the tip of the nose, bright red lipstick).

Information about a student's visual field can also be determined by observing his or her functional behavior during the school day. Does the student consistently bump into objects located in certain areas of his or her visual field? Does the student miss objects located on a certain part of the desk or on a deliberately designed visual display that includes scattered items on a table? Does the student read fluently across a full page and then return to the far left margin to begin reading the next line?

If the student has cerebral palsy or other type of physical disability, it is important that the assessor give the student sufficient time to organize an oculomotor response to the assessment objects or tasks (Good et al., 1994). Otherwise, the assessor may have moved the object past the point at which the student first perceived it and farther into the student's visual field by the time the student's eyes or head turn to acknowledge the object. This will confound the testing results. The assessor not only needs to move the object very slowly, but he or she may also need to bring it to a stop at certain points along the path of the visual field test. It is also helpful to note other responses, such as a smile, a body movement, or a stilling of the body. These physical signs may indicate that the student has seen the object, even though the assessor did not detect any significant eye movement.

Color Vision

Approximately one out of every 12 boys and one out of every 200 girls have some type of color vision deficiency (Patterson, 1980). Heredity plays a significant role in color vision problems. It is important to assess color vision because it can directly affect literacy in the school. For example, in the younger grades, many of the activities center around coloring, cutting and pasting, painting, and making crafts. Some classroom teachers use color-coded charts and activities. Reading a map also involves color discrimination. Color is typically used in the classroom to enhance the environment and to supplement many literacy experiences, as in pictures in books, posters, reward stickers, and the like.

A beginning assessment strategy is to note whether the student demonstrates any preferences for or aversion to specific colors. Preferences might be demonstrated by an increase in visual interest, by how long the student is interested, and/or by the distinct selection of an object of a certain color over the same object of a different color. If a preference for one color is discovered, many literacy-related activities can include that color. For example, if the student seems to prefer the color red, book covers, name tags, and games can be modified so that the color red becomes a dominant color on the item.

The first accurate evaluation of a child's ability to demonstrate color discrimination can be done at a developmental age of 29 to 33 months; this is when children become able to match primary colors (Furuno et al., 1984). Sorting colors is a developmental skill that appears around 33 to 36 months (Furuno et al., 1984). (Assessment of color vision in students who are developmentally delayed may need to make use of the beginning strategies.) Around this age, students can be asked to identify or match color samples collected by the teacher. Color card samples can be made from colored pieces of paper—preferably sturdy and of equal size—paint card samples from the local paint store, fabrics, or painted pieces of white cardboard. If the student is unable to verbally identify the color, he or she may be able to point to a color sample that matches it. Or the student may be able to point to the name of the color—for example, to the word *orange* to label the color orange. Older students can also match or rank light, medium, or dark shades of color samples (Sanford & Burnett, 1997). Another quick method of assessing color vision is to color in quarter-size circles of various colors on a single sheet of white paper and have the student point to the colors requested by the teacher.

The Ishihara Color Plates with the embedded colored trails may be performed by an older preschool-age child who can understand how to trace the color trail. An advanced preschooler or kindergarten-age child will be able to identify the color plates with the embedded numbers. Other tests for color vision include the Farnsworth 15D Test or Quantitative Color Vision Test by Lea Hyvärinen; these tools involve colored chips that can be sequenced in order of chromatic similarity (Wilkinson, 1996).

Students who are cortically visually impaired will often respond favorably to certain colors, such as red, yellow, and orange. Students with this diagnosis may also appear to demonstrate an aversion to certain colors. In either case, the teacher of students who are visually impaired will need to consider the student's color preferences when conducting the rest of the assessment. For example, if the student demonstrates fixation to a red drinking cup, a second red drinking cup could be used to probe shift of gaze skills.

Depth Perception

Depth perception requires binocular, or stereoscopic, vision; that is, both eyes must team together to achieve three-dimensional visual fusion. Depth perception will be affected if there is monocular vision or a significant visual discrepancy between the two eyes. For students who can respond to verbal directions with a physical action or a verbal response, there are tests to determine stereoscopic vision. Some of these tests are performed while the student is wearing three-dimensional glasses. The student is asked to touch the part of the picture that is designed to appear three-dimensional or to indicate which item is closer to him or her. If the student is able to correctly indicate the three-dimensional image, stereoscopic vision is considered to be present.

For students who cannot participate in such testing or if these testing materials are not available, there are many functional opportunities that allow an assessor to observe a student's ability to perceive depth. Eye-hand coordination activities that require precision placement can provide an abundance of information about the student's depth perception, unless a physical disability negatively influences fine motor accuracy. A major sign to look for is accuracy in reaching for an object. Any indication of a consistent overreach, underreach, or hand placement to the side of the object may indicate poor depth perception (Jose et al., 1980).

Another informal testing measure of depth perception is to observe the student's ability to visually decode changes in ground surfaces. For example, does the student consistently miss a step up or a step down? Does the student anticipate oncoming surface changes? However, poor contrast sensitivity and poor visual acuity (discussed later) may also interfere with detecting drop-offs. For example, the student may anticipate a drop when there is none because the color of the floor changes.

Figure-Ground Perception

The ability to discern an object from its background is called *figure-ground perception*. Students with a diagnosis of cortical visual impairment in particular may have difficulty focusing on a visual target located on a busy background. This is an important finding, because it will influence how objects are presented to the student and/or how a communication system may be designed.

Figure-ground perception may be assessed by observing whether a student can find an object positioned on a busy background (such as a multicolored bulletin board), locate a particular item in a basket of objects, or ascertain a detail in a book illustration. Visual acuity and contrast sensitivity will also affect figure-ground abilities.

The teacher should be aware of how materials are presented to the student throughout the functional vision assessment insofar as poor figure-ground discrimination may interfere with the completion of other visual tasks. The teacher's attire may also be visually distracting or confusing to the student. For example, if the teacher is wearing a multicolored geometric design shirt, its design may be in unwitting competition with the assessment activities.

Light Sensitivity and Light-Dark Adaptation

It is important to document the student's sensitivity to light as demonstrated by tearing, wincing, or deliberately shielding the eyes. This condition may occur in both indoor and outdoor environments. Therefore, the functional vision assessment needs to take place in environments that have a variety of lighting conditions. In particular, it is important to note the type and amount of lighting that causes sensitivity. For example, some students may show increased sensitivity to overhead fluorescent lighting but not to incandescent task lighting. Students with certain eye conditions such as albinism may have a global sensitivity to light.

Adaptation to both light and dark conditions can be noted as the student experiences natural illumination changes, such as sudden darkening of the classroom during a film presentation, walking from a classroom to a dimly lit hallway, or leaving the school building on a bright sunny day. It is important to pay attention to how much time it takes for the student to adapt to a decrease or increase in lighting. Typically, it is easier to adapt from a dark to light environment than from a light to dark one (Bishop, 1996). Children with Leber's congenital amaurosis (a degenerative condition of the retina) or other retinal disorders typically display delayed light–dark adaptation.

Light–dark adaptation tests with colored chips (e.g., Precision Vision Cone Adaptation Test) can be used for students who have a diagnosis such as retinitis pigmentosa, in which rod function gradually decreases. The test measures the ability to visually discern specific colors in a dimly lit setting. If such a tool is used, it will be important to budget 30 or more minutes for the procedure in order to allow for enough time for the eyes to adjust to the dark room needed for the test. It is generally best for this type of testing to occur within a clinical setting, where the environment can be controlled optimally and where the results can be interpreted with a high level of expertise. Students with light–dark adaptation difficulties should be referred to an eye care specialist for further testing.

Contrast Sensitivity

The ability to see differences in the brightness of symbols or in objects against their background is called *contrast sensitivity.* Poor contrast sensitivity can cause difficulty for the student who is trying to distinguish details in visual displays (Morgan, 1992). This difficulty may influence the ability to recognize faces; to decode pictures, letters, or words; or to locate one item in a group. For students who ultimately will use a picture or communication board or who will read regular or enlarged print, contrast sensitivity is an important optical consideration. In some situations, absorptive lenses, colored filters, and/or changes in illumination will help a student who has reduced contrast sensitivity to identify a picture, icon symbol, or printed letter (Morgan, 1992). Photocopying material on paper other than white may also increase the contrast for a student with low vision.

While there are commercially available contrast sensitivity tests for children (see the Resources section), this is an area in which the assessor should work in close tandem with the low vision specialist (see Chapter 3). The teacher of students with low vision may be in a better position to follow up on the results (for example, by experimenting with color filters or background contrast) than to do the actual assessment.

Visual Acuity

Visual acuity refers to "the measurement of the sharpness of vision as it relates to the ability to discriminate detail" (Levack, 1991, p. 30). A clinical measurement of visual acuity (see Chapter 1) provides only one piece of information about a student's vision. These numbers, at best, offer a global assessment that provides some expectation of what the child may or may not be able to see. For example, it can be noted that 20/200 denotes legal blindness and probably translates to reduced distance vision. It does not, however, provide true functional information as to what a child with that visual acuity can see. In fact, two students with the same visual acuity may demonstrate very different visual functioning. Such differences may be due, in part, to differences in contrast sensitivity, in the ability to use cognitive clues to decode compromised visual information, and in personal familiarity with a visual situation.

Preferred Viewing Distance

The assessor should note the distance that the student prefers for near and distance viewing during everyday activities and during tasks that are unfamiliar to the student (Erin & Paul, 1996). These observations lend themselves to a better understanding of the student's preferred viewing distance or *comfort* visual acuity.

Too often, eye care specialists and even teachers of students with low vision work hard to help the student achieve the best possible visual acuity on a near or distance acuity chart. The student may be able to read a symbol or row of symbols on an acuity measurement card or chart—but only with great effort. Comfort visual acuity is more important than *blur* acuity, which refers to the best acuity measurement under conditions of visual strain. Achieving a "best acuity" in an eye care specialist's office that is higher than the student's acuity in practice may actually work against the student by rendering him or her ineligible for the services of a teacher certified in the area of visual impairment. Achieving a 20/60 acuity measurement is not a great accomplishment if it eliminates needed services. It also gives the student the message that eyestrain is an appropriate goal. It is better for the student to experience a comfortable viewing distance.

Near and distance visual acuities are determined through a standardized testing process by the medical practitioner. However, informal observation methods can be used to estimate visual acuity. Both processes will be briefly reviewed.

Formal Testing Methods
Near and Distance Acuity Cards or Charts

Tools to measure near and distance visual acuity include picture and symbol optotype tests such as the Snellen chart (see Chapter 1), the Lighthouse Distance Visual Acuity Chart, or Lea Symbols cards or charts (see the Resources section). These tests measure visual recognition acuity, insofar as the student must apply meaning to the image (by giving it a verbal label or making it a visual match). As such, these tests require some level of verbal or voluntary motor participation by the student.

Snellen-type acuity charts are based on high-contrast optotypes. An optotype is a letter, number, or symbol that is used in standardized tests of vision. This mode of testing is not representative of the real world (Mannis, 1987). As already noted, in the wide variety of illumination and contrast circumstances of the everyday world, a student's ability to achieve quality visual resolution may differ considerably from one situation to another.

The Lighthouse Pediatric Visual Acuity cards, for example, have three pictures: an apple, an umbrella, and a house. Children may call one or more of these pictures by a different name. Children in native villages in northeast Alaska, for example, often do not have personal experience with an umbrella. For these children, a name of a flower could be substituted if this was an item familiar to the child. Or a specific familiarity lesson with an umbrella could be offered to the child prior to the assessment. The important factor is consistency in the identification of the symbol. As long as the word *flower* is always used for the umbrella, the teacher has confirmation that the child knew which picture was being presented.

The Lea Symbols cards have four symbols: house, circle, square, and apple. These symbols may be easier for young children to identify, and each is relatively consistent in shape and size from one symbol to another. For students who are nonverbal or who have inconsistencies in their language, a matching exercise can be arranged. Copies of the picture choices can be placed in front of the child on a wheelchair tray or table. When one of the acuity symbol cards is presented at the previously determined testing distance, the student has the opportunity to touch the nearby matching picture. Patience is the key when working with the student who requires time to organize a voluntary body or eye-pointing movement. In order to base the test on the motor capabilities of the student, it may also be wise to consult with a motor therapist prior to the test to determine the best physical layout of the choice cards. Acuity measurements can also be recorded in more functional terms, such as "the student was able to identify one-quarter-inch letters on the Snellen chart from a distance of five feet under the fluorescent lighting of the classroom."

Once single-letter or single-word near acuity has been tested and the student's working distance has been determined, Wilkinson (1996) recommended that students be assessed using a continuous-text card. Continuous-text cards have sentences of three or more words on them. The size of the letters in the sentences are gradually reduced and correspond to Snellen-equivalent sizes.

Forced Preferential-Looking Tests

A forced preferential-looking (FPL) instrument involves a series of card targets that have two visual displays. One of the displays in each card is plain, and one has a striped pattern. The stripes gradually become smaller and smaller, making it more difficult to visually distinguish the plain card from the striped card. The premise is that the child's eyes will involuntarily shift to the more visually complex target. When the visual system can no longer decipher the difference between the two cards, the test is completed. It is important to realize, however, that the preferential-looking tests do not measure whether the child gives meaning to the visual target. They only measure the ability to visually respond to a variety of graded visual targets.

FPL tests provide a means to measure the visual acuity of students who are unable to participate in testing that requires verbal identification or matching pictures, letters, or symbols. FPL tests are typically used with infants or toddlers and with children who are nonverbal and/or multidisabled and who have a developmental level below two years of age (Levack, 1991). One caution, however, is that the test requires a directed eye gaze movement. Consequently, FPL tests may underestimate the visual acuity of students who have visual impairment and cerebral palsy because of their oculomotor difficulties (Good et al., 1994). In addition, the black-and-white pattern of the test may not be visually motivating for some children with cortical visual impairment (Roman, personal communication, 1999). Proper training is required before administering FPL tests to students.

Informal Observation Methods

Functional Acuity Estimate

A functional estimate of a student's visual acuity can be determined in a number of ways. For example, by observing the smallest objects (for example, cereal pieces, cake decoration pellets, dried rice) that a student visually locates from a specified viewing distance, the teacher of students who are visually impaired can make a statement such as, "Billy is able to see half-inch pink cereal pieces on a white background at a distance of 25 inches." For students who display an interest in faces or objects in the environment, such objects or faces may allow more relevant attempts at acuity measurements for many students, including those with cortical visual impairment (Good et al., 1994).

Smith and Geruschat (1996) recommend the practice of determining *awareness* and *identification* visual acuities. These strategies give information about the distances at which a student first becomes aware of an object and can identify the object. For example, a student may first see something on the chalkboard at 20 feet and then identify it as a "list of spelling words" from 6 feet. Information on the object's size, on the viewing distance of the object from the student's eyes, and on the lighting conditions provides a functional perspective on what the student sees. Such information can be used for practical programmatic purposes (Jose, Smith, & Shane, 1980), as it encourages teachers to "visually package" their lessons in a manner suitable for the student's visual abilities.

Current Print Functioning

A teacher-made notebook of reading materials, classroom items (for example, texts, reference books, handouts, rulers, and maps), and environmental print can be used to determine the student's print-functioning skills—that is, the ability to read print. The assessor should incorporate into the assessment a variety of materials that exist in the student's everyday world, such as a locker combination, signs in the hallway announcing pep rallies, numbers in the phone book, food labels in the pantry, and so on. The assessor should document the size of the print, the viewing distance used by the student while reading the print, whether the material is held on a slant, and whether the student moves the print back and forth in front of his or her eyes or uses eye or head movements to read. If the student uses a low vision device such as a stand magnifier or a closed-circuit television (CCTV) for reading, it should be used during the reading tasks. Notes should be made about the student's reading performance with and without the device or devices.

Reading Rate and Comprehension

A complete literacy media assessment (Koenig & Holbrook, 1995) will involve a comprehensive assessment of reading rate and comprehension. However, a baseline check of these skills should be made during the functional vision assessment process. The student's classroom materials and the teacher-made notebook, which will contain a variety of reading materials of different types and sizes, can be used to determine how many words are read aloud and silently during a given period of time. Information should be recorded about the font size of the print, the grade level of the material, the types of reading errors the student makes, and any words that are omitted while reading aloud. Once the student is finished with the selected passages, his or her comprehension of the material should be checked. If the student has a prescribed magnification device, it should be used during the reading evaluation.

Visual Motor Coordination

Visual motor coordination is made up of two areas: *visual fine motor skills* and *visual gross motor skills*. Visual fine motor skills involve coordination of the hands with the eye (e.g., reaching for a visual target) while visual gross motor skills involve moving one's body in relation to a visual target (e.g., kicking a visual target). Factors that may affect the assessment of visual motor skills include the following:

◆ Background contrast.

◆ The presence or absence of visual clutter.

◆ Body position or support.

◆ The position of objects used in the task.

◆ The accuracy of reach or kick.

◆ The tendency to look at or away from the object that is about to be contacted.

◆ The influence of a physical disability.

Students who have both sensory and physical disabilities may demonstrate poor fine and gross motor accuracy. The challenge for the team is to sort out what influence the motor disability has upon these skills from the influence of the visual disability. Focusing on a reduction of the physical complexity of the task and the possible use of assistive technology will help with deciphering this information.

Visual Fine Motor Coordination

The skills of visually directed reaching, stacking, opening, closing, and inserting and removing objects are included in the visual fine motor category. The teacher can observe the student performing everyday activities that involve fine motor coordination, such as inserting coins in a vending machine, turning a combination lock, and picking up a thin object such as a pencil. Visual fine motor activities specifically related to literacy include coloring within lines, drawing shapes, cutting out shapes, tracing shapes/letters/numbers, copying letters and numbers from a model, and printing or writing letters and numbers (Sanford & Burnett, 1997).

Handwriting skills should also be assessed with students who are in academic programs. One or more handwriting samples should be taken. It is helpful to note the legibility of the student's handwriting, whether the student can read his or her own handwriting, and the working distance the student generally maintains when writing. It will be beneficial to have a variety of writing instruments and types of lined paper to determine whether the student has a preference for or demonstrates improved legibility with a particular paper and writing tool combination. A variety of black-lined writing papers may be purchased at local office supply stores and/or specialty catalogs. In some cases, books and pads of black-lined paper with increased space between lines can be created and mass produced by the school district's printing facilities.

Visual Gross Motor Coordination

Examples of visual gross motor skills include visual navigation during travel routes, kicking a ball, and negotiating steps. This is an area that may be completed in conjunction with the O&M specialist and/or the adaptive physical education teacher.

Visual-Cognitive Skills

Visual-cognitive skills are made up of three general areas: visual imitation of movement; identification, matching, sorting, and classification of objects and pictures; and visual sequencing. Tasks may be set up differently for students of varying functional vision abilities and age groups. The academic learner, for example, may engage in matching words of different sizes and placing complex pictures into their proper sequence, while the nonacademic learner may match an object to a picture or discriminate his or her name tag from a group of name tags on the tabletop. Tasks that require movement by the student (for example, pointing to a picture, or copying a shape or word from the chalkboard) should be adjusted to meet the needs of students with physical disabilities. That is, if the student is unable to hold a pencil and is asked to draw the exact shape drawn by the assessor, the task should be altered so that the student is able to indicate, from a predrawn array of similar shapes, the one that matches the assessment item.

Visual Imitation of Movement

The assessor can model different movement behaviors for the student at various distances. Notes should be made on what kinds of movements the student can decipher from various distances and on whether they can be replicated. For example, can the student imitate the gross motor movements of a gym teacher during a period devoted to floor exercises? Can the student follow the actions involved in daily living tasks? For younger children, the game "Simon Says" is a fun way to test vision imitation and movement.

Identification, Matching, Sorting, and Classification of Objects and Pictures

Visual identification of people, common objects, pictures, and words may be demonstrated by a student in many ways. For example, when responding to a question printed on the chalkboard (a task that is designed to assess a student's ability to read print in the distance), the student may respond to it verbally, by using sign language, by pointing to pictures on a picture symbol board, by using tactile symbols to label an object, or by writing a response on a separate piece of paper.

Matching occurs when a student is given a model of what objects go together and can repeat the "match" using other visual stimuli. Matching is initially completed with pairs of familiar objects. More complex matching activities—such as putting an actual object and its corresponding picture together (for example, a comb with a picture of the comb), matching an item with its counterpart (for example, putting a tube of toothpaste with a toothbrush), or matching a word and its corresponding picture (for example, the word *hamburger* with a picture of a hamburger)—can be used to assess a student's ability to match. Care must be taken to avoid assuming that a child's errors are the result of his or her visual impairment. Rather, it may be that the *type* of matching activity was inappropriate for that particular student because he or she is not old enough, does not have the cognitive ability to complete the task, or lacks the cultural reference to make the task meaningful.

Finding pairs or groups of similar objects, pictures, or words without a model is an example of sorting. During the functional vision assessment, students may be asked first to find all of the pictures of cows (pictures that have been scattered randomly on a table surface) and then to place them in a box. Then the assessor may ask the student to locate all of the chickens and place them in a different box, and so on. The same type of sorting task can be accomplished using real objects, line drawings, and words.

Placing items into groups according to a particular function (for example, used for eating, used for grooming) is an example of *classification*. Again, assessment activities can include classifying objects, line drawings, pictures, and words. In some cases, younger children who do not have established literacy skills may need to pick up each word card, bring it close to their face, read it letter-by-letter, put the word together as a whole, and then determine into which category it fits.

Visual Sequencing

Visual patterns produced by stringing beads together or by arranging pictures so that they create a story are examples of activities students might engage in during a functional vision assessment. The assessor may string together a series of beads of different shapes, colors, and sizes and then ask the student to reproduce the pattern. Or the teacher may ask the student to copy a series of upper- and lowercase letters (or words) on a piece of paper. Some of the things that should be considered when assessing visual sequencing skills are:

◆ The familiarity of the objects and tasks used.

◆ The novelty of the tasks and testing items, and the overall complexity of the tasks.

◆ The student's developmental level.

◆ The amount, type, and positioning of the lighting.

Visual Perception Skills

Visual perception skills include the following:

◆ Visual closure abilities.

◆ Part–whole relationships.

◆ Pattern recognition.

◆ Figure-ground discrimination.

◆ Spatial orientation.

Visual closure involves the ability to "identify and recognize objects or symbols with incomplete representation" (Hritcko, 1983, p. 123). There are several excellent tests of visual perception, including instruments that do not require a motor response (see the Resources section). Testing of visual perception skills is also the domain of an occupational therapist and classroom teacher. It may be helpful to work as a team on this aspect of assessment.

ENVIRONMENTAL ANALYSIS AND CONSIDERATIONS

Because both the features of the environment as well as the student's own visual abilities play a role in a student's visual performance, the teacher of students with low vision needs to be alert to what environmental conditions seem to assist in or interfere with the student's functional vision skills. One of the best ways to analyze the student's environment is to view the setting under a simulated visual loss. A simulator that mirrors the student's visual impairment as much as possible (see the Resources) can provide valuable insight into what environmental features may be helpful or distracting to the student. It is also important to analyze the environment with regard to the tasks that are completed within that setting (Smith and Geruschat, 1996).

Commercial forms, such as the Environmental Layout Checklist from *The South Carolina Functional Vision Assessment* (South Carolina Department of Education, 1992) can be used to outline the design and content of the setting. If the forms are not used, the assessor can draw a map of the target setting. Once the layout and contents of the room have been identified, the primary areas to be evaluated include lighting, glare, color and contrast cues, the amount of visual clutter, and ambient noise (Smith & Geruschat, 1996). Each area will be reviewed briefly.

Lighting

The type, amount, and position of lighting all contribute to the ease or difficulty of a visual task. These features should be noted throughout the functional vision assessment activities. The teacher of students with low vision should record lighting preferences. Does the student prefer incandescent task lighting compared to fluorescent lighting? Does the student's pace slow down or accelerate when walking through a hallway that suddenly becomes more dim or illuminated? Do any changes in the classroom environment over the course of the day, such as morning or afternoon sunlight, make a difference in the student's visual skills? Is lighting equally distributed throughout the setting? Is it possible to regulate the light—for example, using a rheostat or window blinds—or introduce task lighting?

Glare

Glare is one of the most common complaints of individuals with low vision. Glare is caused by the angle of lighting on reflective surfaces. It can also be produced by light scattering in the eye in conditions such as cataracts. Thus, it can be created by both external and internal factors. There are different types of glare. *Discomfort* glare "is light that because of its intensity, misdirection, or exposure time causes discomfort or fatigue" (Brilliant, 1999, p. 272). This type of glare does not usually interfere with visual performance; however, some students may find that it does make some tasks more difficult. *Disability* glare typically does interfere with visual performance. Disability glare reduces visual functioning due to a blinding or dazzling effect of light rays. While it is not critical to distinguish the type of glare in all situations, it is important to understand when a student is unable to complete a task due to impossible conditions of glare.

Classroom environments should be analyzed for glare during the times of day that the student is in that particular room. Sources of glare should be noted. For example, does the classroom have a chalkboard or a white marker board? Is there a gloss finish to the desks or lab tables? If there are computers or a CCTV in the room, are the monitors free of glare? Shiny surfaces are more reflective than matte finish surfaces. Is it possible to cover shiny surfaces? Does supplemental task lighting or colored acetate filters over a book text or paperwork help to reduce glare problems? If glare is a chronic problem and if the student has not been referred for a light absorptive lens evaluation, the teacher of students who are visually impaired should consider referring the student to a low vision clinic for evaluation (see Chapter 3).

Color and Contrast

If the teacher uses a white marker board, can the student see all of the marker colors on the board? Is there adequate contrast between the chalk and the chalkboard? Is there good contrast between the classroom furniture and the floor color that will allow the student to navigate around objects more easily?

Visual Clutter

"In general, the more complex the environment, the lower the proficiency of functional vision" (Smith & Geruschat, 1996, p. 311). This often describes the typical classroom environment. Visual clutter may dramatically influence some students' ability to visually decipher classroom activities and/or materials. Students with cortical visual impairment may be especially sensitive to extraneous visual information. If the student is affected by visual clutter, is it possible to ensure that the student's workspace is free of unnecessary materials?

Ambient Noise

The noise level of the environment may be disruptive to a student who is visually impaired. Some students may need a quiet environment for visual concentration. The background noise level of the setting should be recorded. If a student is also hard of hearing, it will be important to complete a full acoustic analysis of the environment. If the student uses an assistive listening device, is it in good working order each and every day? An audiologist or teacher certified to work with students who are deaf or hard of hearing can assist with ensuring an optimal listening environment for the student.

WRITING THE FVA REPORT

A sample of a completed report of a functional vision assessment appears in Appendix 2.B at the end of this chapter.

An FVA report should be concise, informative, and factual. It is a tool for parents, teachers, and eye care specialists to learn about the everyday visual performance needs of a student. If it is too lengthy, the reader may lose interest. On the other hand, it should not be so short as to make it impossible for the reader to glean a perspective of the student's functional vision. Observations should be written in a format that truly informs the reader about the student's functional vision. For example, it does not help the reader to know that the student has poor figure-ground perception. Rather, a behavioral example of poor figure-ground perception should be offered, with a specific recommendation of how to assist the student.

While a report should be factual, it should also be personalized to the student. The opening paragraph sets the tone of the report. Rather than inundating the reader with the medical history of the student in the first paragraph, it is important to set the stage by giving some indication of the person whose information will be reviewed. A narrative might begin with a brief biographical sketch about the student that includes personal hobbies, interests, and highlights. For example, it might say, "Sara is an active high school senior. In addition to maintaining a 3.6 grade point average, she is active in the Latin Society, and she works on the high school yearbook." The narrative can then address the student's visual impairment.

The narrative should note the purpose of the FVA—for example, whether it was to help determine the student's primary literacy media or to identify possible classroom adaptations that would ensure optimal access to the regular education curriculum. Stating the purpose of the FVA also alerts the reader to what areas will not be covered, such as travel skills in an outdoor environment.

The report should credit the persons who were interviewed during the FVA. The writer should refrain from calling parents "mom" or "dad" in a report. A parent's name (e.g., "Wanda" or "Mrs. Benolken") should be used, thus adopting the same format that is used for naming other professionals in the report.

The report should have the date(s) of the assessment and the completion of the report. It should be professionally written and formatted. Subtitles will help the reader organize the information. Information highlighted by bullets may be easier to read and decipher.

If recommendations directly follow student-specific observations, the reader is more likely to understand why an adaptation is suggested. A helpful tool designed by Sanford and Burnett (1997) offers a menu of recommendations that correspond to a particular visual behavior.

Inferences should not be made about the student's visual potential. The report should consist of actual observations. Details about the lighting conditions, the size of objects, viewing distances, and other pertinent environmental information should be reported. Observations can be written in the past tense to indicate that the behavior was observed during a particular assessment period.

Observations should be documented in a positive framework. Report what a student can do, not what the student cannot do. If a negative phrase is essential to the report, include a positive statement first. For example, the report might say, "Elsa was able to copy a sentence from her textbook, but she had difficulty copying a line of text from a photocopied sheet." If a student completed a task using another sense besides vision, this technique should be framed as an important strategy. The writer should take care to avoid any reference that might lead the reader to think that there is a sensory hierarchy (e.g., the student "had to" complete the task using tactile cues).

Reported medical information should be pertinent to the current situation of the student. If medical terminology is used, it is important to provide brief definitions of words that may not be readily understood. This is also true of educational vocabulary. As a general rule, professional jargon should be kept to a minimum. Also, acronyms should be spelled out the first time they appear in the report, followed by the acronym in parentheses [e.g., American Foundation for the Blind (AFB)]. A test of a good report is that it can be read by people who do not have specific training in visual impairment.

SUMMARY

Completing a functional vision assessment is an important task of a teacher of students who are visually impaired. The information collected through medical reports, personal interviews, student observation, and formalized assessment procedures will help to build a perspective of a student's functional vision.

It will be important for the assessor to understand a student's medical diagnosis, what factors might influence a student's visual performance, and what assessment components are pertinent to each individual child. Over time, the assessor will develop a personal repertoire of preferred instruments and activities that he or she can use to observe and assess a student.

A functional vision assessment involves a combination of science and art. The science involves the technical aspects of an assessment process: what behaviors are being assessed, what tool(s) to use, the sequence of visual development, the practical implications of specific eye conditions, and so on. The art emerges in the keen observation of a student's visual skills and in the engineering of an environment that results in optimal visual performance. The assessor's interwoven roles of scientist and artist become refined with practice and experience.

REFERENCES

Anthony, T. (1993a). Functional vision assessment for children who are young and/or multi-disabled. In Linda B. Stainton & Eugene C. Lechelt (Eds.), *Proceedings of the eighth international conference on blind and visually impaired children* (pp. 73–94). Edmonton, Alberta: Canadian National Institute for the Blind.

Anthony, T. (1993b). Program development for young children with visual and physical disabilities. In Linda B. Stainton & Eugene C. Lechelt (Eds.), *Proceedings of the eighth international conference on blind and visually impaired children* (pp. 335–350). Edmonton, Alberta: Canadian National Institute for the Blind.

Bishop, V. E., (1988). Making choices in functional vision evaluations: "Noodles, needles, and haystacks." *Journal of Visual Impairment & Blindness, 82,* 94–99.

Bishop, V. E. (1996). Causes and functional implications of visual impairment. In A. L. Corn and A. J. Koenig (Eds.), *Foundations of low vision: Clinical and functional perspectives* (pp. 86–114). New York: AFB Press.

Black, P. D. (1980). Ocular defects in children with cerebral palsy. *British Medical Journal, 281,* 487–488.

Brilliant, R. L. (1999). *Essentials of low vision practice.* Boston, MA: Butterworth Heinemann.

Erhardt, R. (1980). *Developmental visual dysfunction: Models for assessment and management.* Tucson, AZ: Communication Skill Builders.

Erin, J. N., & Paul, B. (1996). Functional vision assessment and instruction of children and youth in academic programs. In A. L. Corn and A. J. Koenig (Eds.), *Foundations of low vision: Clinical and functional perspectives* (pp. 185–220). New York: FB Press.

Farrenkopf, C., McGregor, R. D., Nes, S. L., & Koenig, A. J. (1997). Increasing a functional skill for an adolescent who has cortical visual impairment. *Journal of Visual Impairment and Blindness, 91,* 484–493.

Fieber, N., & Robinson, C. (1974). *Some relations of oculomotor coordination to postural control and interventions in cerebral palsied and multihandicapped children.* Paper presented at the annual meeting of the American Academy of Cerebral Palsy, Denver, CO.

Furuno, S., O'Reilly, K., Hosaka, C., Inatsuka, T., Zeisloft-Flbey, B., & Allman, T. (1984). *HELP checklist—ages birth to three years.* Palo Alto, CA: VORT Corporation.

Good, W. V., Jan, J. E., DeSa, L., Barkovich, A. J., Groenveld, M., & Hoyt, C. S. (1994). Cortical visual impairment in children. *Survey of Ophthalmology, 38*(4), 351–364.

Hritcko, T. (1983). Assessment of children with low vision. In Randall T. Jose (Ed.), *Understanding low vision* (105–137). New York: American Foundation for the Blind.

Jan, J. E., Farrell, K., Wong, P. K. H., & McCormick, A. Q. (1986). Eye and head movement of visually impaired children. *Developmental Medicine and Child Neurology, 28,* 285–293.

Jan, J. E., & Groenveld, M. (1993). Visual behaviors and adaptations associated with cortical and ocular impairment in children. *Journal of Visual Impairment & Blindness, 87,* 101–105.

Jose, R. T., Smith, A. J., & Shane, K. G. (1980). Evaluation and stimulating vision in the multiply impaired. *Journal of Visual Impairment & Blindness, 74,* 2–8.

Koenig, A. J., & Holbrook, M. C. (1995). *Learning media assessment of students with visual impairments* (2nd ed.). Austin, TX: Texas School for the Blind and Visually Impaired.

Levack, N. (1991). *Low vision: A resource guide with adaptations for students with visual impairments.* Austin, TX: Texas School for the Blind and Visually Impaired.

Mannis, M. (1987). Making sense of contrast sensitivity. *Archives of Ophthalmology, 105,* 627–629.

Morgan, E. (Ed.). (1992). *The INSITE model: Resources for family centered intervention of infants, toddlers, and preschoolers who are visually impaired.* Logan, UT: SKI*HI Institute.

Nelson, L., Rubin, S., Wagner, R., & Breton, M. (1984). Developmental aspects in the assessment of visual function in young children. *Pediatrics, 73*(3), 375–381.

Patterson, J. H. (1980). *Visual screening techniques: A practical guide for the determination of the visual status of children.* Anchorage, AK.

Physician's Desk Reference for nonprescription drugs and dietary supplements. (1999). 5th Ed. Revised. Montvale, NJ: Medical Economics Data Production Company.

Roman, C. (1999). Personal communication.

Sanford, L., & Burnett, R. (1997). *Functional vision and media assessment for students who are pre-academic or academic and visually impaired in grades K-12* (3rd ed.), Hermitage, TN: Consultants for the Visually Impaired.

Smith, A. J., & Geruschat, D. R. (1996). Orientation and mobility for children and adults with low vision. In A. L. Corn & A. J. Koenig (Eds.), *Foundations of low vision: Clinical and functional perspectives* (pp. 306–321). New York: AFB Press.

Smith, A. J., & O'Donnell, L. M. (1992). *Beyond arm's reach: Enhancing distance vision.* Philadelphia, PA: Pennsylvania College of Optometry Press.

South Carolina Department of Education. (1992). *The South Carolina functional vision assessment.* Columbia, SC: South Carolina Department of Education.

Taft, L. (1984). Cerebral palsy. *Pediatrics in Review, 6*(2), 35–45.

Wilkinson, M. E. (1996). Clinical low vision services. In A. L. Corn and A. J. Koenig (Eds.), *Foundations of low vision: Clinical and functional perspectives* (pp. 143–175). New York: AFB Press.

Yates, C. (1989). *Positioning and handling. ADAPT-A-STRATEGY booklet series for parents and teachers of infants/young children with multiple disabilities.* Hattiesburg: University of Southern Mississippi.

Factors That Can Influence Visual Performance

BY TANNI L. ANTHONY

When the teacher of students who are visually impaired conducts a functional vision assessment on a student, the factors that can affect the student's visual performance include, but are not limited to, the student's visual condition. Among the other factors the teacher needs to be aware of are other physical and emotional conditions that the student may have as well as conditions in the surrounding environment at the time the student is observed.

PHYSICAL FACTORS

Visual Diagnosis

Simply knowing about the student's eye condition can help the teacher of students who are visually impaired anticipate some of the student's needs that may arise during the functional vision assessment. The vast majority of visual diagnoses have lighting implications. For example, a student with retinitis pigmentosa (RP) may demonstrate great variability in visual skills depending on the amount of environmental illumination. Individuals with RP have poor rod (peripheral photoreceptors in the retina that function in dim lighting) function and cannot accommodate quickly to sudden changes in lighting, such as walking under the shade of a tree from a sunny area or entering a sunlit hallway after being in a dim room. Other examples of expected functional vision implications of eye conditions include loss of color vision for the student who has achromatopsia (color blindness) or central field loss associated with Stargardt's disease. The latter condition is a form of macular degeneration that is characterized by rapid central visual acuity loss (Bishop, 1996). Students with cortical/cerebral visual impairment (CVI) present yet another example because they may exhibit dramatic changes in visual performance from situation to situation.

Students who have CVI typically have difficulty with environments that have too much visual information (visual clutter) (Jan & Groenveld, 1993). Simplicity of the visual task or environment, color consistency, and the use of familiar, motivating, functional objects or tasks can result in improved visual functioning by students with CVI (Farrenkopf, McGregor, Nes, & Koenig, 1997).

Other Medical Diagnoses

Other medical diagnoses can also affect visual performance. For example, if a student has an uncontrolled seizure disorder, the ability to achieve and sustain visual attention may be compromised significantly. Certain anticonvulsant medications may further contribute to poor visual functioning. Phenobarbital has a possible side effect of blurred vision, in addition to physical fatigue (Physician's Desk Reference, 1999). Another common anticonvulsant, Tegretol, has possible side effects such as visual hallucinations, diplopia (double vision), poor oculomotor (eye movement) function, and reduced distance vision. Anticonvulsant or other medications that need to be taken on a daily basis should be monitored closely because they may contribute to the development of glaucoma, cataracts, or other health-related complications. Finally, it is beneficial to monitor whether a medication may lead to dizziness, poor balance, or reduced auditory responsiveness.

In general, students who have multiple disabilities have a high incidence of associated visual challenges. Either cerebral palsy or reduced postural tone can also influence visual functioning. It has been estimated that 40 to 75 percent of individuals with cerebral palsy have some form of visual impairment (Black, 1980). Visual problems may include a high incidence of refractive error (e.g., nearsightedness, farsightedness), strabismus (eye muscle imbalance), and visual field loss. Oculomotor difficulties are also common in children who have cerebral palsy (Fieber & Robinson, 1974); and a significant percentage of individuals with hemiparesis (a type of cerebral palsy that affects either the right or left side of a person's body) have *hemianopsia* (Taft, 1984), a field loss in either half of an individual's visual field.

If a student has poor postural stability due to cerebral palsy or to other conditions that result in reduced postural tone, it may be difficult to demonstrate periods of sustained visual concentration (Levack, 1991; Anthony, 1993b). Students who have significant postural tone or orthopedic challenges require careful assessment procedures, insofar as many will ultimately use a visual means of communication such as an object or picture board. If visual challenges are not identified, a student's capacity to use and benefit from a communication system may be compromised greatly. For example, a student who has a field loss and limited head movements may be unable to visually access the entire display of a communication board.

Assessment strategies should include attention to the position of the student and the presented visual targets, waiting for the student to organize a motor response (commonly referred to as "wait time"), providing accessible materials within the student's reach and visual field, and establishing several assessment opportunities to get a complete picture of the student's capabilities.

Positioning

Because of the importance of posture and stability, attention to the student's physical positioning may help to increase visual performance during the functional vision assessment. Anytime the student is in an unstable position, he or she may feel insecure and be unable to concentrate on the task. Simply put, the first priority should always be postural security. It may be too challenging for a child with a physical disability to hold him- or herself upright and demonstrate a visual response. Imagine yourself trying to read a book while maintaining your balance on both tiptoes at the edge of a cliff! Although you may be able to read for awhile, it is unlikely that you would understand much of what you read because of the physical stress of maintaining your balance.

According to Yates (1989), there are four general guidelines for positioning a student who has multiple disabilities:

- The student should be visually symmetrical and should not be leaning off-center.
- The student should have positioning support for the bony parts of the body for physical comfort.
- The student should have support where it is necessary, but not at the expense of voluntary freedom of movement.
- The student should be positioned in a way that does not reinforce an abnormal muscle pattern.

Even if a student does not have a physical disability, attention to positioning is important during tasks which involve sustained visual attention. An important component of the functional vision assessment is to determine whether the student would benefit from a reading stand (thereby reducing stress on the neck and shoulder muscles) or a lowered or elevated desk seat so that the student's feet can be flat on the floor with a neutral hip position (to avoid the need to slouch). Consequently, it is important to consult with an occupational or physical therapist and the individual student to determine individual ergonomic needs and preferences.

Stress and Illness

If a student is experiencing anxiety or is not feeling well, visual performance may be altered. Stress and illness may cause a student to be distracted from the task at hand. For example, if a student is preoccupied with peer pressure, problems at home, academic challenges, and so on, it may be impossible for him or her to perform at his or her best. Some students experience stress about being pulled out of their regular classrooms for special programming. Missing out on what the rest of the class is doing may be difficult, especially for young students because they enjoy playing with their peers. Stress may also contribute to poor sleeping habits, which may further complicate the ability to concentrate visually.

Illness may also weaken the student's physical ability to complete visual tasks. A student who has just recovered from the flu may still not be functioning up to par. Watery eyes and light sensitivity typically accompany a cold or sinus infection. These factors will likely interfere with the student's ability to maintain visual concentration.

ENVIRONMENTAL FACTORS

Familiarity

A familiar environment will present less of a challenge than an unfamiliar one. A student will not need to work as hard to locate an object visually in a known setting, because cognitive and motor memory will assist with the process. For example, the student may know that the pencil sharpener is located on the back wall of the geography classroom, but the same visual location task may be more difficult in a new classroom where the sharpener is located somewhere else.

Lighting, Color, and Contrast

Environmental conditions such as lighting, color, and contrast contribute to a student's visual reactions to different settings. For example, the afternoon sunlight through a classroom window may limit a student's ability to see the classroom teacher's writing on a chalkboard or white marker board. Some overhead transparencies may be easier to distinguish than others because of the size of the font, the spacing between words, the amount of written text, and/or the use of color. It is important for the student and classroom teachers to understand why visual performance may be altered from morning to afternoon, from one transparency to another, and so on.

Functional Vision Assessment

Student:	Andrew Holt	**DOB:**	September 19, 1984
FVA Dates:	January 24–27, 2000	**Report Date:**	January 28, 2000

Background Information

Andrew Holt is a tenth grader at Benjamin Franklin Senior High School. His family is new to the state. He is an avid sports fan with a penchant for professional football. He divides his free time between watching sports and playing the clarinet for his high school band. Andrew is active with his church group and has a 3.4 grade point average. His post–high school plan is to attend college and study music education.

Andrew is legally blind due to oculotaneous albinism. His last eye examination was October 10, 1999 by pediatric ophthalmologist Dr. J. Stein, who indicated the following key points:

- ◆ 20/600 distance visual acuity in the right eye.

- ◆ 20/200 distance visual acuity in the left eye.

- ◆ Compromised depth perception and binocular vision.

- ◆ Photophobia (light sensitivity).

- ◆ Eyeglasses prescribed for moderate nearsightedness (3.25 diopters, both eyes).

- ◆ Tinted lenses for photophobia.

- ◆ Normal visual field.

Andrew has not had a recent low vision evaluation. One has been scheduled for February of this year. Andrew had an audiological evaluation in September 1999. The school audiologist indicated that his hearing is within normal limits. Andrew does not take any medication and does not have any health concerns other than his sensitivity to the sun. He uses sunscreen when he is outdoors for any extended period of time.

F. M. D'Andrea and C. Farrenkopf, Eds., *Looking to Learn,* New York: AFB Press, 2000. This form may be copied for educational use.

A functional vision assessment was completed during the days of January 24–27, 2000. The purpose of the functional vision assessment was to prepare for a March triennial evaluation meeting and to review Andrew's educational needs. Andrew was observed in his school environment, including several different classroom situations. Most classroom settings were set up with about 35 desks facing a green chalkboard. Three out of six of his classrooms have access to natural lighting. Andrew is not enrolled in a gym class this semester. Andrew and several teachers were interviewed during the assessment period. Their input has been infused into this assessment report.

Functional Vision Assessment Results

Appearance of Eyes: Andrew has beautiful blue eyes. Both eyes are equally aligned. Nystagmus was evident with increased intensity during tasks requiring sustained visual concentration. Andrew wears tinted glasses.

Muscle Balance: A Corneal Reflection Test indicated equal eye alignment. This was confirmed with a cover-uncover test.

Eye Preference: Andrew showed a left eye preference when he was asked to look through a monocular. When he was asked to maintain fixation while covering one eye at a time, his right eye showed a marked increase in nystagmus when his left eye was covered. Andrew described his left eye as his better eye.

Eye Movement/Teaming: Andrew occasionally squinted when he was asked to look at small visual targets, thereby shutting out the vision in his right eye. The acuity discrepancy between both eyes interferes with binocular viewing. Andrew demonstrated full-range ocular motility skills. He was able to cross midline when following a moving object such as a person walking across the room from 10 ft (3 m). Andrew compensated for poor eye teaming skills by using accompanying head movement to follow a moving target into either periphery. This was especially evident with targets moving into his far right visual field. Andrew demonstrated good scanning skills in an "eye spy." That is, Andrew was asked to visually locate and verbally identify a number of objects that were placed throughout the room (high on the walls, on the floor, in corners, etc.).

Visual Field: Confrontational field testing did not indicate any evidence of field loss. This is consistent with the ophthalmologist's findings. Further field testing is, however, suggested in future orientation and mobility evaluations where Andrew's visual field can be evaluated in dynamic postures.

Color Vision: Andrew has been tested with the Ishihara Color Plates in previous assessments—there are no concerns with color discrimination.

Depth Perception: This is an area of concern for Andrew since he has a significant acuity difference between his right and left eyes. He has learned to judge depth and is a competent traveler in the familiar environment of this school. However, he did hesitate when he approached the stairs in the building. The O&M specialist is working with Andrew on both indoor and outdoor cane travel.

Sensitivity to Light: Andrew is highly light sensitive. This was noted in several classrooms where overhead fluorescent lighting was present. Andrew has learned to accommodate for this by shielding his eyes or keeping his head in a bent-forward position. When he is outdoors, he typically wears a baseball-styled cap with a brim. His tinted glasses did not appear to sufficiently screen out bright lights. This was an important area of discussion with Andrew's teachers because many were not aware of the influence of lighting on Andrew's visual performance.

Sensitivity to Glare: This is an area of considerable concern in many of Andrew's classrooms. Colored acetate sheets were used during the assessment to determine whether they helped to reduce the effects of glare on Andrew's reading material. He reported that a light yellow sheet appeared to help. He indicated a willingness to experiment with a number of colors over the course of the next month.

Near Visual Acuity: Andrew readily identified 1–2 in. (3–5 cm) objects such as a small pencil, eraser, paper clip, and rubber band at a distance of 5 ft (1.5 m) in a classroom environment with overhead fluorescent lighting. He was able to identify all denominations of coins and bills in this setting. People and common objects in photographs or color illustrations were identified from a distance of 6–12 in. (15–30 cm). Several factors contributed to Andrew's visual identification ease or difficulty: area illumination, contrast, organization of the materials, size of the item, and the brightness of the colors.

Andrew was able to identify 18-point font (.5 cm) symbols at 16 in. (40 cm) with a Lighthouse Near Vision Test. His preferred near range acuity was 18-point font at a self-regulated viewing distance of 10 in. (25 cm).

Distance Visual Acuity: Andrew's visual performance changed considerably in response to the lighting conditions. As the illumination increased, his distance vision decreased. Under typical classroom lighting conditions (overhead fluorescent lights), Andrew was able to locate the wall clock from about 15 ft (4.5 m), though he could not tell the actual time unless he was seven feet from the clock. Andrew identified facial expressions and gross body movements (waving hand, lifted foot) from a distance of 10 ft (3 m) in an indoor setting with typical overhead lighting.

Andrew could identify that there was something written on the chalkboard from 10 ft (3 m). At approximately 3 ft (1 m), he could decipher the written information. For best viewing results, the board needs to be clean and free from glare, and the writing must be neat. White chalk is better than pink or yellow chalk. Andrew takes notes from class lectures and often will ask a friend to share the notes from the chalkboard. He can read from an overhead projector when the writer uses dark colors and large print or script. It is helpful if the classroom lighting is dimmed when the overhead projector is used.

When a television monitor (19 in./47 cm) is used in the classroom to show a film, Andrew prefers to sit within 5 ft (1.5 m) of the screen. At home, where the screen is slightly larger, he reports that he sits about 2 ft (60 cm) from the television set.

Andrew identified the 20/600 symbols with his right eye and 20/200 symbols with his left eye using the Lea Symbols Distance Acuity Chart.

Print Size and Reading Speed: Andrew was able to look up a requested listing in the phone book. This task was done in an environment with good task lighting and from a viewing distance of 3 in. (7.5 cm). He read the front-page newspaper headlines from a distance of 8–10 in. (20–25 cm). Andrew's textbooks are in large print. In a timed passage, he read aloud 125 words per minute and 154 words during a silent reading passage. Both passages were in 18-point type. Andrew reported that he fatigues easily when completing reading assignments.

Andrew is reading at grade level, though he finds it difficult, at times, to keep up with the amount of reading required for his coursework. He occasionally reads for pleasure and is generally not interested in books on tape, unless it is a story about a sports figure. Andrew can read most menus at a close viewing distance. He does not like to ask his friends to tell him what is on the menu. Oftentimes, he orders what the person before him orders, if he does not know the content of the menu.

He uses a CCTV at home for some of his homework assignments and a CCTV in his algebra class at school. Andrew uses a screen enlargement program on the computer called CloseView. He uses ClarisWorks for word processing and is able to enlarge the font to 18-point type. One challenge with the computer is the brightness of the computer screen. Andrew tires after 30–45 minutes at the computer. He can type 40 words per minute based on a recent typing assessment.

Handwriting: Andrew's dominant hand is his left hand. He prefers to print rather than use cursive writing. He was able to read back his notes from a class lecture given four days ago. His preference was to use pens with black ink. Blue ink and pencils are difficult for him to visually decipher. He uses regular lined paper.

Summary and Recommendations

Andrew was fun to be with over the course of the assessment period. He is very engaging and has a good sense of humor. He is doing well in school because of his diligence. There are important next steps in determining how best to support Andrew's visual performance. All media should be evaluated on an ongoing basis to give him a range of literacy options.

Andrew has a basic understanding of his eye condition. During the assessment session, he was asked to explain both the cause of his visual impairment and what helped or hindered his visual performance. He was able to describe albinism in general terms. When asked if he would like more information about albinism, he said he would like to read more about it and maybe meet a few other people with the same diagnosis. He was less confident of how to describe his vision, other than to say that he preferred low lighting situations. He expressed an interest in learning more about ways to help improve his visual functioning when he attends the low vision evaluation clinic next month. His only concern was to have devices that would not make him look "weird" in the eyes of his fellow students. He did like the idea, however, that a monocular might help his travel independence and ability to watch field sports.

Recommendations include:

1. Andrew is a great candidate for a low vision evaluation. His teacher, who is certified in the area of visual impairments, will accompany Andrew and his parents to the February exam. A list of questions will be drafted for the eye care specialist. In particular, it is important to learn whether Andrew will benefit from low vision devices for reading and distance tasks. Another area of discussion will be what type of light absorption eyeglasses might assist him with both indoor and outdoor light sensitivity. In addition, the low vision exam will help to address mobility and task lighting needs. Suggestions from the exam will be reviewed for their implementation in the home, at school, and in community environments.

2. Follow-up training will be necessary for prescribed devices. If a magnification device(s) is prescribed for reading tasks, it will be important to reassess his reading rate with a variety of print sizes. Reading efficiency is critical to Andrew's ongoing success with schoolwork and in his future employment.

3. A learning media assessment will be conducted after Andrew's visit to the low vision clinic to help determine his most appropriate and efficient learning media. Andrew should continue to have a variety of literacy options: large print, books on tape, use of a CCTV and screen enlargement programs, low vision aids, and so on.

4. Andrew would benefit from a comprehensive technology evaluation in the near future.

5. All work written on a board should be verbalized. The chalkboard should be clean and white chalk should be used, as possible. Dark-colored markers are easiest for Andrew to see when the overhead projector is used.

6. Glare and lighting factors should be addressed in each classroom. Light absorption lenses may help considerably. Andrew should be encouraged to pick seats that best meet his needs, depending on the environmental features of each classroom. Colored acetate sheets can be used on

Andrew's reading material over the course of the next month to see if they are beneficial.

7. It is great that Andrew is interested in learning more about albinism. Information will be gathered on the diagnosis of albinism, including literature on NOAH (National Organization of Albinism and Hypopigmentation). There are opportunities for annual conventions that might be of interest to Andrew and his family. He will also be invited to the State Teen Workshop that will be held on the campus of the School for the Blind in June. There will be other students with visual impairments at the workshop.

If there are any questions about the content of this report, please contact me at (555) 555-5555.

Reported By:
Janet Shepard, M.A.
Teacher of Students with Visual Impairments

Working Effectively with a Low Vision Clinic

BONNIE SIMONS AND DEBORAH J. LAPOLICE

THE PURPOSE OF A CLINICAL LOW VISION EVALUATION is to provide functional, usable information about the visual abilities of an individual who has low vision. The focus of the evaluation is usually on verifying the individual's visual acuity and on finding ways to enhance his or her visual functioning. Whereas medical ophthalmologists generally focus on curing and improving visual impairments with surgical or medical intervention, low vision clinics approach visual impairments from the aspect of enhancement of functional vision—that is, how the individual is able to use his or her vision in real-life situations. An ophthalmologic exam seeks to define the nature, degree, and progress of ocular disease while determining possible surgical or medical interventions, which may improve a student's visual functioning. The clinical low vision evaluation is conducted in order to gather information on the student's levels of visual ability (or functioning) as they relate to everyday tasks such as reading and writing, while seeking to identify optical and nonoptical tools that will increase the student's ease of completing such tasks. Visual comfort and efficiency are of primary concern to the clinical low vision evaluator while conducting the evaluation. Enhancement of visual functioning may be accomplished through the use of both optical and nonoptical devices and accommodations. The teacher of students who are visually impaired will be concerned specifically with a student's access to literacy materials in school.

Typically, a visit to the low vision clinic should provide the following:

◆ Information and clarification about a student's visual impairment.

◆ Explanations of how optical and nonoptical devices improve visual functioning.

◆ Trial use of optical and/or nonoptical devices.

◆ An explanation of the need for follow-up training and visits to the clinic for the student, if appropriate.

This chapter will provide information about the process of a clinical low vision evaluation so that teachers of students who are visually impaired can adequately prepare their students and students' families for a visit to the low vision clinic. The teacher of visually impaired students plays a unique role in the successful outcome of a visit to a low vision clinic by ensuring that the persons involved communicate and collaborate to find solutions to the particular visual challenges with which the student is presented.

A clinical low vision evaluation can provide information that is critical to the kind of educational programming that is needed by students who have low vision. The evaluation, in combination with a functional vision assessment (FVA) and a learning media assessment, may provide information that will allow a student with low vision access to more types of reading materials and to a wider range of literacy options; it may also result in an overall increase in independent functioning for the student.

All students with low vision should have regular low vision evaluations in order to assist them in their efforts to improve their visual functioning as well as to provide useful information for educational and vocational planning. The low vision specialist will determine the frequency of regular check-ups; however, the student, teacher, or family must feel free to recommend additional visits if there are changes in vision, visual performance, school or home settings, or circumstances in which visual performance has not been previously addressed.

IMPORTANCE OF THE LOW VISION EVALUATION

The importance of a clinical low vision evaluation for students with low vision is generally accepted, although such evaluations are not always implemented. The clinical low vision evaluation has been the primary means of determining the need for optical and nonoptical devices for students with low vision, and for informing caregivers and schools of the student's proper use of such devices. Caregivers and schools are sometimes unaware of the assistance that can be provided to the student with low vision, or may see it as mainly appropriate for older individuals only. It is not uncommon for a student with low vision to lag in concept development and literacy skills throughout the school years (Koenig & Farrenkopf, 1997). These delays may be caused by the lack of sensory input in areas such as distance perception, color skills, or near recognition of letters and numbers. Optical and nonoptical devices can provide a student with low vision access to visual information that can be invaluable to learning and development. For example, telescopic devices may be used to teach preschool children about animals in a field, airplanes in the sky, and other distance concepts, while they may help the older student understand the concepts of street corner intersections and distance measurements.

Research of students with low vision indicates that about 70 percent of these students would experience an improvement in visual functioning and increased access to a wider range of literacy materials if prescribed the correct optical and/or nonoptical device in a low vision evaluation (Hofstetter, 1991). It is also generally true that the earlier the student's exposure to low vision devices and device training and experimentation, the easier it will be for teachers to integrate the optical and nonoptical devices into the student's classroom and everyday life. A visit to the low vision clinic is an opportunity for the student, family, and teachers to have myriad questions answered about functional vision, particularly during critical periods of change or development.

WHEN TO VISIT THE LOW VISION CLINIC

As already noted, all students with low vision should have regular check-ups in the low vision clinic. Sidebar 3.1 outlines the times at which the teacher, family, or student might request a visit to the low vision clinic to help refine or define aspects of a student's classroom modifications and his or her functional use of aids. Sidebar 3.2 provides suggestions for finding low vision services for students.

It is appropriate to consider a low vision evaluation when a child with low vision exhibits difficulties in an area of concept development. For example, a child who is unable to recognize similarities and differences in shapes or positional relationships, who has difficulty recognizing familiar objects or family members, or who seems unaware of things in distant environments (for example, streets, corners, crosswalks, and signs) may benefit from the use of simple low

---

Sidebar **3.1**

When to Visit the Low Vision Clinic

- When a young child exhibits difficulty in acquiring concepts in school.

- When the student experiences difficulty when participating in classroom activities.

- When the student enters a grade in which the print size changes.

- When a student's reading speed decreases.

- When a student has problems tracking or following lines of print smoothly.

- When the student experiences physical discomfort in reading and writing tasks.

- When a student is moving into a grade in which reading, writing, and/or boardwork demands will increase.

- When a student is preparing to make college, career, and vocational training plans.

- When a student experiences difficulty with new print formats or styles.

- When a student has difficulty traveling in school or home environments.

- When teachers or other school personnel express concerns regarding the student's vision.

- When a learning media choice needs to be made (e.g., appropriate print sizes, or combined-media choices).

---

vision devices. The low vision specialist may find that a combination of a visor to block light and guided-exploration of the environment with a low-powered telescope will help the child receive better-quality visual information, thereby improving the child's understanding of these concepts.

A visit to the low vision clinic may be necessary if a student in kindergarten experiences difficulty when trying to discriminate letters, complete worksheets, color, or participate in group activities with the class such as changing the calendar or engaging in shared reading of "big books." Additional lighting, bookstands and easy-to-use magnification devices can be tried in a clinical setting to determine the child's ability to benefit from such devices.

When a student with low vision is about to enter a grade in which print size or formats change, teachers will wish to know how best to prepare the student for the change. Textbook print can decrease two point sizes between primary (kindergarten to grade two) and elementary grade levels (grade three to grade five) and print formats found in charts, maps, graphs, and tables in science and social studies textbooks can be visually challenging for the student with low vision, particularly when moving into higher grades. It is important to ensure that the student has access to a variety of literacy materials in the classroom during such a change. The low vision specialist can identify handheld magnifiers that might be useful for the student. He or she might also suggest the use of a

---

How to Find Low Vision Evaluation Services

There are a wide variety of low vision services available to students needing this specialized service. Low vision clinics are frequently attached to academic eye centers at universities, and a school of optometry may have clinics that provide training for the school's students under the supervision of an experienced optometrist. These programs frequently bring low vision services to rural areas within a specific radius of their centers, and such programs can travel to a central location in the rural area if enough low vision students are available for the optometry students to evaluate. Adult rehabilitation agencies will also know of or run their own clinics, but they may have limited experience with young children and with the range of devices available for school-related tasks. The teacher of students who are visually impaired should contact the agency to see if it is appropriate for a young child to go to such a clinic for a low vision evaluation.

City hospitals may have a clinic or a department with optometrists who have experience in evaluating students with low vision. Many areas have private practitioners who have similar experience in their training or current practice. The teacher of students who are visually impaired can contact individual practitioners and/or verify information received from others who have been to the practitioner for this purpose. Teachers may find it useful to search through the *AFB Directory of Services for Blind and Visually Impaired Persons in the United States and Canada* (1997), which has a listing of low vision centers by state as well as a comprehensive listing of other services that may be of assistance.

If a teacher wants to find a center that specializes in conducting low vision evaluations on students with multiple disabilities, there are several avenues for investigation. Sometimes, a specific person in a low vision clinic will specialize in testing students with multiple disabilities. Teachers should make sure they know who it is and schedule the appointment when that person is available. It may also be helpful to contact a college or university program that prepares teachers to teach students with other disabilities or multiple disabilities. Such programs frequently know of local or nearby specialists who are successful in evaluating students with special needs. Residential schools for students with visual impairments usually have students with low vision and with multiple disabilities and will sometimes provide low vision evaluations on-site for these students. These schools may be contacted about providing this service for students not enrolled at the school, or they may know of clinics that can provide such specialized evaluation.

---

combination of media that might be beneficial to the student. For example, if the print size and graphic format in charts, maps, graphs, and tables in science and social studies books is visually challenging for a student with low vision, the combination of a large-print social studies textbook used with a handheld magnifier may work for reading the information in a regular-print atlas, or the student may actually find the combined use of print and braille materials to be helpful.

A visit to the low vision clinic might also be helpful for a student with a central visual field loss or cortical visual impairment (CVI) whose reading speed reaches a plateau due to difficulty with tracking and scanning (see Chapter 2).

The low vision specialist might be able to identify scanning techniques the student can practice to increase reading speed, or the specialist may provide specific information about field loss that would help in identifying the best position for reading materials. Proper illumination combined with high contrast materials may also help the student with cortical visual impairment, since there is evidence that increased light enhances visual attention in such students (Padula and Shapiro, 1996). A low vision specialist can evaluate the usefulness of such devices as high-intensity lamps and closed-circuit television systems (CCTVs) for such students (see Chapter 7).

When a student with low vision and a physical disability is moving into a grade in which copying from the board will be required, the teacher of students who are visually impaired and the physical and occupational therapists will want information on which low vision devices may help the student. This will help them to devise the proper modifications for positioning and support and to decide on adaptive technology that may be useful.

A student who is being followed by an ophthalmologist due to a sudden change in vision may also need to visit the low vision clinic to have current optical devices reevaluated or to try new devices because of reduced visual acuity. The low vision specialist can help identify the combination of media and devices which will most benefit a student who experiences a decrease in vision.

The visual demands on the student with low vision may increase at any time in school. There will be times when students are required to move through print material quickly to get information, for example, by scanning tables, graphs, maps, and indexes. Students may also have increased demands on their vision because of new print formats presented in their grade, such as horizontal math problem alignment features or more complicated graphic pages in textbooks. A low vision evaluation can help the student find techniques and new devices that can make getting information in these formats easier, such as a line guide or a typoscope—a nonoptical device consisting of a piece of black cardboard or plastic with an opening wide enough to view only a single word or line of print. Such a device helps one to maintain one's place, and it increases contrast.

A student with low vision who is moving into higher grades in which the visual demands of reading and boardwork increase may benefit from a low vision evaluation to determine if additional devices would be useful. This may also be an age at which students with low vision can benefit psychologically from such a visit because it may help them better understand their visual impairment; it will allow them to discuss vocational or higher education goals related to functional vision; and it will enable them to share their concerns about the use of optical and nonoptical devices. The low vision specialist can reinforce the importance of the use of devices and, if appropriate, allow the student to practice with state-of-the-art electronic devices.

It may also be helpful for the student with low vision who is having difficulty traveling in typical school or home environments to have a low vision evaluation. The low vision specialist can help the teacher of students who are visually impaired and/or the orientation and mobility (O&M) specialist to identify optical devices that will increase the student's ability to travel independently, read street signs and addresses, identify obstacles, and move comfortably and safely. If school administrators have expressed concern about the student's ability to travel safely at school, it is particularly important for a formal low vision evaluation to take place along with an O&M evaluation.

Every student with low vision is different, but evidence exists that the reading speed of students who use regular print with optical devices continues to increase through the grades, whereas students who use large print alone have reading speeds that tend to reach a plateau (Corn, 1981). Some schools may have the expectation that every student with low vision needs large print. A low vision evaluation helps the teacher of students who are visually impaired educate schools on efficient ways to increase a specific student's access to print materials through the use of handheld and stand magnifiers when recommended in a clinical low vision evaluation. For a student who has been using large print, a low vision evaluation can help determine whether this accommodation continues to be appropriate.

PREPARING TO VISIT THE LOW VISION CLINIC

Information about the purposes and procedures of evaluation at low vision clinics should be introduced to family, teachers, and support staff as early as possible in the teacher's work with a student who has low vision. It is important to discuss the need for a comprehensive low vision evaluation as opportunities arise, giving examples of how optical and nonoptical aids can benefit the student in upcoming grades. One of the most powerful ways for the teacher of students who are visually impaired to encourage families and schools to support evaluations at low vision clinics is to attend the appointment with the student and parents, caregivers, or other family members.

Since schools are required to conduct vision screenings on school-age children, school personnel generally are aware of the role and importance of vision in classroom learning. The teacher of students who are visually impaired can build on this basic understanding to explain and promote the need for low vision evaluations of students with low vision. He or she can address the concerns of classroom teachers by clearly and accurately explaining the functional aspects of the visual challenges that students face, as well as the basic optical principles of low vision devices, and he or she can describe or demonstrate a variety of optical and nonoptical aids.

Preparing Questions

Before visiting the clinic, it is helpful for teachers, family members, and other support personnel to meet to develop a comprehensive list of goals and questions regarding the student's functional vision, especially if this is the first visit for the student and family. A sample prescreening questionnaire that the teacher may use to question the family and student at this time can be found in Appendix 3.A of this chapter.

The teacher of students who are visually impaired can assist the student, family, and school to prepare questions that will assist the low vision specialist in addressing all concerns. The teacher may direct older students to keep journals or notes regarding vision fluctuations or times of fatigue during the day. With younger students, the majority of the information will be obtained from the classroom teacher, and this information will focus on the student's difficulty in functioning and on his or her fluctuations in performance; however, the student should not be left out of the process. Even young children have concerns regarding why they are unable to complete visual tasks in the same manner as their sighted peers. It will be up to the teacher of students with visual impairments to help the student voice these concerns and to be sure that they are covered during the evaluation. Sidebar 3.3 lists the types of questions students and their families typically will want to have answered by the low vision specialist, as well as the questions often asked by classroom teachers and teachers of visually impaired students.

The family needs to understand the importance of providing specific examples to the low vision specialist, examples concerning the student's daily use of vision at home and school. An hour spent with the family discussing how the student uses vision for specific tasks will help everybody better understand what functional vision is (see Chapter 2) and how the clinical evaluation can enhance the student's functioning. The teacher can create a short list of some of the functional vision activities the teacher has observed the student performing and give it to the family members so that they can review it before visiting the clinic. This information can also be used to develop specific questions

Sidebar 3.3

Typical Questions About Students' Visual Functioning

Students who are visually impaired, members of their families, their teachers, other professionals who work with them, and school administrators all have many questions about the student's abilities and visual functioning that the teacher of students who are visually impaired can help to answer. These individuals may not always be able to articulate all their questions, however. When the teacher meets with these individuals, he or she may want to refer to the following list, which includes some of the questions most frequently asked by each group, to make sure that all the important issues are addressed.

STUDENTS

- Why can't I see the information on the chalkboard or overhead projector?

- Why is reading the dictionary and other reference materials in the library so difficult for me?

- How will I be able to read labels and price tags when shopping?

- Is there a way for me to be able to read family's, teachers', or friends' handwriting?

- How can I read my own handwriting more effectively?

- Is there a way that I can decrease the fatigue or neck pain, for example, that is related to using my vision?

- Why do I see better on some days and not on others?

- Will I be able to drive?

- Is there some way I can use the computer to do the same things as my friends?

- How can I go out with my friends at night when I can't see well in the dark?

- Is there a way I can recognize my friends in the halls or outdoors?

FAMILY MEMBERS

- What materials will my child need to succeed in school?

- How will my child get information from phone books and dictionaries?

- How will my child read street signs, dials, gauges and measurement markings?

- How will my child read his or her mail, fill out forms, and the like?

- Can my child use household appliances such as stoves and washing machines?

- How can we make sure my child is using and maintaining optical devices correctly?

- How long will these devices work for my child?

- Should my child be able to complete tasks to live independently, such as writing checks, reading recipes, and doing household chores?

- How will my child be able to function independently in a college or university?

- How will my child be able to function independently at a job and in a career?

TEACHERS OF STUDENTS WHO ARE VISUALLY IMPAIRED

- Where should the student sit in the classroom?

- What is the student's lens prescription, and when should eyeglasses be worn in school?

- What aids might increase the student's access to more print and/or literacy materials in school?

- What lighting should this student use?

- Would window shades help this student?

- Does the student have any blind spots that affect reading ability?

(continued)

- What aids might help the student travel more efficiently within school environments and on community-based field trips?

- What signs should we look for that would let us know that low vision devices are no longer working and that we should return for a follow-up?

- How will the student view movies and videos, particularly in dark rooms?

- Are there any new visual skills that need to be taught to the student as a result of the low vision evaluation?

- Have the student's needs been addressed in the IEP?

CLASSROOM TEACHERS

- What devices will the student use?

- Should the student use those devices all the time?

- Should the student wear eyeglasses all the time?

- Why doesn't the student wear eyeglasses if he or she is visually impaired?

- What do I need to do to my materials so the student can use them?

- Should the student sit in a particular place?

ADMINISTRATORS

- Are there safety concerns that the school should address?

- How long will it be before the student is independent with these optical devices?

- Are there adaptive devices the school should be purchasing?

- Who is responsible for the care and maintenance of the optical and nonoptical aids?

OTHER PROFESSIONALS (PHYSICAL AND OCCUPATIONAL THERAPISTS, ORIENTATION AND MOBILITY SPECIALISTS, ADAPTIVE TECHNOLOGY SPECIALISTS, ETC.)

- Are there any aids or devices that will help this student with tasks requiring eye-hand coordination?

- What distance devices would help this student travel in the community more efficiently?

- Would this student benefit from a glare screen on a computer?

- Are the eyeglasses this student wears comfortable when he or she uses the computer?

for the low vision specialist. Families will also find it helpful to understand the differences between low vision evaluations and ophthalmological exams.

It is also a good idea to review the current eye report with the family before a visit to the low vision clinic, as well as the results of the functional vision assessment (FVA) (see Chapter 2); this will ensure that the family members have an understanding of the diagnosis and treatment, and it gives them the chance to clarify any misunderstandings. This also provides an opportunity for everyone to discuss the family's concerns and questions regarding the student's use of his or her vision. Any questions regarding the medical information on the eye report should be noted and addressed (see Chapter 1).

Gathering Information

To assist the low vision specialist in accurately assessing the student's performance in a variety of situations, the teacher of students who are visually impaired should collect the following information prior to the exam; such information should then be shared with the low vision specialist:

- ◆ The most recent eye report and/or low vision evaluation report.

- ◆ Functional vision assessment report or materials, and learning media assessment results, with updates and recent observations where needed.

- ◆ A prescreening form and/or a list of concerns or questions by interested professionals.

- ◆ Report of other disabilities.

- ◆ Educational data such as grade level, math and reading levels, and support services, etc.

- ◆ Typical classroom materials used by the student, including samples of the various print sizes and styles the student is expected to use.

Gathering together these reports and materials will ensure that all members of the team—teachers, low vision specialist, family, and other evaluators—have the same information on the student's current functioning. Depending on the evaluator's preference, this information should either be sent to the low vision specialist prior to the exam or brought to the evaluation.

The student's school program and individualized education program (IEP) should also be reviewed with the family as well as with the school personnel involved in the student's program. The focus should be on the student's visual functioning in order to prepare questions to be answered at the low vision evaluation. IEP objectives may need to be rewritten after the low vision evaluation to include information on training and the use of low vision devices. School personnel will need to be aware of these changes. For example, an IEP objective may state, "The student will retrieve homework assignments from the board by using a telescopic device," or "The student will use an optical aid to increase access to reference materials."

Current information and concerns about the student's classroom visual functioning should be addressed by both the teacher of students who are visually impaired and the classroom teacher together. They should spend time observing the student completing a variety of activities in order to develop questions that can be presented to the low vision specialist. Information should be obtained regarding adaptive behaviors the student uses to complete classroom tasks, such as head tilting to view materials, and repositioning materials. Current methods the student uses to increase visual efficiency in the classroom, such as increased illumination, use of place markers, color and contrast changes in materials should be noted also. The student's use of vision to travel in the classroom, cafeteria, and outdoors and around school in general should also be observed and discussed with the teacher.

The teacher of students who are visually impaired should also obtain current information about the student's sustained reading rate and the duration of this rate before fatigue becomes a problem. Also, information regarding comprehension of both silently read material and material read aloud by the student will provide clues to the success of the student's current method of visual functioning. This should have been addressed in the functional vision assessment (see Chapter 2) and learning media assessment, but it may need to be updated prior to the low vision evaluation, especially for younger students whose reading skills may change quickly and dramatically in the early school years.

Preparing the Student for the Evaluation

Some students may be comfortable and familiar with the specialized procedures and instruments used during the visit to the low vision clinic, but most need to be prepared in some manner, particularly if it is a new experience for them. Some students want as much information as possible to prepare them for new experiences, and others prefer just a brief familiarization beforehand.

Familiarization with specialized procedures and instruments used in a low vision evaluation should be done in many situations. The process and rationale for such an evaluation should be addressed in formal individual educational planning (IEP) meetings when appropriate, particularly in the initial team meeting in which a student is identified as having an educational visual impairment, and the results of the FVA and learning media assessments are reviewed by the teacher of students who are visually impaired. The teacher can bring a sample of optical aids and devices to the meeting, or a catalog of aids, perhaps. Many states require that the FVA and learning media assessment reports address the need for a clinical low vision evaluation for the student. In preparation for a visit to the low vision clinic, students can be presented with explanations of the procedures involved in a clinical low vision evaluation over many sessions. It is helpful to have an older student or adult with low vision discuss the process with the student and caregivers, relating his or her first-hand experiences with the evaluation.

Students should be helped to appreciate that the reason for the examination is to enable the low vision specialist to better understand their vision and to help them use it. The teacher of students who are visually impaired needs to explain the purposes and operation of the special tools that the low vision specialist will use in terms the student can understand. (These tools and procedures are described later in this chapter.) Cartoonlike drawings of the instruments can make the tools seem more friendly and helpful to young children. Older students may enjoy learning about the technical aspects of the instruments. This information is easily integrated into science and math learning or even career education study. Some students may wish to have the action of the eye drops that will be administered explained (they keep the focusing parts of the eye from moving when the light comes in). Others will not want to be reminded of the drops before the clinic visit because they dislike getting them, and they will need to be distracted when the drops are administered in the clinic. The teacher of students who are visually impaired will need to be sensitive to the wishes and needs of the student.

Preparing Oneself

It is very important for the teacher of students with low vision to be prepared to facilitate the sharing of information at the low vision evaluation. Frequently in a clinical evaluation, students and families are not easily able to share information that may be critical to providing effective evaluation and treatment. The teacher of students who are visually impaired plays a critical role in presenting the evaluation in a positive light to the student, family, and school, as well as in helping them communicate clearly with the low vision specialist. Additionally, the teacher should help the family and student understand the purposes of and options presented during the evaluation. Unless communication is honest and open, friendly and helpful, a practical plan of treatment will not be developed. The teacher may be able to assist the low vision specialist in establishing rapport with the family and student—and so, should help clarify information regarding educational and home concerns.

The teacher should check to see if the student and family understand what is being evaluated at each step of the assessment, and he or she should provide clarification if necessary. This should not be done in a manner that is disruptive to the low vision evaluator. Most low vision specialists are highly skilled at establishing rapport quickly with patients and families, and they are very familiar with the kinds of school-related tasks that students are presented with in the classroom. However, the teacher should remember that the low vision specialist might sometimes need educational concerns and tasks explained. This explanation should be given briefly and clearly, with specific examples if possible. For instance, if a parent asks a general question (such as, "How is Emilio's distance vision?"), the low vision specialist might respond with an acuity level. The teacher might clarify, saying, "Emilio will have to take notes from an overhead projector in many of his classes next year." Asking the right questions is important. The teacher might follow up by asking, "Are there any devices or aids that could help him do this?" This will give the low vision specialist a specific situation to address when formulating a response to the parents' question.

Finally, the teacher of students who are visually impaired needs to review appropriate ophthalmalogical and optometric terms related to the student's visual impairment before going to the clinic; this review will enable the teacher to clearly understand the information given by the low vision specialist during the exam. Although the teacher is required to have a certain level of understanding of ophthalmological terms and tests, the low vision evaluation can frequently be a learning experience for the teacher too.

THE CONTENT OF A LOW VISION EVALUATION

The focus of the low vision evaluation will depend upon the questions brought to the clinic by the student, family, and teachers. The exam should be oriented toward the concerns of all involved. Sidebar 3.4 lists areas typically covered in a low vision evaluation, which are explained in detail throughout this section. However, the teacher and the family can help the low vision specialist decide which areas may need more attention. For example, if glare is the main area of difficulty for a student, more testing time might be devoted to evaluating the student's acuity under a variety of lighting conditions or to trying out various lens tints and filters.

Depending on its purpose, the visit may be a complete initial evaluation or a shorter, follow-up visit related to a specific question posed by the student or to a problem he or she is experiencing. The clinic personnel can explain, for example, the various components of the optics of the student's current eye condition while describing how optical and nonoptical devices may improve visual

---

Sidebar **3.4**

Components of the Low Vision Examination

• Case history.	• Visual fields and perimetry.	• Refraction and conventional lenses.	• Contrast sensitivity, light sensitivity, and illumination needs.
• Ocular health.			
• Visual acuity.	• Color vision.	• Binocularity.	• Low vision devices.

functioning. The low vision specialist accumulates a great deal of information about the student's functional skills through observation during testing. He or she will be observing the student's visual attention, eye preference, tracking ability, attention to central and peripheral targets, scanning ability, mobility skills, and null point in nystagmus (see Chapter 1).

In addition to the low vision specialist, low vision clinics vary in the variety of personnel they employ (see Sidebar 3.5.). Some clinics employ mobility specialists to train in basic mobility techniques, whereas others have occupational therapists or vision trainers to provide assistance and training in the areas of device usage and daily living skills. Many clinics, particularly those found in medical centers, offer social work or counseling to assist with referrals to outside agencies or adjustment counseling. Although this section refers to the low

---

Sidebar **3.5**

Clinic Personnel and What They Do

The low vision personnel involved in the evaluation of a student will vary depending on the student's low vision needs at the time of evaluation. These personnel function as a team to determine which aspects of student functioning need to be addressed during the comprehensive assessment or after it is completed. It may be appropriate, for example, for a high school student planning to begin in a work experience program in the community to spend time with the low vision clinic's O&M specialist in order to evaluate optical aid use for travel to and from the work site. For a student who has experienced a recent loss of vision, a more thorough evaluation in daily living skills may be needed, or the student may require assistance from a social worker to identify the support needed for the student and the family.

• **Low Vision Specialist**—The individual who conducts the evaluation in the clinic may be an ophthalmologist, optometrist, or someone with a degree in vision who is working with a physician. This person is responsible for completing the examination and may or may not be the person who provides training with low vision devices.

• **Rehabilitation Specialist**—This individual may be a person with a university degree in the rehabilitation of individuals who are visually impaired, an occupational therapist, or someone with training courses in completing activities of daily living. This individual may provide training in optical device use or training in daily living skills.

• **Orientation and Mobility (O&M) Specialist**—This individual has completed a university or college program in orientation and mobility. This person is certified to teach travel skills to individuals with low vision or blindness. His or her training may include sighted-guide techniques, cane travel, or working with individuals using dog guides.

• **Technicians**—A Certified Ophthalmic Technician/Assistant (COT/COA) might be used to conduct the refraction on students. Technicians may also provide training on optical device use for students with low vision.

• **Social Workers**—Social workers are used in many clinics to conduct initial intake and to complete a patient history, as well as to provide resource information and adjustment counseling.

vision specialist in describing the procedures carried out during the low vision examination, the actual personnel who conduct the different sections of the evaluation may vary, depending on the clinic and the needs of the student.

The experience with low vision devices which a family will bring to a visit to the low vision clinic may range from a handheld magnifier a grandparent uses to read the television guide to an appreciation of the technology available in current electronic devices.

Case History

The visit to the low vision clinic generally begins with a discussion among the low vision specialist, the student with low vision, the parents, and the teacher of students who are visually impaired that focuses on the specific questions that brought the student in for the evaluation. The family is asked to verify the medical history and information from the last ophthalmological exam. This will help the low vision specialist to review pertinent information, discover the family's level of understanding of their child's visual impairment, and begin to formulate goals and purposes to be addressed during the evaluation. The family is asked about the onset of the visual impairment, eye surgeries and dates, current treatments and medications, and perhaps their child's general health—a particularly important factor if the student has additional disabilities. If the student is older, it is appropriate to let him or her answer some of these questions.

The low vision specialist will also ask questions regarding the student's independent functioning at home, in the community, and in the classroom. He or she will interview the student briefly about which eye functions better, about whether the student is bothered by light, and about which optical and nonoptical aids or other adaptive materials and devices he or she uses. A student with low vision may also be asked to describe any recent changes in vision.

If information from a previous low vision evaluation is available, it may be reviewed. This is an ideal time for the teacher of students who are visually impaired to share information about the functional vision assessment, including the following:

◆ The student's current reading rate and duration before fatigue, with preferred print size.

◆ A sample of the student's handwriting skills.

◆ Whether the student has any problems with light sensitivity or glare.

◆ The student's current use of optical and nonoptical devices, if not covered by the student.

Ocular Health

The low vision specialist will use several instruments to evaluate the general condition of the structures of the eyes at the beginning of the clinical exam in order to determine the nature and extent of the visual diagnosis. The low vision specialist may discuss his or her observations while viewing the structures of the eye with specialized instruments such as the ophthalmoscope. (Sidebar 3.6 provides definitions of a number of the instruments used in the eye examination.) It is possible that previously undetected eye problems may have been seen, although this is unlikely. The low vision specialist may be able to explain the student's visual impairment more thoroughly than the teacher of students who are visually impaired and can describe related visual conditions not previously noted. For example, the low vision specialist may discover that a student who comes to the low vision clinic with a diagnosis of iris coloboma (an incomplete iris) also has restricted visual fields and may have an underlying nystagmus and sensitivity to light.

Visual Acuity

The low vision specialist will assess visual acuities both with and without correction. Each eye is assessed separately, and then both eyes are assessed together in order to determine the preferred eye, the difference between the eyes, and the functional use of each eye. The examiner may use a variety of low vision acuity charts to determine these acuities (see Chapter 1 for additional details and definitions).

Distance acuity is always measured first and is usually measured at a distance of 10 ft (3 m), rather than the standard 20 ft (6 m), to allow the student to achieve some success on the initial test and to provide the evaluator with more defined visual acuities between 20/100 and 20/400 which are not available on the standard 20-ft (6-m) charts. During this testing, the examiner may observe the student's scanning skills and viewing patterns to make an initial assessment regarding field loss. The same distance acuity can be recorded as 5/200, 10/400, or 20/800, depending on the distance at which the test is given. These acuities may differ from the testing done in the ophthalmologist's office with a standard projection chart due to differences in distance and contrast factors. For determining legal blindness, the standard 20-ft (6-m) projection-chart results should be used.

After the distance acuity has been measured, near-point vision is evaluated. The near acuity test is often the major emphasis of the exam since increasing access to reading media is a major goal in low vision rehabilitation. Various charts are available that measure single letters, pictures, numbers, words, or phrases and

Sidebar 3.6

Low Vision Evaluation Instruments

BIOMICROSCOPE (OR SLIT-LAMP)

The biomicroscope, or slit-lamp, is used to view the cornea, iris, lens, and vitreous—the parts of the eye that bend light. It is a microscope on a stand that looks somewhat like a robot with eyes, and it sends out an intense beam of light. The examiner uses a metal frame in the back on which to rest his or her chin and on which to align his or her eye when using the microscope.

KERATOMETER

The keratometer measures the shape of the cornea and corneal distortions. The instrument is about 16 in. (40 cm) high and has a laser-gun type of appearance. It uses a fluorescent tube light incorporated into the keratometer to measure the overall dimensions of the cornea. This measurement is written in a lens prescription, if needed, as a number in millimeters for sphere and axis in the lenses.

OPHTHALMOSCOPE

This tool is usually used to view the optic disk, retina, macula, and choroid in the back of the eye. It is a handheld instrument shaped like a wand, with a special halogen light and a series of up to 48 lenses which are used to look at the structures of the eye from the front to the back. The student will hear a clicking or sliding noise when this tool is used, as the examiner moves one of two dials to choose different lenses or apertures. The light is bright but somewhat diffuse.

PHOROPTER

The phoropter is routinely used to measure the refractive error in the eyes. It looks like a superlarge pair of eye glasses hanging from an armlike support. The device has a series of spherical and cylindrical lenses which the clinician uses to perform a refraction on the patient. Patients with low vision may have difficulty with this type of correction as it prevents eccentric viewing.

RETINOSCOPE

The retinoscope is a handheld, wandlike instrument that shines a light into the eye. By viewing the movement of the light, the clinician is able to determine the presence of any refractive error. Putting different lenses in front of the eye and reevaluating the movement pattern of the light allows the examiner to determine the best refractive correction. This test does not require a response from the patient, so it can be used with infants, small children, and others who cannot answer questions during evaluation.

TRIAL FRAME AND LENSES

A trial frame is used when performing a refraction and is particularly helpful in determining the correct lens prescription for the student with low vision. The trial frame has the appearance of typical eyeglasses, which the student wears during this part of the exam. The examiner slips handheld lenses of varying strengths into openings in the top of each eye frame to determine which are best for the student. Trial frame testing is a closer simulation of the actual way lenses will be positioned in front of a student's eyes, thereby allowing the examiner to produce the best prescription for the student and one that allows for natural head posture and movement for visual tasks.

TONOMETER (OR TONO-PEN)

This is an instrument used to measure the intraocular pressure—"IOP" in medical shorthand. An applanation tonometer is a handheld wandlike instrument with a small disk, which is placed lightly on the student's anesthetized eye for a brief period. The eye pressure is measured by the displacement of weight created in the instrument while resting on the eye. It is quite common now for clinical low vision evaluators to use the Tono-pen to measure intraocular pressure during testing. The Tono-pen uses a puff of air to measure eye pressure, so it may be easier for children to tolerate. Younger children may still back away from this tool as it comes directly toward their eye to deliver the puff of air.

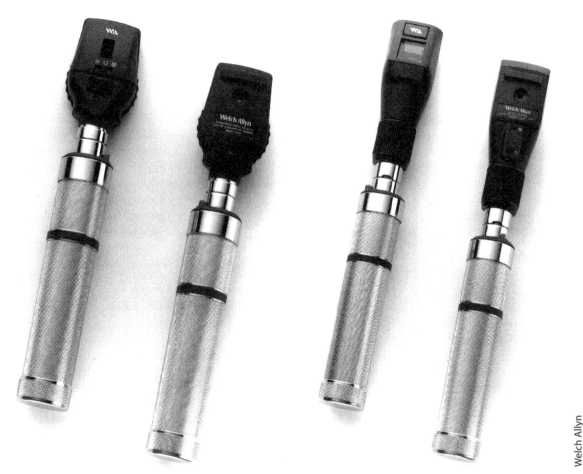

Welch Allyn

The ophthalmoscope (the front and back are shown at the left) is used during the clinical eye exam to examine the structures of the eye. The retinoscope (the front and back are shown at the right) is used to measure the refractive error in the eye.

sentences (see Chapter 1). A standard distance of 16 in. (40 cm) is used. However, the low vision specialist will allow the student to choose the distance he or she is most comfortable with in order to get an idea of functional near ability and to make an initial judgment as to the type of low vision device to use. If the test is given at the standard 16 in. (40 cm), it may be converted to an equivalent distance acuity. It is important to remember that this may differ significantly from the results of the distance acuity test, because it assumes a correlation between near and distance vision that does not necessarily exist. Other near-point tasks may also be used to assess near acuity, particularly with very young children and with students who are unable to respond verbally or who cannot identify common letters, numbers, or symbol names. Materials such as small objects, pictures, and school materials may be used to estimate levels of acuity for such students.

Deborah Lapolice

A trial frame is a lens holder that is used when performing a refraction.

Visual Fields and Perimetry

Tests of the central visual field and perimetry, including the Goldmann Visual Field Test, the Humphrey Visual Field Test, the tangent screen, and the amsler grid, provide information regarding visual field defects and scotomas (see Chapter 2), and give an overall picture of "available vision." The computer-generated tests, such as the Humphrey and Goldmann tests, provide a more detailed mapping of the visual fields than the noncomputerized tests and are usually done as part of an ophthalmological exam. These tests are also used to assist in diagnosing the disease process in such visual impairments as retinitis pigmentosa, macular degeneration, or glaucoma. Visual skills testing, although not as formalized, provides functional information as to where the areas of best potential vision are located. Such testing will assist the low vision specialist in developing a training plan.

Color Vision

Testing of color vision is especially important for students, insofar as it provides useful information regarding functional abilities in sorting, mobility, and the completion of daily tasks. Color vision tests will also provide useful information regarding the student's contrast abilities. This may be done by presenting color matching activities with objects in the environment or by using standard tests such as the Farnsworth Panel D-15 or the Ishihara Color Plates. Lighting is an important issue when testing color vision since the full range of reflected light must be available in order for the appropriate cone function to take place. The results of color vision testing may not be used in prescribing low vision devices, but they will be very useful in directing a student's academic and vocational training.

Refraction and Conventional Lenses

The low vision specialist will test for refraction to determine the optimal amount of correction possible with conventional lenses (see Chapter 4 for a more detailed discussion of refraction and low vision devices). Full refraction for students with low vision warrants the use of trial frames and lenses with an initial retinoscopy. Typical refractive errors like myopia (nearsightedness), hyperopia (farsightedness), or astigmatism (curvature of the cornea) can often be corrected with refraction and lenses. This best-corrected distance acuity can then be used to determine the level of magnification needed for a low vision distance device. It can also be the starting point for assessing the magnification needed for near devices. Near-acuity testing may be redone at this time to determine whether the addition of a bifocal will increase the ability of the student to read 1 meter (1M) size print. If the bifocal is warranted, fitting will be done to ensure that it is in the proper position to ensure optimal usage. The low vision specialist will provide a prescription for these conventional lenses.

Contact lenses may be used to improve the acuity in students with irregular cornea surfaces or with high refractive errors. These contact lenses may be prescribed during the visit or may require fitting by an optometrist or contact lens specialist.

Binocular Vision and Oculomotor Skills

Most students with low vision use one eye primarily (monocularity). The low vision specialist can determine the potential for sustaining binocularity (use of both eyes). This is done using a variety of tests and observations: the Hirshberg test to determine whether motor misalignment is present (see Chapter 2); the Worth four-dot test to determine the presence of sensory fusion; the binocular contrast sensitivity test; comparison of monocular visual acuity; and student functioning. Both tests for fusion and for contrast sensitivity are noninvasive. In fusion tests, students are asked to wear a pair of lenses that will provide a three-dimensional optical image of testing materials, which may include a fly, dots, or animal pictures. The student's ability or inability to recognize the three-dimensional image provides information as to the amount of fusion present. With contrast sensitivity testing, the student is asked to view a series of pictures or circles with decreasing contrast. This test is done using only the student's standard correction and results are evaluated by the number of correct responses. The results of these tests will have an impact on the prescription of the low vision device and training.

Oculormotor skills such as fixation and tracking may be assessed. The low vision specialist may ask questions about the student's ability to move his or her eyes from one object to another and whether the student loses his or her place when reading, is able to follow the teacher or a moving object in the classroom, and is able to follow the action at sports events and in physical education class. The low vision specialist will evaluate the student's viewing patterns, scanning abilities, head position, and visual motor abilities.

Contrast Sensitivity, Light Sensitivity, and Illumination Needs

Good sensitivity to the contrast between an object and the surrounding area will increase the visibility of the object. This area is initially assessed using contrast sensitivity tests such as the Pelli-Robson or the Bailey Hi-Low Contrast Acuity chart. These tests provide information on the degree of loss of the ability to detect patterns at low contrast, thus providing information about the problems that may be encountered when engaging in certain tasks. High-frequency losses which prevent discrimination of fine detail at maximum contrast often indicate the need for good lighting, while mild and low losses often correspond to difficulties with mobility and object viewing. If the student performs poorly on the contrast sensitivity tests, more attention will be given to the issues of lighting, glare, and contrast.

Lighting and glare should be evaluated in a variety of settings that match the problem areas mentioned by the parents, student, and teacher of students who are visually impaired. Various types of filters may be used to decrease glare, including such options as Corning CPF blue-blocking lenses, NoIR photochromatic lenses, tinted lenses, or antiglare film (AR coating). These filters may be incorporated into the standard prescription or provided as lenses which fit over the student's current correction. Environmental modifications, such as decreased or redirected lighting, re-orienting the work area, or adjusting the angle of material presented, will also be explored at the low vision clinic as needed.

Low Vision Devices

The low vision specialist will choose possible low vision devices for a student on the basis of both the particular goals for that student and his or her visual acuity outcomes. The specialist then needs to evaluate the student's ability to use those devices on the basis of motor, visual, and cognitive ability. Training is provided on each device, dealing with *focal distance* (the distance between the lens and the point at which light rays converge, the optimal distance from the lens to the viewing material), tracking skills, and practical usage. Numerous training sessions may be necessary in order to make the student feel comfortable with the device. Clinics vary greatly in the methods used for training students. Although some provide the device only after the student has mastered its use, others provide only initial instruction and expect the teacher of students who are visually impaired to provide the training in the skill areas of tracking and scanning. It is always best to discuss the most appropriate way to meet the student's needs with the low vision specialist. Teachers who do not feel comfortable providing this training should express any needs or concerns that they have to the clinician. The teacher of students who are visually impaired may try to request an extended training period when at the low vision exam if one is not offered. This is typically done if the teacher is unfamiliar with the device and usage, if the student exhibits significant difficulty with the device, or if numerous devices are being recommended for trial at the same time. (Chapters 5, 6, and 7 discuss in detail training in the use of various low vision devices.) If further trials with the loaned optical or nonoptical devices are recommended, the teacher of the visually impaired should ask about the conditions under which the device should be used and the length of the trial for each device.

The low vision specialist will prescribe devices for near, intermediate, and distance activities. The choices of these devices are based on the visual acuity levels, visual impairment, visual fields, and the necessity of increased performance in school. Input from the family, teacher of students who are visually impaired, and the student with low vision will provide information as to whether these devices are functional in the actual classroom setting.

By the end of the low vision evaluation, the student, family, and teacher should have received clearly explained information. Too much information can be discouraging to a family and student, making it difficult to implement recommendations. The teacher of students who are visually impaired should try to review the important points of the evaluation toward the end of the session and avoid overwhelming the family with data.

The specific problems that can be addressed with optical or nonoptical aids should have been identified. It is important to provide devices for the everyday problems the student encounters in order to ensure adequate practice with devices. It is also important to provide the least restrictive and most efficient device for the task. For example, a handheld magnifier can allow students access to many materials and is easy to carry and learn how to use (see Chapter 6). High-powered reading lenses are portable and provide many students with limited access to regular print information in a variety of settings. Portable CCTVs provide options for use in a variety of places and are less cumbersome than full-size CCTVs on roller carts (see Chapter 7).

The student should feel comfortable with the devices that were recommended. He or she should have received some training and feel at least somewhat competent in using them. The simple act of nicknaming a monocular or magnifier (for example, "Maggie") can help make the first step in the use of an optical aid a positive one for a young child. It is important that the family and teacher also feel comfortable with the device because the student will look to them for guidance in its use.

At the completion of the initial visit, a recommendation for devices is usually made. In some clinics, loaner devices are sent home with the student for trial use, whereas other clinics recommend additional visits for device training and only prescribe the device after the student has mastered use of it within the clinic. Expectations that the student, teacher, and family will continue to work with this device are assumed. Each clinic and school district will vary in its actual provision of the device. In some districts, schools request that the low vision evaluator train the student with the device and provide the device to the student from the clinic. Other districts may provide the recommended device and training from their own resources. Communication between the family, student, teacher, and clinician is of the utmost importance in determining the number of return visits, and in assuring that the student's needs for training are met.

EVALUATING STUDENTS WITH MULTIPLE DISABILITIES

Evaluation of a student with multiple disabilities is usually considered to be an ongoing process. The results should be used to maximize the student's use of vision in the classroom and home settings for functional tasks. Times for referral may include:

◆ When changes in the educational setting occur.

◆ When changes in visual behaviors are noted, such as changes in gaze, lack of visual attention, or increased difficulties with mobility.

◆ The period before speech or occupational therapy devices are prescribed in order to allow for the maximum to be gained visually from each new device.

◆ When consistent visual performance cannot be obtained from a student.

The goals of a low vision evaluation for the student with multiple disabilities often need to be specifically related to tasks being worked on in his or her functional environments. Clinic staff should be told before the low vision evaluation takes place of the kinds of demands that are placed on the student's vision at home, at school, and in the community. It is helpful if a separate statement describing these daily tasks is added to the prescreening low vision referral form. It may also be helpful if low vision clinic personnel can see the student with multiple disabilities performing daily tasks. The teacher of students who are visually impaired may ask the clinic staff if a slightly longer time can be scheduled when bringing a student with multiple disabilities to the clinic. This will allow the teacher and/or parent to demonstrate the student's use of actual everyday materials, such as selecting items from a menu, looking through a favorite magazine, putting together a puzzle, or communicating using a specialized communication board. It is also helpful if the low vision specialist can know before testing begins how the student communicates best—for example, by pointing, gesturing, sign language, or picture symbols—in order to facilitate the testing process and help the clinic provide an accurate evaluation.

Typical information to be gained during the evaluation of a student with low vision and additional disabilities includes:

◆ The best position for presenting visual information.

◆ The correct size and position for picture symbols or speech devices.

◆ Activities and positions that increase localization and tracking skills.

◆ Information about the reason for head tilts and unusual eye gazes, along with suggestions for decreasing the negative effects of each.

Suppose, as an example, a five-year-old boy with quadriplegia and an undetermined visual impairment has recently begun exhibiting an upward gaze. The teachers, therapists, and family are concerned about his current visual functioning in this position, and they all want to find a way to decrease the behavior. The low vision specialist will evaluate the student's ability to track and visually attend to objects, as well as his body positioning, his ability to shift to a downward gaze, to place objects, and to display eye-muscle balance.

During the evaluation, it will be important for the teacher of students who are visually impaired and the family to provide information regarding the student's educational placement, all medical conditions and treatments, times and tasks in which the student displays visual difficulties, physical limitations, behavioral changes, and related services the student receives. With many of these students, formalized acuity or visual field testing cannot be completed, although the Teller acuity test is used in some clinics for estimating distance acuity. The Teller acuity test is a preferential-looking distance vision test that uses the subjective judgment of the examiner to determine if the student displays a fixation eye movement when presented with a gradient-patterned visual test target. If eye fixation movements are noted for a card, an estimated acuity is determined to exist based on the particular card's level of discriminability. The examiner will usually conduct testing through observation, with the student completing a variety of tasks initiated and aided by the teacher or a family member. The low vision specialist will provide information regarding the potential reason for head tilts or gaze positions, and he or she will provide suggestions for maximizing the student's visual functioning. Clinic personnel vary in their ability to assess children with severe multiple disabilities. It will be up to the teacher of students who are visually impaired to contact the clinic prior to making the appointment to inform the clinician of the child's additional disabilities and goals for the evaluation. This will ensure that the person conducting the evaluation is comfortable with assessing the student and making recommendations.

IMPLEMENTING RECOMMENDATIONS FROM THE LOW VISION CLINIC

The clinical low vision evaluation and report are important tools to help the student with low vision obtain the proper classroom modifications and equipment that will increase the student's academic success. The low vision report provides medical support for any findings and recommendations that may have been cited in a functional vision assessment and learning media assessment by the teacher of students who are visually impaired. The low vision specialist generally writes the low vision report, but the report may contain information from all evaluations, trainers, and consultations conducted at the clinic by various personnel. It is a complete record of the visit and contains specific recommendations as they relate to the evaluation, training, and consultation. Original copies are usually sent to caregivers and the teacher of students who are visually impaired, and an additional copy may be sent to the head of the agency or department paying for the evaluation.

The results of the low vision evaluation should be communicated in clear terms to the professionals involved in the student's program. The teacher of students who are visually impaired and the student's parents should request a team meeting to discuss the evaluation results. They can take that opportunity to have the student display any low vision devices that have been prescribed or loaned in order to demonstrate their use. The other team members may be able to help clarify how the information presented in the low vision report can be applied to enhance the student's functioning in school. Parents will need to know how to implement the recommendations at home as well as how to reinforce literacy activities, and they will benefit from specific recommendations and suggested activities for practice at home with the low vision device.

Occupational therapists will be particularly interested in information provided in a low vision report about a student's fine motor skills and eye-hand coordination. They can help to implement appropriate adaptive technology, such as reading stands and writing slant boards, as well as to develop strategies for improving hand skills (e.g., in handwriting or in the manipulation of toys and switches). They may also use the information to develop effective feeding strategies for students with low vision and with additional disabilities.

Physical therapists will be able to use information from the low vision report to help provide both structural seating plans and positioning support for students, particularly those who have multiple disabilities, to help them maximize the use of their vision in all tasks.

Speech therapists will benefit from certain information in the report if the student is using a special communication device or board. For example, the layout, contrast, and print or picture size are factors that need to be considered by the speech therapist in the overall design of the communication board.

O&M specialists may be involved in training the student in the use of an optical device recommended by the low vision specialist. Community-based outings during mobility lessons are excellent times to reinforce and introduce skills in highly motivating situations. For example, using a telescope to read a fast food menu sign on the wall is a functional activity for most students. State-certified educational evaluators will need to know what types of aids or devices are needed by the student with low vision during academic, achievement, or comprehensive testing in order to ensure nonbiased test results.

Principals, counselors, and other school personnel will need to be made aware of the introduction of optical and nonoptical devices to their school. Many low vision devices are expensive, and the school will feel a responsibility in their safe use while in the student's possession in school. It is usually best for the student to demonstrate the device and its use, allowing administrators and other school personnel to show their support of the student's use of such adaptive equipment in school. School staff are usually happy to be informed of what new things students are doing and will generally show acceptance and enthusiasm to the student with low vision who takes the time to share such information.

The school program and the IEP will need to be reviewed in light of the low vision evaluation, and IEP objectives will have to be written to include training in the use of low vision aids or devices that were recommended in the low vision report; this can be done at the same time. Objectives may need to be written to provide training to a student in how to use a low vision device. The goal of such training is to teach the student how to get information from the overhead projector during class lectures (see Chapter 5) or how to use a hand-held magnifier (see Chapter 6) efficiently with library reference materials. Time-lines for skill acquisition should be included, along with persons responsible for implementing the training as well as reinforcing the skills (see Chapters 5 and 6 for examples of IEP statements).

The teacher of students with low vision may establish a time to meet the classroom teacher, the parents, or the staff most involved with the student. It is best to meet during times when the aids will be used in order to conduct a mini-training session in the use of the device. After the lesson is completed, specific functional situations can be identified in the classroom or at home, situations in which the student can use the aid and in which the family or teacher can reinforce its use. Progress in the use of aids should be monitored regularly, and a record should be kept. Skills should be retaught when necessary.

SUMMARY

A visit to the low vision clinic provides unique opportunities for those involved in collaborating on evaluating and designing ways to help the student with low vision function independently in a variety of everyday settings. Literacy issues will be of prime importance to the teacher of students who are visually impaired. This is also a time when a team of people concerned with a student's daily school functioning can work together to ask important questions and receive information that will help the student in a variety of ways. When specific functional questions are asked, when specific information is given, and when training programs relevant to a student's needs are designed, current and future functioning will be enhanced. When students are successful in using low vision aids and devices, independence is also enhanced. Early evaluation at a low vision clinic can set a standard for programming for students with low vision that will be of benefit to them during the critical school years as well as help them later in adult life.

REFERENCES

AFB directory of services for blind and visually impaired persons living in the United States and Canada, 25th edition. (1997). New York: AFB Press.

Cole, R. G., & Rosenthal, B. P. (1992). *Problems in optometry: Strategies and management of low vision.* Philadelphia: Lippincott.

Corn, A. (1981). Optical aids in the classroom. *Journal of Visual Impairment & Blindness, 12,* 114–121.

Cowan, C., & Shepler, R. (1990). Teaching techniques for teaching young children to use low vision devices. *Journal of Vision Impairment & Blindness, 84,* 419–421.

Goldberg, S. (1991). *Ophthalmology made ridiculously simple.* Miami, FL: MedMaster, Inc.

Hofstetter, H. W. (1991). Efficacy of low vision services for visually impaired children. *Journal of Visual Impairment & Blindness, 85,* 19–22.

Holbrook, C. (Ed.) (1996). *Children with visual impairments: A parents' guide.* Bethesda, MD: Woodbine House, Inc.

Jackson, N. E., & Roller, C. M. (1993). *Reading with young children* (RBBM 9302). Storrs, CT: The National Research Center on the Gifted and Talented, University of Connecticut.

Jose, R. T. (Ed.) (1983). *Understanding low vision.* New York: American Foundation for the Blind.

Koenig, A. J., & Farrenkopf, C. (1997). Essential experiences to undergird the early development of literacy. *Journal of Visual Impairment & Blindness, 91,* 14–24.

Lowenfeld, B. (1981). Effects of blindness on the cognitive functions of children. (1948). In B. Lowenfeld (Ed.), *Berthold Lowenfeld on blindness and blind people.* New York: American Foundation for the Blind.

Padula, W. V., & Shapiro, J. B. (1996). Head injury and the post-trauma vision syndrome. *RE:view, 24,* 153–158.

Swallow, R. (1977). *Assessment for visually handicapped children and youth.* New York: American Foundation for the Blind.

Low Vision
Prescreening Questionnaire

Name _____ Date of Birth _____

Prior low vision exam?   Date _____   Location _____

Does the student wear eyeglasses?   ☐ Yes   ☐ No

   To complete what activities?   ☐ Reading   ☐ Mid-distance tasks   ☐ Distance tasks

Does the student currently use low vision devices?   ☐ Yes   ☐ No

If so, what devices and how often are they used?

   ☐ Magnifier: Strength _____   Activities _____

   ☐ Telescope: Strength _____   Activities _____

   ☐ Other _____

Visual history _____

_____

Other significant health impairments _____

Grade _____

Extracurricular activities _____

_____

Reading Level _____

Reading Media: ☐ Regular Print   ☐ Large Print   ☐ Braille

School's concerns _____

_____

Parents' concerns _____

_____

Student's concerns _____

_____

Goals for low vision examination _____

_____

Task Analysis: Circle the appropriate response

N/A = Not Applicable   N = No Problem   M = Mild Problem   Y = Major Problem
O = Patient Objective

Distance Tasks
Do you have difficulty:

Seeing the board or overhead?	N/A	N	M	Y	O
Getting around people/objects?	N/A	N	M	Y	O
Seeing curbs/stairs?	N/A	N	M	Y	O
Seeing faces?	N/A	N	M	Y	O
Traveling in familiar places?	N/A	N	M	Y	O
Traveling in unfamiliar places?	N/A	N	M	Y	O
Seeing street lights?	N/A	N	M	Y	O
Crossing streets?	N/A	N	M	Y	O
Participating in physical education?	N/A	N	M	Y	O
Other	N/A	N	M	Y	O

Near Tasks
Do you have difficulty:

Reading headlines?	N/A	N	M	Y	O
Reading large print?	N/A	N	M	Y	O
Reading newspapers/magazines?	N/A	N	M	Y	O
Reading phone numbers?	N/A	N	M	Y	O
Reading books/textbooks?	N/A	N	M	Y	O
Seeing price tags and labels?	N/A	N	M	Y	O
Reading maps?	N/A	N	M	Y	O
Reading the dictionary?	N/A	N	M	Y	O
Other	N/A	N	M	Y	O

Writing Tasks
Do you have difficulty:

Signing your name?	N/A	N	M	Y	O
Writing in print?	N/A	N	M	Y	O
Writing in cursive?	N/A	N	M	Y	O
Writing on printed lines?	N/A	N	M	Y	O
Transferring information?	N/A	N	M	Y	O
Other	N/A	N	M	Y	O

Lighting
Do you have difficulty:

Tolerating the sun?	N/A	N	M	Y	O
On cloudy/rainy days?	N/A	N	M	Y	O
Seeing in dim light?	N/A	N	M	Y	O

Do you wear sunglasses?	N/A	N		Y	
Are the sunglasses effective?	N/A	N		Y	
Does a bright light help you to see better?	N/A	N		Y	

Other tasks
Do you have difficulty:

Using a computer?	N/A	N	M	Y	O
Seeing to play games?	N/A	N	M	Y	O
Seeing to complete art activities?	N/A	N	M	Y	O
Completing worksheets?	N/A	N	M	Y	O
Matching colors?	N/A	N	M	Y	O
Telling time?	N/A	N	M	Y	O
Seeing food on your plate?	N/A	N	M	Y	O
Participating in your hobbies?	N/A	N	M	Y	O
Other	N/A	N	M	Y	O

Low Vision Devices: An Overview

MARK WILKINSON

DURING THE VISIT to the low vision clinic (see Chapter 3), the subject of low vision devices can be addressed. The focus of this chapter will be to provide an overview of the various low vision devices available, what they do, how they are used, and how they can help children with visual impairments acquire and maintain literacy skills. An optical low vision device is part of the array of tools used by students who are visually impaired to meet their educational, vocational, and day-to-day functional literacy needs.

For example, low vision devices used in an education setting can assist the student in many ways. Material presented on an overhead projector or on a chalkboard can be made accessible to the student with low vision by using a monocular telescope (see Chapter 5). Bifocal spectacles can help the student view material up close and then refocus on the teacher for the discussion portion of the class.

In a vocational setting, the student with low vision can use low vision devices to meet the demands of the workplace. A stand magnifier can be used in the industrial arts class to examine a machine manual while actually working on the machine.

Day-to-day functional literacy needs, or literacy tasks that are of practical significance in a student's daily life, can also be met using low vision devices (Koenig, 1996). When functional literacy is achieved, the student is able to use skills or tools to gain independent access to regular print—for example, when literacy tasks require communication with others in this medium. Functional literacy tasks include such things as using reference books; completing admission or registration forms; reading periodicals, maps, classified ads, and labels on bottles; paying bills; telling time; filling out a credit card application form; writing a check; reading menus in restaurants; and voting. Using a low vision device is one of the most commonly employed strategies used by students in their attempt to gain independent access to print.

LOW VISION SERVICES

As detailed in Chapter 3, comprehensive low vision services provide an assessment of visual functioning and recommendations concerning low vision devices. These provide the starting point for the educational team working to help the student with low vision achieve functional literacy. For this reason, low vision services must be an integral part of the ongoing care provided for children with visual impairments. Members of the low vision team who may work with a child who has a visual impairment include the following:

- The primary eye care practitioner.
- The low vision specialist (optometrist or ophthalmologist).
- The teacher of students with visual impairments.
- An educational consultant.
- A technology consultant.
- An orientation and mobility (O&M) specialist.
- Classroom teacher(s).
- Parent(s).

This team works together to assess the strengths and weaknesses of the student with respect to his or her educational, vocational, and avocational pursuits. They will work with the student and other members of the team to help the student function at his or her highest potential during his or her formal education years—and also later, as an adult.

Low vision devices can be acquired or purchased from a variety of different sources, including low vision specialists, primary eye care specialists, optical shops, closed-circuit television (CCTV) dealers, and mail order catalogs (see the

Resources section). However, it must be stressed that it is essential that a low vision specialist prescribe optical low vision devices. Well-intentioned teachers, family members, or friends may suggest or offer a low vision device to "help" the student with low vision, but these individuals have neither the training nor the experience to prescribe such aids. More harm can result than good. Low vision specialists, unlike many other sources, will typically provide the user with an extended trial of the recommended device(s) to determine their efficacy on a day-to-day basis before the device is purchased. A list of low vision providers in each state or province should be available through the state or provincial optometric and ophthalmological associations. It should also be noted that not all low vision specialists have experience in dealing with the special needs and educational considerations of children with visual impairments or children with multiple disabilities.

REFRACTION

As mentioned in Chapter 2, performing a refraction is an essential component of determining what device or devices may assist a student with low vision. A refraction is the process of determining and correcting refractive errors that prevent images from being brought into focus on the retina. If you consider the eye as a camera, the focusing elements of the eye are the cornea and the lens. The film of the camera is analogous to the retina. Because of the length of the eyeball and/or the curvature of the cornea, light rays may converge in front of the retina (myopia), behind the retina (hyperopia), or on more than one plane (astigmatism). (See Sidebar 4.1.)

High refractive errors are those over ±6.00 diopters. A diopter is a unit of measurement that indicates the power of a lens that refracts or bends light. By performing a refraction, the low vision specialist is then able to determine if spectacles or a spectacle lens change will improve visual functioning for distance and/or near-vision tasks. To correct refractive errors, a plus (+) lens, which is convex (thick in the middle), bends light rays inward (converges); a minus (−) lens, which is concave (thick on the edges), spreads light rays out (diverges). (See Figure 4.1.) Once a refraction has been performed, the need for additional low vision devices can be determined.

It should be noted that the degree of correction does not always predict how well the student will see when wearing spectacles or contact lenses. The lenses simply focus the image on the retina, the "film" in the "camera." From there, the photoreceptor cells of the eye (rods and cones) must register the image. These photoreceptor cells then send a signal through the optic nerve to the occipital lobe (visual cortex) of the brain, where the image is seen. Problems

---

Sidebar **4.1**

Common Refractive Errors

Hyperopia (farsightedness). With this condition, the eye is either shorter than normal, or the cornea and lens of the eye do not have enough power to focus light rays on the retina. As a result, the image is focused on a point behind the retina (see Figure 4.1). Things are blurry up close and less blurry in the distance. To correct for hyperopia, a plus (+) lens is generally needed to provide the eye with the extra focusing power it is lacking to ensure that the image is focused directly on the retina.

Myopia (nearsightedness). With this condition, the eye is either longer than normal, or the cornea and lens of the eye have too much power to focus light rays on the retina. As a result, the image is focused in front of the retina (see Figure 4.1). Things are blurry in the distance and less blurry up close. To correct for myopia, a minus (−) lens is typically needed to take away the excess focusing power of the eye to ensure that the image is focused directly on the retina.

Astigmatism With astigmatism, the cornea and lens of the eye are not round—they are more football shaped. This results in two different powers for the eye, which are 90 degrees apart from each other. The more curved part of the eye is less hyperopic or more myopic than the less curved part. A toric or cylindrical lens is needed to correct for astigmatism. A toric or cylindrical lens has two different powers that compensate for the two different powers of the eye.

Presbyopia Presbyopia occurs as the lens of the eye ages. This causes the lens to become less elastic, which results in difficulties when trying to focus for reading and other near-point tasks. This condition affects most people by their mid-forties, resulting in the need for reading glasses or bifocal lenses. However, a teenaged student with low vision who holds reading materials at 5 inches, for example, will often require reading glasses or bifocals in his or her teens because of the increased accommodative demands placed on the eyes by this closer working distance.

---

with any of these components of the visual system—the retina, the optic nerve, or brain—can result in decreased visual functioning that cannot be fixed with eyeglasses.

For students with high refractive errors or anisometropia (a discrepancy of visual acuity between the two eyes), contact lenses can be helpful in improving overall visual functioning, and they are often cosmetically more appealing than thick spectacles. Students with nystagmus or distorted corneas may see significantly better when they use contact lenses because the contacts provide a clearer optical image to the retina than a comparably powered pair of eyeglasses. Contact lenses can be colored to reduce photophobia by creating an artificial pupil that will decrease the amount of light entering the eye. Additionally, such a contact lens can provide a better cosmetic appearance for students with conditions such as aniridia and iris coloboma (a condition in which the normal iris is absent or incomplete). Students who have had cataract surgery—without an intraocular lens implant—may experience a larger field of view with contact lenses than with eyeglasses.

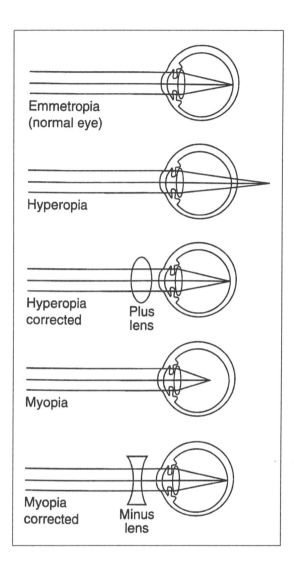

Figure 4.1

**Refractive Errors and Lenses
Used for Correction**

Source: Reprinted, with permission, from "Anatomy and
Physiology of the Eye," in *Foundations of Low Vision:
Clinical and Functional Perspectives* (p. 76), edited by
A. Corn & A. J. Koenig, 1996, New York: AFB Press.

MAGNIFICATION

When a child needs help to read print visually, there are several options the low
vision specialist should review with the student, with input from the teacher
of students with visual impairments. All of these options improve visual functioning by providing magnification that results in a larger image on the retina.
Each type of magnification provides different methods for enlarging print, as
shown in Sidebar 4.2.

Relative Distance Magnification

Relative distance magnification is the easiest way to magnify an object. Relative
distance magnification occurs when an object is brought closer to the eye. For

---

Sidebar **4.2**

Magnification Options for Reading Print

Type of Magnification	Method of Enlarging Print
Relative distance magnification.	Hold the materials closer to the eye.
Relative size magnification.	Enlarge the print.
Angular magnification.	Use a low vision device.
Electronic magnification.	Use a CCTV or computer software.

---

example, if an object being viewed at a 16-in. (40 cm) working distance (that is, the distance from the eye to the object being viewed) is brought closer to the eye so that it is now viewed at 4 in. (10 cm), the relative distance of the object to the eye has been decreased by a factor of 4 (16 in. ÷ 4 in. = 4). Therefore, the image will appear four times larger (4×).

Relative Size Magnification

Relative size magnification occurs when the object is enlarged while maintaining the same working distance. This is the type of magnification used in large-print materials.

Angular Magnification

Angular magnification occurs when an object has not changed in position or size, but an optical device is interposed between the object and the eye to make the object appear larger. Telescopes and hand magnifiers are used in this type of magnification. An example of angular magnification is the change in the object size noted when viewing football players on the far side of the field with a pair of binoculars as opposed to using one's regular vision.

Projection or Electronic Magnification

Another category of magnification is electronic or video magnification. Electronic magnification has the advantage of providing greater levels of magnification with a larger field of view than can be provided by a conventional optical device, such as a magnifier; in addition, electronic magnification is able to provide contrast enhancement.

LOW VISION DEVICES

Near Vision Optical Devices

Regular size print can be too small for some students with low vision to see clearly or to read comfortably. Near-vision optical devices such as reading spectacles, prisms, magnifiers, head loupes, and telemicroscopes are designed to bring near-point activities (e.g., reading and writing) into focus. Near-vision devices, like other low vision devices, should be prescribed only by a qualified eye care specialist, such as an optometrist or ophthalmologist, at a low vision evaluation center.

Reading Spectacles

When a child begins to have more difficulties with sustained near-point activities and complains of headaches, eyestrain, or fatigue, the need for a reading correction device or bifocal should be reviewed by the low vision specialist (see Chapter 3). During the low vision evaluation, if the teacher of students with visual impairments or the child's parents have additional questions or concerns about the student's reading abilities when using the prescribed low vision devices, additional evaluations can be requested. Additional evaluations could include a learning media assessment (Koenig & Holbrook, 1995) to determine whether or not there has been a change in the primary literacy medium, another functional vision assessment (FVA), or a review by the student's primary eye care specialist.

All children have considerable ability to accommodate (focus their eyes for near-point tasks) when they are younger. This accommodative ability allows students with visual impairments to function comfortably at the closer working distances required for them to read regular sized print. Additionally, they can sustain the accommodative effort needed for closer working distances for an extended period of time without eyestrain or fatigue. Because of this ability, a reading correction is often not needed until the second decade of life for children who are visually impaired. Beginning at approximately 10 years of age, the accommodative abilities of the eyes start to decrease. This decrease is more noticeable for students with visual impairments because of the closer working distances they naturally adopt for near-point tasks such as reading. When accommodation becomes more difficult to sustain, reading glasses are needed for the eye to focus clearly and comfortably. This decrease in accommodative ability occurs whether the child is using eyeglasses or contact lenses. For this reason, reading spectacles are often needed to complement the use of contact lenses for best near-point visual functioning as the student gets older.

Mark Wilkinson

Students with low vision often need reading glasses as they get older to allow them to function comfortably for extended periods at the close working distances they naturally adopt.

As the strength of the reading spectacles is increased to provide greater reading power, its focal length—the distance between the lens and the point where the light rays entering the lens are brought into focus—becomes shorter. Therefore, the working distance—the distance between the eye and the object being viewed—is also reduced. Reading spectacles do not magnify by themselves, but they do so because they allow the object to be positioned closer to the eye. A closer working distance increases the person's ability to read small print as a result of relative distance magnification.

If binocular vision (both eyes working together with similar visual functioning) is present, it is possible to maintain binocularity with the use of base-in prisms (the base is the thickest part of the prism) in the person's reading spectacles to powers of 10–12 diopters. Prism lenses are triangle-shaped lenses that redirect light rays entering the eye, thereby changing the place where the image lands on the retina. Prism lenses are incorporated into the regular lenses of the spectacle. Base-in prisms allow the two eyes to work together more comfortably because the eyes do not have to converge (turn in) as much as they would if the prism were not present. The teacher of students who are visually impaired can easily tell if the student is wearing prism glasses because if the glasses are held at an angle, the teacher can see the rainbowlike colors on the surface of the spectacles.

For those students who need even more magnification (greater than 10–12 diopters), they must learn to perform near visual tasks monocularly (with just one eye). Often, students with low vision have significantly better vision in one eye than the other, or they are only able to use one eye at a time. This is because their eye condition has significantly affected one eye more than the other. However, this lack of binocularity typically does not create a problem in reading tasks for the student.

Reading spectacles come in three designs: half eye (sometimes called "granny glasses"), which allow users normal distance vision when they look over the top of the frame; full frame; and microscopic. Microscopic spectacles are monocular spectacle corrections in higher powers. Optically, because of their aspheric design (special design of the lens that minimizes the distortion produced by the peripheral areas of the lens), they provide a clearer image than would be seen with a standard spectacle lens design of similar strength.

Advantages of Monocular or Binocular Reading Spectacles

◆ They offer the widest field of view.
◆ They allow the wearer to keep both hands free.
◆ They are relatively inexpensive.
◆ They are relatively inconspicuous.

Disadvantages of Monocular or Binocular Reading Spectacles

◆ They require a closer working distance.
◆ Because of the closer working distance, they can lead to arm fatigue and increased head movement when reading.
◆ They can be uncomfortable for the person using them for sustained near-point activities.

Magnifiers

A wide variety of magnifiers exists. (See Chapter 6 for a detailed discussion of magnifiers.) Magnifiers can be handheld or mounted on a stand that eliminates

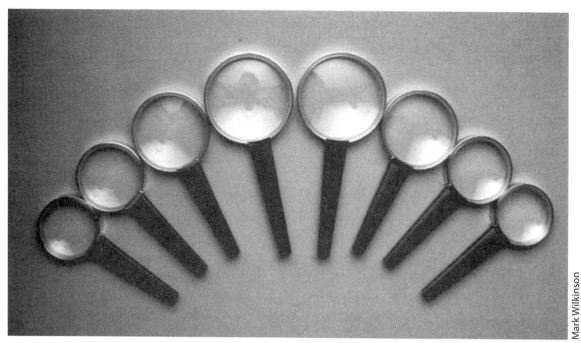

Mark Wilkinson

Handheld magnifiers may be used for a variety of near-vision tasks, such as spot checking small print in dictionaries or f-stop settings on cameras.

the need to hold them. Some have built-in light sources, and some are fixed to flexible arms.

A source of confusion about hand and stand magnifiers is the problem of lens size versus magnification power. Often, students want a large, high-powered magnifier. However, the optics of lenses dictates that as the power of the magnifier is increased, the diameter of the lens decreases. The smaller lens size and resulting smaller field of view can be frustrating for students who need a higher-powered magnifier.

Advantages of Hand/Stand Magnifiers

◆ They are helpful for specific activities, such as reading small print on maps, exponent notations in math books, accents on letters, selective reference materials, or when setting the exposure and/or aperture of a camera.

◆ They are easy to use for people with eccentric fixation.

◆ They are portable.

◆ They are flexible.

◆ They are relatively inexpensive.

◆ Stand magnifiers may be helpful for individuals with hand tremors because they do not require the individual to maintain a specific working distance.

Disadvantages of Hand/Stand Magnifiers

◆ It can be difficult to use a hand or stand magnifier when writing or playing a musical instrument.
◆ The total field of view is decreased when using a hand or stand magnifier.
◆ Reasonably good eye-hand coordination is necessary.
◆ During lengthy periods of reading, arm fatigue can also become a factor.

Head Loupes

Head loupes are simple convex (plus) lenses for magnifying that can be used in monocular or binocular form when mounted in front of the eye. Head loupes can be attached to regular spectacle lenses and moved in front of the eye as necessary, or they can be worn over spectacles as a separate unit. Head loupes are most useful for viewing small objects at a very close distance (e.g., repairing electronic circuitry, or checking negatives, prints, or slides).

Advantages of Head Loupes

◆ The lens can be moved in and out of the line of sight, as necessary.
◆ They allow both hands to remain free.
◆ They are relatively inexpensive.

Disadvantages of Head Loupes

◆ They have a negative cosmetic appearance.
◆ A close working distance is required (1.5–10 in.).

Telemicroscopes

Telemicroscopes are intermediate and near-vision telescopes that provide additional magnification to a student's existing visual system. They can be helpful for individuals who need a longer working distance as well as hands-free magnification. Telemicroscopes are prescribed for students who cannot function comfortably at the closer working distance required by other spectacle mounted systems, such as reading spectacles. A telemicroscope could be used when working on a computer or reading music while playing a musical instrument.

When the visual acuity between the two eyes is essentially equal, using a binocular telemicroscope system is the logical approach. If the visual acuity of the two eyes is not equal, the better eye should be fitted with the telescope.

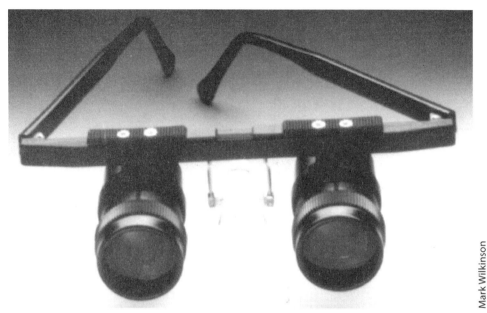

Mark Wilkinson

Telemicroscopes are useful for students who need to view small features from a greater distance and must have both hands free.

Advantages of Telemicroscopes

◆ They can be set for any working distance desired.

◆ Arm fatigue is not a factor.

◆ The student's hands are kept free to do various manipulative tasks (writing, typing, keyboarding, and so on).

Disadvantages of Telemicroscopes

◆ They may not be focusable.

◆ They are more conspicuous than other reading devices.

◆ They are more expensive than other reading devices.

◆ They involve a smaller field of view than other reading devices.

◆ The weight of the system can limit the length of time a student can use them.

◆ Spectacle mounted systems require additional head movement (because of their smaller field of view).

◆ They may be considered less cosmetically appealing than handheld devices.

Distance Vision Devices

Telescopes

Telescopes can be handheld or mounted on eyeglasses, monocular or binocular. They are also adjustable to varying viewing distances from 10 in. (25 cm) to infin-

Telescopes are used for intermediate and distance tasks. They come in a wide variety of styles, such as monocular (top), spectacle (center), and binocular (bottom).

ity. Telescopes are useful for students who need to be able to spot an object in the distance but do not have the ability to get closer to the object. For example, a student trying to read the menu behind the counter at a fast-food restaurant could use a telescope to locate the appropriate section of the menu and then make a choice. (See Chapter 5 for a detailed discussion of training students to use a monocular telescope.)

Advantages of Telescopes

◆ They are helpful for such tasks as orientation and mobility, reading the chalkboard, and reading street signs.

◆ They are relatively inconspicuous.

◆ They are flexible for use in a number of tasks, such as viewing the signs in the aisles of the grocery store and then reading the labels of the items on the shelves.

Disadvantages of Telescopes

◆ They have a smaller field of view.

◆ They may be difficult to use if eccentric fixation is present.

For driving purposes, bioptic telescopes (small Galilean telescopes mounted in the upper portion of a pair of glasses) can be used legally in many states to provide enhanced distance resolution ability for briefly spot checking distance targets (for example, reading road signs). That is, the student can shift back and forth from a standard prescription spectacle to the telescope as needed. This capability can allow some individuals with low vision who are carefully screened and who receive appropriate driver's education to drive a vehicle.

Binoculars

Binoculars are another type of distance optical device. Binoculars have two lenses (one for each eye) that increase the field of view because both images are projected onto the retina to form a "whole" picture. Binoculars can be two telescopes mounted on regular spectacle lenses or they can be handheld units, like the binoculars used to go bird watching or when attending the opera. Binoculars are typically used to watch plays, sporting events, and other activities in the distance.

Advantages of Binoculars

◆ They provide a wider field of view than a monocular handheld telescope.

◆ They may be easier to manipulate and focus than a monocular handheld telescope.

Disadvantages of Binoculars

◆ They are heavy.

◆ They are large.

◆ Inability to focus at intermediate and near distances.

◆ Typically need two hands to hold them up to the eyes.

Electronic or Projection Magnification Devices
Closed-Circuit Televisions (CCTVs)

CCTVs are electronic devices that provide magnification by the use of a video camera that projects the enlarged image onto a television monitor (see Chapter 7 for a detailed discussion of CCTVs). CCTVs are the only optical devices that provide both contrast enhancement and magnification in addition to a larger field of view than any other optical device of similar strength. Students with very limited vision, who use auditory or tactual approaches as their primary learning modality, may find it helpful to use a CCTV for reading maps, reference materials or worksheets that cannot be easily scanned or transcribed into braille.

Advantages of CCTVs

◆ The amount of magnification can be varied.

◆ The image can be reversed to allow the viewer to see black letters as white letters on a black background.

◆ They are available in both black-and-white and color models.

Disadvantages of CCTVs

◆ They are expensive.

◆ They have a relative lack of portability.

Computer Magnification

Another form of projection magnification is enlarged text on computer screens (see also the section on Technology later in this chapter). The number and type of programs and equipment available are constantly changing and are beyond the scope of this book. Such systems are typically not provided through a low vision evaluation. Students who may benefit from this type of magnification should be evaluated by their educational system's technology consultant or team or by a rehabilitation program that specializes in assistive technology devices.

Absorptive Lenses and Filters

Absorptive lenses or filters are colored lenses that are prescribed on the basis of reported symptoms of photophobia (light sensitivity) that can occur both indoors and out. There are almost an unlimited number of colors available. Clinically, the perception of the effect of the filters by each individual weighs heavily in the decision as to which absorptive filter is best. There are no one or two colors that work best for most children or for a specific eye condition. This

Absorptive lenses improve this student's visual function in bright lighting conditions.

is why individual trials of the various filters are critical when trying to determine which will work best for a given child. Children with conditions such as albinism, aniridia, achromatopsia, and iris coloboma can be highly photophobic, although this is not universally the case. Absorptive lenses may be placed in frames with shields on the tops and sides to prevent extraneous light from entering the eye.

Field Expansion Systems

If the teacher of students who are visually impaired has a student with a field loss and if this student is having difficulties with reading because of the field loss, field expansion techniques may prove beneficial in helping the student be more aware of the materials being presented in his or her missing field of view. According to Faye (1984), there are three options available to an individual who wishes to compensate for a large area of missing peripheral field:

◆ Compress the existing image to include more of the available area.

◆ Provide prisms that relocate images from the blind area into the seeing area.

◆ Use a mirror to reflect an image from the nonseeing area (this option can sometimes be helpful for independent travel but does not usually have applications for literacy activities).

Fresnel lenses and prisms are a brand name of pliable, soft plastic lenses that can be attached temporarily to regular spectacles. One of the most common uses of prisms, aside from their use discussed earlier in the section regarding reading spectacles to maintain binocularity, is in the treatment of field loss. In this case, Fresnel prisms arc placed on an area of the lens that brings objects into view that were otherwise not visible to the student because of the field loss. Fresnel prisms in powers of 10–20 diopters are placed with the base in the direction of the field loss. The prism is often presented over the temporal (outer) half of the lens on the side of the field loss. When the student directs his or her eye into the prism area, a low contrast image from the missing field will come into view. Because of the decrease in visual acuity as a result of the reduced contrast, most students will reject Fresnel prisms as a permanent solution for field enhancement. However, a trial is helpful to see if the student will benefit from having a prism incorporated into his or her spectacle correction.

In the past, reversed telescopes have been used to compress the existing image in order to enhance the effective visual field for persons who have concentric peripheral field loss (tunnel vision). With this technique, the individual looks through the objective end of the telescope (end closest to the object when being viewed) rather than the ocular end (the part of the telescope normally placed up to the eye). Although the field of view has increased, the image has become smaller. Therefore, this device has no use for literacy tasks because the image being viewed will be minimized—and therefore it will be more difficult to view. This device can be helpful for individuals with small visual fields who are having trouble with independent travel.

OTHER METHODS OF VISION ENHANCEMENT

Optical low vision devices are of great benefit to many students with visual impairments. However, there are a number of additional methods of enhancing visual performance, including contrast, body posture, lighting, nonoptical devices, and auditory assistance.

Nonoptical Enhancements

A number of nonoptical devices and accessories can assist the visual performance of students who have low vision under a variety of circumstances. For example, felt-tipped pens are helpful for writing activities because they provide a darker

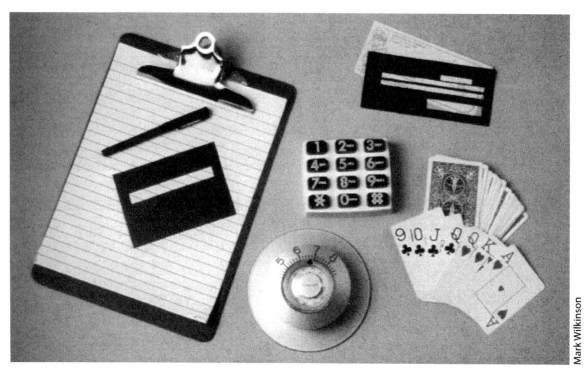

Mark Wilkinson

A number of nonoptical devices can be useful to students with low vision, such as bold-line paper and felt-tip pens, large-type telephone dials and playing cards, raised markings on dials, and signature guides.

and thicker line for the student to see than most ink pens or pencils. Reading stands and copyholders are useful for both reading and keyboard work because they allow the student to maintain a more normal body posture while moving those materials to be viewed closer to the eye. Such devices also enable the student to use both hands to work on other activities, such as reading books or transcribing materials to a computer while viewing the material on the copy stand. Large print and assistive devices such as auditory watches, talking clocks, and talking calculators are other options available to support the assistance being received from optical low vision devices.

Technology

Technological advances that assist students with low vision include computer speech synthesis and variable size fonts, to name a few. Many high quality computer speech synthesis programs are now available. This software, combined with a sound card or speakers, enables the computer to say aloud what is on the screen. Variable size font programs enlarge whatever is visible on the monitor to various sizes. This enables the student to sit farther back from the monitor and still see the screen. The teacher of students who are visually impaired, along

Table **4.1**

The SETT Framework for Evaluating Assistive Technology

S Student	E Environments	T Tasks	T Tools
◆ Eye condition. ◆ Low vision evaluation findings. ◆ Functional vision information. ◆ Consideration of other impairments.	◆ Home. ◆ School. ◆ Vocational. ◆ Community.	◆ Activities with which the student may require technology.	◆ What are needed by the student to function as independently, efficiently, and competitively as possible.

Source: Adapted from The SETT framework: Critical issues to consider when choosing and using assistive technology, by J. Zabala, 1995, Minneapolis, MN.

with the technology team (if one exists in the school or school district) or rehabilitation specialist, will review with the educational team the options that are appropriate for a given child. The expertise of a technology consultant is invaluable in answering questions regarding access to technology and the use of technology to increase visual functioning.

When appropriate, the technology consultant reviews assistive technology designed to improve current visual functioning. The technology consultant considers a range of solutions, from low-tech to high-tech; facilitates access to technology; and makes referrals for local follow-up or provides follow-up in the student's home, school, and community. Review of technology options should be part of the ongoing process to determine what additional learning and literacy media will best meet the needs of students with visual impairments. Table 4.1 outlines factors that the technology consultant may consider when using the SETT framework (Zabala, 1995); SETT refers to the *s*tudent, the *e*nvironments in which the student functions, the *t*asks to be performed, and the *t*ools available to assist the student.

Lighting

Quality and quantity of illumination are critical for optimum visual functioning. When performing prolonged near-point tasks (for example, reading a novel), the light source should be positioned to avoid glare problems. Many students find that a light angled over the shoulder (nearer the better seeing eye), with adjustments in the positioning of the materials to be viewed (for example, holding the material on an upward angle or using a reading stand), helps to reduce glare. An adjustable lamp with an incandescent indoor floodlight bulb of 60–75 watts is usually effective in controlling task illumination and enhancing contrast. When watching television, someone sitting close to the screen can experience increased illumination of the images and enlargement of those images.

SUMMARY

Ongoing, comprehensive low vision services are an essential component in the education of students with visual impairments. This is especially true for students with visual impairments, because their visual needs are constantly changing as they advance through school and work to become more independent. Simply providing the student with a hand magnifier or a CCTV, without having his or her specific visual abilities and needs assessed, may result in the child not being able to perform at his or her highest level of functional literacy. A low vision refraction on a regular basis is important in order to find uncorrected or undercorrected refractive errors. Without the appropriate spectacle correction, the student's overall visual functioning may be reduced. With ongoing low vision services, children with visual impairments can develop their literacy skills to a higher level than they would if they were only provided with large-print materials. Optical devices can be helpful tools to add to the repertoire that a student needs to be successful.

REFERENCES

Faye, E. E. (1984). The effect of eye condition on functional vision. In E. Faye (Ed.), *Clinical low vision, (2nd ed.).* Boston: Little, Brown.

Koenig, A. J. (1996). The literacy of individuals with low vision. In A. Corn & A. J. Koenig (Eds.), *Foundations of low vision: Clinical and functional perspectives* (pp. 53–66). New York: AFB Press.

Koenig, A. J., & Holbrook, M. C. (1995). *Learning media assessment of students with visual impairments (2nd ed.).* Austin, TX: Texas School for the Blind and Visually Impaired.

Ward, M. E. (1996). Anatomy and physiology of the eye. In A. Corn & A. J. Koenig (Eds.), *Foundations of low vision: Clinical and functional perspectives* (pp. 69–85). New York: AFB Press.

Zabala, J. (1995). The SETT framework: Critical issues to consider when choosing and using assistive technology. Presented at Closing the Gap Conference on the Use of Assistive Technology in special Education and Rehabilitation, Minneapolis, MN, October 1995. Available online at http://sac.uky.edu/~jszaba0/JoySETT.html.

Activities and Games for Teaching Children to Use Monocular Telescopes

CHRISSY COWAN AND RENAE SHEPLER

HROUGHOUT THEIR DAY, students with visual impairments are required to perform countless visual tasks in order to be included in academic, social, recreational, and daily life activities. Teachers often need to provide modified methods and materials to such students to ensure educational access, yet it is a tremendous challenge to keep up with the sheer volume of visual information presented daily in the classroom.

Historically, teachers of students with visual impairments have been trained to provide a wide range of modifications for students in the environment and in the materials they use, in addition to suggesting such strategies as using peers as note takers, providing carbons of notes, asking classroom teachers to provide copies of materials presented at a distance (for example, the chalkboard), or recommending special seating arrangements. While these methods may be helpful in some situations, they also have some disadvantages. For one thing, they can force the student into a passive role, one in which the responsibility for

Some material in this chapter is from "Techniques for Teaching Young Children to Use Low Vision Devices," by C. Cowan & R. Shepler, 1990, *Journal of Visual Impairment & Blindness, 84,* pp. 419–421. Adapted with permission.

Mark Wilkinson

Monocular telescopes can help students access information in the community as well as in school.

getting information and material lies with someone else. Furthermore, these modifications and strategies do not teach skills that transfer to environments other than those that involve specific classroom tasks. Students with low vision also need access to bulletin boards, visual educational prompts, body and facial language, demonstrations, interactive teaching presentations, and activity in the lunchroom or on the playground. Outside of the school environment, students typically have no strategies for accessing information such as scoreboards, movies, menus at fast-food restaurants, and thousands of general concepts which occur at a distance.

As an alternative to providing modified materials and teaching techniques, teaching the use of a monocular telescope that has been prescribed by a low vision specialist (see Chapter 3) enables students to be included in the full scope of activities which contribute to a diverse and independent life. As part of the array of compensatory skills taught to students with visual impairments, the use of monocular telescopes requires specific training to ensure success in the classroom as well as in the transition to diverse settings.

LAYING THE GROUNDWORK

The introduction of assistive technology devices such as a monocular telescope to students who are visually impaired will depend on a number of factors, including coordination, interest level, medical and physical considerations, and the availability of consistent training (see Sidebar 5.1).

A thorough evaluation by a professional low vision specialist (see Chapter 3) should occur before the teacher of students with visual impairments begins a training program with monocular telescopes. This step is critical, as a low vision specialist will be able to provide essential information regarding such issues as the presence of scotomas (blind spots) and eccentric viewing angles, which may affect the student's performance with a monocular telescope.

Some teachers of students who are visually impaired may choose to present lessons aimed at familiarizing the student with monocular telescopes even before referring the student for a low vision evaluation. These lessons are brief and exploratory—the teacher can simply present a variety of telescopes (for example, 2.5×, 4.0×, 6.0×) for the student to try in a range of typical activities. The purpose of these miniexposures is neither to teach the skills required to effectively use the devices nor to prescribe the device itself (which is the job of the low vision specialist). Rather, it gives an idea of the student's motivation for and aptitude in using the device. For example, upon his or her first exposure to a monocular telescope, a student will not know how to focus or locate a target.

Sidebar **5.1**

Factors that Lead to the Successful Use of a Monocular Telescope

- Initial exposure to telescopes at a young age.

- Desire for independence.

- Desire to participate in the same activities as one's peers.

- Positive attitude toward using a device.

- Support from the family.

- Specific training that involves many environments.

- Availability of the device, including a replacement device.

- The coordination of efforts between the teacher of students who are visually impaired, the student's family, and other professionals.

- The ability to maintain stability and motor coordination.

- Orientation for educators regarding appropriate situational usage.

- Orientation for peers to provide exposure to the device.

However, if the teacher of students with visual impairments starts by demonstrating the exciting capabilities of this tool by pointing out something they typically have not been able to see, most students quickly see the benefit and are anxious to begin to learn more. This attitude assists both the teacher and low vision specialist in determining the appropriate device to begin a training program. Furthermore, most low vision specialists will ask the student to read acuity charts using the monocular telescope while participating in the low vision evaluation. If the teacher of students with visual impairments has already introduced the monocular telescope to the student so that he or she has some basic locating skills and possibly even focusing skills, the low vision specialist will be able to conduct a more accurate evaluation and suggest appropriate devices.

SKILLS AND TRAINING TECHNIQUES

Students with low vision need to learn a number of skills (listed in Sidebar 5.2) to be able to use the monocular telescopes. Although these skills are not presented in a strict hierarchy, students typically respond most successfully when the skills are presented in the order listed. It is appropriate to teach these skills to students of all ages; however, some adjustments need to be made for different age groups. For example, when first introducing the monocular telescope to an older student, a more sophisticated overview of the mechanics of the

---

Sidebar 5.2

Skills for Using Monocular Telescopes

- Appropriate positioning for optimal viewing.
- Awareness of the dominant eye.
- Scanning to find stationary objects without magnification.
- Locating and verifying an object with the telescope.
- Using a systematic technique to spot desired targets.
- Focusing and adjusting the focus to allow for a variety of planes.
- Copying symbols, words, and sentences.

- Scanning with the telescope to find objects in a variety of planes.
- Tracking targets which move across a consistent focal distance.
- Locating, focusing, and tracking targets which move through more than one focal plane.
- Developing skills to store and handle the device in a responsible manner.
- Communicating to others the uses and purposes of the device.
- Independently initiating the use of the telescope in a variety of settings.

device might be more appropriate, whereas initial orientation to the device for the younger student would be based on experimentation and discovery.

Students' ability to learn to use the monocular telescope vary widely. Some students will pick up a telescope for the first time and be able to focus it, scan, and locate objects within 30 minutes, whereas others will require a structured approach, with multiple opportunities to develop their skills. Focusing and locating, in particular, seem difficult for some students, especially for those who lack the visual framework to interpret what they see at a distance or for those who lack the concept of what "clear" (i.e., in focus) means. Therefore, as the teacher of students who are visually impaired proceeds with systematic training in the use of the monocular telescope, he or she should be directed by the student's individual needs and skill levels while offering specific activities for practicing weaker skills.

The following sections outline the process of training young students in the various skills involved in using a monocular telescope. Appendix 5.A at the end of this chapter provides ideas for activities and games that reinforce the different skills and help make this training interesting and varied for the student.

Positioning

Appropriate positioning for optimal viewing is the first step in training a student to function with the monocular telescope in various environments. To learn the best place for their own optimal viewing through the telescope, students need to learn to be aware of such obstacles as physical barriers (such as a VCR placed in front of the chalkboard that is blocking the student's view), glare from windows and lights, and sharp angles (for example, sitting near the front, right side of the classroom while trying to view something written on the far left side of the chalkboard). Instruction on physical positioning (such as using a desk to stabilize the arm) will reduce muscle fatigue as well as reduce extraneous movement while the student is trying to view through the telescope.

Leaving nothing to chance, start by showing the student the correct end of the telescope, the end he or she should look through. The student will then need to stabilize his or her body in a comfortable position in which the back and the arm holding the telescope are well supported. In a classroom situation, the student typically sits in a chair at a desk, with his or her elbows resting on the desk and the hand holding the telescope resting against the cheekbone of the dominant eye (that is, the eye the student prefers to use for distance viewing). The physical location of the desk must be such that the arm using the telescope can be supported. Facing the chalkboard is ideal; however, in some classrooms, desks are arranged in groups, with the student turned sideways. In

Resting the elbows on a flat, hard surface ensures steady viewing with a monocular telescope.

this case, simply position the student within a seating arrangement which allows support for the arm holding the telescope. When working on positioning, the teacher should be sensitive to obstructions between the telescope and the target as well as to the viewing angle. The student needs to be taught to recognize and articulate the conditions that are optimal for him or her to see while using the telescope. Avoid changing natural seating arrangements if at all possible because this can isolate the student from peers and may inhibit participation in social interactions and group-learning activities.

When initially teaching students to be comfortable using their monocular telescope, teachers need to be aware that wearing prescriptive lenses will affect the use of the device. The field of view is reduced when using a monocular telescope in conjunction with eyeglasses because the monocular telescope is further away from the eye. However, there are several options. If a student is able to use a monocular telescope while wearing his or her eyeglasses at the same time, the student can readily change from distance to near tasks (as is necessary when copying notes from the board) simply by removing the monocular telescope. Depending on their prescription, some students prefer to remove their eyeglasses while using the monocular telescope, while others will temporarily nudge the glasses up with the monocular telescope as they view material placed at a distance. The issue of whether or not eyeglasses should be worn during monocular telescope activities should be covered during the clinical low vision evaluation.

Dominant Eye

Teaching awareness of the dominant eye involves helping the student determine the best eye for the most efficient use of his or her vision with the telescope. Eye reports seldom note the child's dominant eye. This is not necessarily the eye in which the vision is clearer, but rather the eye the child prefers to use when looking through a monocular telescope. Teaching awareness of the dominant eye provides a good opportunity to incorporate the student's medical information, such as visual acuity, within the context of a functional activity, such as reading a clock on the wall. Most people are not aware of their dominant eye until they experiment with this concept. See Chapter 2 for additional information on eye preference.

One technique for identifying dominance is for the teacher to prefocus the telescope, select a target within a 10–20 ft (3–6 m) range, and then ask the student to look at the target, experimenting with first one eye and then the other. If the student can communicate a preference, that information should be included in a collaborative decision-making process (between the teacher of students with visual impairments, the student, and the low vision specialist) when determining the most efficient eye for monocular telescope tasks. If the student cannot communicate at this level, the teacher should closely observe the student's behavior and responses within an activity that is motivating, as well as use input from the low vision specialist. Behaviors that might indicate that the student is using his or her dominant eye include an instant placement of the telescope to the same eye repeatedly, as well as a positive identification of specified targets once the student looks through the telescope with this eye.

Using the dominant eye and corresponding arm is often an automatic gesture when the student first peers through the telescope, but some students will need guided practice. Students will not always use the arm on the same side as the dominant eye, however, and should be allowed the flexibility to use whatever combination suits their personal style.

Scanning without Magnification

Scanning to find stationary objects without magnification (see Chapter 2) is a skill which the student may or may not be able to perform, depending on the student's motivation, visual acuity, and experience. A few activities to assess or develop this skill are necessary so that subsequent telescope training is successful. Because a monocular telescope reduces the field of vision (depending on the power of the scope), the teacher should ask the student to point to a desired target placed at a distance before looking through the telescope. This helps the

This student points to a bulldozer at the construction site next to the playground to help locate the object as he uses his monocular telescope to scan for it.

Renae Shepler

student use full visual fields to locate the object before having to reduce the field with a telescope. It is not uncommon for students who have not been expected to see at distances to "shut down" their visual behaviors beyond reaching distance. For example, adults have a tendency to point out many interesting sights to the developing child who has typical vision by saying such things as, "Look at the cows in that pasture!," "Here's the street we need to turn on," "Did you see that raccoon run across the road?" However, it is not uncommon for adults and friends of children with visual impairments to avoid calling attention to objects at a distance they know the child won't be able to see. For this reason, the child has not had sufficient opportunity to access information beyond a few feet, at best. Practicing scanning will help students utilize their vision more efficiently both with and without the telescope, and to better develop concepts which require distance viewing. For a more in-depth discussion on teaching this skill, with sequential lessons and teaching strategies, see *Beyond Arm's Reach: Enhancing Distance Vision* by Smith and O'Donnell (1992).

Locating and Verifying

Locating and verifying an object with the telescope is an exciting opportunity for exploring the advantages of using a distance device. For some students, this will be the first time they ever see with clarity an object that was typically out of range. Enthusiasm on the part of the teacher is critical in order to help students realize the opportunities the telescope opens for them.

At this stage, the teacher of students with visual impairments should pre-focus the telescope for the student. The teacher may begin by standing about 10 to 20 ft (3–6 cm) directly in front of the student, and he or she should hold an object that cannot be easily identified without magnification. By standing in front of the student and moving the object close to his or her face, the teacher of students who are visually impaired will be able to verbally guide the student toward the target while determining where he or she is looking. When the telescope is properly positioned by the student, the teacher should be able to see down the barrel of the scope. Some students will experiment with eccentric viewing (see Chapter 2) until they learn how to shift the angle of their eyes for optimal viewing. Learning to use a telescope when a student has eccentric viewing patterns may require many guided practice sessions with the teacher of students who are visually impaired. The low vision specialist may also be able to offer suggestions and techniques for the use of a telescope for students with eccentric viewing.

Systematic Scanning with a Monocular Telescope

Using a systematic scanning technique with a monocular telescope to spot desired targets is another skill many students will not automatically engage in because they lack experience with this skill. Systematic scanning techniques enable students to reduce the time and effort needed to spot objects and information. Learning to scan from left to right, top to bottom, or by using a reference point is more efficient than randomly searching for a desired target.

One method a teacher may use to teach systematic scanning is to use a wide, fixed plane (such as a chalkboard) and to point out the structure of the board using terms such as "left," "right," "top," and "bottom" while the student watches the teacher through the telescope. Next, the teacher can draw a large shape in the upper left corner of the board and in the lower right corner. The next step is for the teacher to draw a pattern, one which connects the top to the bottom and imitates a typical reading pattern as illustrated here:

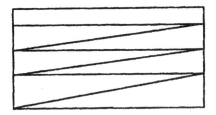

The student should visually trace this pattern using the monocular telescope. This search pattern can then be transferred to a variety of environments, from another fixed visual plane (such as reading a fast-food menu located on the wall) to highly sophisticated tasks (such as locating a bird in a tree).

The next skill is to teach the student to use a larger landmark to help locate a smaller target. Starting with a fixed plane (such as a wall), the teacher stands next to a small target and instructs the student to locate him or her. The teacher points to the target and instructs the student to track along the teacher's arm to find the target at the end of the pointing finger. The teacher should also explain the concept of using a larger object (for example, the teacher's body) to find a smaller one located close by. This concept can be transferred to all kinds of landmarks (for example, finding a door first and then locating the room number or finding a swing set first and then looking to see if the swing is occupied).

Focusing

Focusing and adjusting the focus to allow for a variety of planes (distances) will be an automatic skill for some students, but others will require intervention and instruction in precise techniques. To continue progress in other skill areas simultaneously while learning how to focus, the teacher can set the focus for other specific tasks beforehand.

To teach a student how to focus a telescope, start with the concept of "in focus" (or "clear") and the general mechanics of the telescope. At this point, allow the student to twist the barrels of the telescope, pointing out that it gets longer or shorter depending on the direction turned. There is also a point at which the barrels should not be forced any farther because they have been turned as far as they can go. Explain that an elongated telescope is useful for targets at a closer range, whereas a shorter telescope is used for greater distances. Once the student knows how to carefully manipulate the telescope, explain that the focus will need to be changed depending upon the distance between the scope and the target.

Before continuing with lessons on verifying a focus with the telescope, the teacher of students with visual impairments should help to teach the concept of "clear" using an overhead projector (without the telescope). Place a transparency with very simple black, bold line drawings on the projector, which is placed relatively close to the projector screen. Demonstrate how to turn the knob on the projector to change the clarity (or focus). Start by setting the target in the best possible focus and asking the student to look at it, getting as close as necessary to the screen. While he or she watches the target, the teacher can turn the knob to blur the image and explain what is happening. Turn the knob back until the image is clear again. Throughout this process, the teacher should emphasize the terms *clear* (meaning "in focus"), *blurry,* and *focus* (as a verb).

Once these concepts are established, they may be transferred to the monocular telescope. The same images used on the overhead projector screen can be used again, except now the student moves farther away from the target. The teacher hands a prefocused monocular telescope to the student and has him or her view the desired image. The student is taught how to turn the barrel of the monocular telescope to blur the image while viewing through it. The teacher asks the student to experiment with moving the barrel to regain the better image, and then discusses what actions were needed to obtain the clearest image.

If after the teacher prefocuses the monocular telescope for the student, the student consistently reports that the initial focus was blurry and needs to refocus, either the teacher or student may have a refractive error which would require corrective lenses. If it is indeed the student who has the refractive error, this information should be shared with the student's parents, family, or other caregiver for referral to the eye doctor.

The following steps can help a student who is learning how to use a telescope to focus it accurately each time he or she uses it:

1. Start by "closing" or "turning down" the monocular telescope to its shortest length.

2. Put the monocular telescope up to the eye. Slowly "open" or turn the barrel while looking at the target.

3. When the image is clear, slowly turn past this point to blur again, and then turn back to the clearest image. (This step is a self-check.)

The teacher can discuss with the student the fact that the monocular telescope needs to be refocused to accommodate different distances from targets. Furthermore, if the plane being focused on is a large expanse, such as the chalkboard, the focus will change from the far right, center, and far left. Advanced and highly coordinated students will be able to learn to focus using one hand only while holding the monocular telescope up to their eye.

Copying

Copying symbols, words, and sentences within a variety of formats with a telescope would be a primary literacy goal for students participating in the general education classroom curriculum. It is possible to start with children as young as preschool age, modifying the material to motivate younger students. The student has completed this goal when a paragraph can be copied from a distance with speed and accuracy.

In preparation for teaching this skill, the teacher of students with visual impairments should prepare materials in advance on lined chart tablets. This not only facilitates transporting teaching materials, but it also preserves them for future use. Drawings, words, and sentences should be clearly made using black, brown, dark green, or purple markers. Leaving a blank sheet between pages on chart tablets will help avoid confusing "shadow" images from showing through.

The materials to display on the chart will depend on the age, reading ability, and interests of individual students, and they should be consistent with the language arts program for students at the elementary level. Suitable chart materials for a young prereader, for example, include shapes, numbers, and letters in isolation. Simple pictures that have been cut from coloring books and magazines that the student has selected can also be used. The young student is instructed to "Draw [copy] what you see." Depending on the age and ability of the student, he or she would then progress from copying short words to sentences and, finally, paragraphs. Copying materials that can be used to motivate more advanced students might include:

◆ Poems, limericks, tongue twisters.

◆ Sentences pertaining to an interesting topic.

◆ Recipes, especially when followed by an actual food preparation activity.

◆ Instructions on how to make something.

◆ Directions to finding a location where a treat is hidden.

◆ Personal notes from the teacher to the student.

Appendix 5.A lists additional activities that use the same skills.

Sidebar 5.3 outlines the steps involved in teaching the progression from single symbol copying (such as shapes, numbers, and letters in isolation) to copying entire paragraphs. Once the student is able to copy a paragraph with a

Sidebar 5.3

Teaching a Student to Copy Using a Monocular Telescope

In teaching students to copy material from the chart or the chalkboard, the teacher usually starts with individual symbols and progresses to individual letters, words, phrases, sentences, and paragraphs. The following steps suggest how this gradual progression can be accomplished.

1. Start with a chart page containing symbols in a column, one per line. Place the chart far enough away so that the student has to use the monocular telescope to see clearly. Orient the student to the parameters of the chart and encourage a systematic scanning technique that allows the student to get an idea of how much material is presented. Once the student is oriented to the chart, instruct the student to draw or copy the symbols.

2. When the student is able to locate the chart, read and copy simple shapes and symbols in a column format, and progress from copying symbols to copying letters.

3. Next progress to a chart page containing short words at the student's independent or instructional reading level (see Koenig & Holbrook, 1995); this chart should be organized in one numbered column of up to 10 words. Avoid using two columns at this time. Instruct the student to find the number *1*, to write a number *1* on his or her paper, and to copy the word next to that number. At this point, the student will probably copy only one letter at a time.

4. Once the student is able to copy short words letter by letter, he or she is ready to progress to copying short words at a glance. Instruct the student to begin copying all 10 words. Time the student with a stopwatch. Many students will copy each word letter by letter, which will slow him or her down. When the student has finished the list, remark on the time it took, and then suggest that he or she try to copy a new list with fewer glances needed per word. The goal is to reduce the time needed to copy by reducing the number of glances. After the student has copied the second list, present the times for the two attempts so that the student can compare them. If the student began this exercise by naturally copying one or more words per glance, simply discuss how this practice increases efficiency.

5. The next goal is to copy multiple words and short phrases. To make it interesting, include phrases and sentences which are appealing, such as riddles, jokes, lines from favorite movies, or personal messages. Instruct the student to copy the sentences, and this time allow him or her to manipulate the stopwatch. After taking an initial timing, instruct the student to copy a new page of the chart by remembering more than one word at a time. Then compare the times again.

6. While the student is copying sentences, introduce the concept of accuracy. If it can be assumed that words and sentences are being used which are within the student's ability level, the students should be expected to proofread their material and correct capitalization, spelling, and punctuation errors. It helps to make a record such as the following for the student to chart his or her progress (include the date, amount of material copied, time it took to copy, and number of errors):

DATE	# OF WORDS COPIED	TIME	# OF ERRORS
10/6/00	10	3 min.	6
10/9/00	10	2 min.	3

minimum of glances and errors, the goal has been met. This progression will take some time to complete, with 1–3 hours per week direct instruction required by the teacher of students with visual impairments. Some children will learn quickly, whereas others will require more time. The student who is at grade level will likely develop this level of skill within three months. A student who does not read or does not read well is not likely to advance all the way to Step 6. The age and literacy ability of the student will determine how far training will advance.

While learning how to copy while using a monocular telescope, the student should not be expected to use this skill in the general educational setting. Rather, the student should continue to use modifications such as taping lectures or copying from another student's notes as a backup during the monocular telescope training process. Once the goal of copying a paragraph with a minimum of glances and errors has been achieved, the student is ready to apply this skill to actual classroom tasks such as copying homework assignments, sentences,

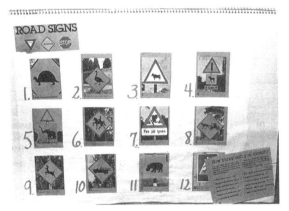

Chrissy Cowan

Teachers can create charts such as these to help students practice using monocular telescopes. Each chart presents a different activity at the appropriate grade level for each student.

math problems, and special directions from the chalkboard, charts, and over-head projector screen.

Scanning in a Variety of Planes

Scanning to find objects in a variety of planes with the telescope is different from scanning on a fixed plane. The student will need to learn the more sophis-ticated skill of moving the telescope (with the body stationary) in a systematic scanning pattern while incorporating focusing techniques that accommodate for a variety of distances.

Begin by reviewing with the student the basic techniques for scanning and locating (discussed previously). Place objects or note cards in a variety of places at various distances throughout the room. Ideas for objects include pieces of a puzzle, Lego® pieces which can be assembled, action figures, or note cards with written messages or jokes. Instruct the student to locate the targets by using the scanning patterns and focusing skills learned previously. Once the student can spy the object, ask him or her to use landmarks to describe where the object is so that the teacher can retrieve it. Continue in this manner until all objects have been accumulated, and then the student can assemble the puzzle or Lego® fig-ure or read the messages on the cards. Transfer this sequence to increasingly larger environments such as the library, gym, cafeteria, outdoor school envi-ronment, and stores.

Tracking Moving Targets

Tracking targets which move across a consistent focal distance is a skill used every day in the classroom. Typical examples include following along with a demonstration at the front of the room, watching as the classroom teacher writes on the board, and watching videos. The quality that these targets share is move-ment across a relatively fixed plane, requiring minimal refocusing but advanced ability to move the head and body to keep up with the target.

Training students to use the monocular telescope to track these types of targets might require intervention within actual contexts. For example, the teacher of students with visual impairments would sit behind a preschool stu-dent and assist the child in watching the classroom teacher during story time as he or she holds up the picture book for all to see. Or the teacher of students with visual impairments might accompany a student to a school play to demon-strate tracking the actors as they move across the stage. As the teacher demon-strates the skill of tracking, he or she would first show the student how to place the monocular telescope up to the eye, then ask the student to set the focus for the distance at which the action is taking place. Once the telescope has been focused, the teacher of students who are visually impaired would show the student how to move the head from left to right to scan the space in which the action occurs, then ask the student to describe details of what he or she is viewing. The student should be assisted in finding a comfortable position for maintaining consistent tracking. This type of viewing, when done in natural contexts, is highly motivating and provides many opportunities to increase concepts that would not be accessible without the telescope.

The task of locating, focusing on, and tracking targets that move through more than one focal plane ties together all the skills that enable the student to access most environments and visual materials that are within the range of the telescope and the individual's visual efficiency. At this stage of training, the teacher will want to expand the student's experiences with the monocular telescope beyond the school environment in an effort to transfer the device's capabilities to a variety of recreational and vocational settings. Encourage the student to use the monocular telescope at home, on field trips, and during vacations to maximize experiences and skill development. Instruct the student to keep a journal of the things and events he or she was able to access with magnification. Keeping a journal about one's visual experiences serves two critical purposes. It enables the student to build an awareness of new concepts he or she is learning, and, most importantly, the journal enhances the student's self-concept as a "visual" learner who is capable of accessing information independently of others. Keeping a journal provides a springboard for further conversation to help bridge the gap between misconceptions the child may have had about visual information and the reality.

Students with Multiple Disabilities

When considering the use of telescopic devices for students with multiple disabilities, the teacher should be aware of the fact that teaching within the context of meaningful routines becomes particularly crucial due to the reduced ability of the student to transfer knowledge from one setting to another. In this case, the educational team, including parents and student, should consider the student's schedule—from waking up to going to bed. Within the framework of this schedule, make a list of activities and specific routines that are meaningful and motivating for the student. Examples of meaningful routines include participation in selecting the wardrobe for the day, in setting the table, in preparing a snack, in decisions on grooming needs, in eating out activities, and in family recreational outings.

Once the team has decided upon a schedule of routines, its members would need to perform a task analysis on specific routines (that is, breaking down an activity into the individual steps required to complete it) to determine points at which the student may benefit from using a telescopic device. For example, if the teacher would like the student to participate in a trip to the grocery store, teach the skill of using the shopping cart as a support for the arm holding the monocular telescope so that the student can use the device to scan the snack food section for a desired product. This allows the student to get a broader picture of what's available, and gives him or her a sense of independence in making a personal selection.

INTEGRATING THE USE OF TELESCOPIC DEVICES

The intent in teaching students to use an optical device is to enable them to participate in activities which span across all environments. Some students transfer information and methods easily from a structured classroom training session to situations outside the classroom. However, a significant part of the training should include working with the student on a wide range of tasks, which can be accomplished by using the telescope, and in a variety of settings.

As the teacher of students with visual impairments introduces the concept of using magnification to enhance the environment, the student can be surveyed about distance tasks he or she would like to perform visually but is currently unable to do with ease. Offering a checklist of tasks typically performed by children in the student's age group helps the student and family to specify activities which are currently difficult for the student (see Sidebar 5.4). Such a checklist also gives students some ideas of possible training goals which, once achieved, will open up many new opportunities. Once a survey of desired visual abilities has been conducted, the teacher should include training within the context of these activities. For example, if the student would love to be able to watch a football game, the teacher might want to provide telescope practice at an actual game and reinforce skills such as scanning to locate the scoreboard, focusing to read the scores, and scanning to follow the action around the football on the field. It helps to prepare the student in advance by performing a task analysis of the visual skills needed for activities before reinforcing the necessary integration of monocular skills.

When introducing the use of a monocular telescope, consider the coordination and dexterity of the student. The teacher should work with the occupational and/or physical therapists to determine additional modifications or methods if necessary. Progression through the monocular telescope training skills may need to be modified to enable the student to achieve success within individual activities. Skills may need to be simplified for some students, depending

---

Sidebar 5.4

Examples of Typical Visual Tasks

Giving students and their families a checklist of activities involving distance vision that are typical for the student's age group and that students might like to do themselves will help them understand the possibilities and give them ideas about the kinds of goals they might want to work toward. The following list provides a sample of activities students might like to perform, but the teacher will want to provide suggestions that are appropriate to a particular student's age and interests, such as:

• Looking out the window on car trips.

• Reading street signs and house numbers.

• Reading menus on the wall at fast-food restaurants.

• Watching television.

• Playing video games.

• Observing wildlife.

• Flying a kite.

• Watching assemblies and performances.

• Seeing the sights at zoos and amusement parks.

• Observing activity in the lunchroom.

• Locating departments in a clothing store.

• Looking at objects in glass cases at museums and stores.

• Checking out the booths at a fair.

• Participating in group story time.

• Finding shelved materials in a library.

• Getting food in a cafeteria line.

• Locating a seat in a theater, auditorium, cafeteria, or other public place.

• Reading signs above the grocery store aisles.

• Reading movie times on signs at theaters.

• Observing activity at a swimming pool.

• Engaging in people-watching.

---

upon individual needs and ability. Students who will only be using the telescope to view a fixed plane at a fixed distance (for example, the distance between the student's desk and the chalkboard, or the distance from a checkout counter to the snack bar menu) may benefit from markings made with colored paint pens on each side of the barrel. When the markings are aligned, the monocular telescope will automatically be focused for a specific task.

In addition to including parents in the telescope training program, the teacher will want to work with related service personnel—in particular, the orientation and mobility (O&M) instructor. O&M instructors typically use distance devices during mobility training, both inside and out of school settings. These devices may be a stronger power than those used in the classroom, depending on the distances and objectives of the student and O&M instructor.

Making sure that the educational team routinely discusses a student's goals, objectives, and progress in monocular telescope skills will encourage him or her to expand the use of the device to a variety of settings. In some situations where the student with a visual impairment has additional disabilities which require intervention from a variety of related service personnel, an integrated IEP helps ensure coordination of programming and gives the student multiple opportunities for skill development. An integrated IEP is written by the student's educational team, typically following assessment that is also carried out as a team. For example, the educational team may have determined that the student needs to be able to ride a bus to a job in the community. Rather than having each professional write a separate IEP for the skills this task requires, the team would write an IEP that integrates specific discipline skills within the context of this one goal of riding the bus. The teacher of students who are visually impaired would include an objective regarding the use of the monocular telescope to identify a bus number and landmarks, the O&M instructor will add an objective about safely locating the bus stop and walking into the building, and the speech therapist may write an objective that involves communicating the destination to the driver. All of these skills may actually be taught by a job coach, after learning specific methodology from each specialist.

A continuing program with built-in incentives and rewards will facilitate integration of the monocular telescope across environments. The student's IEP should include goals and objectives similar to those listed in Sidebar 5.5 with the ultimate goal of using a monocular telescope to access as many environments as possible, both in and out of the school building.

The classroom teacher should also be involved in skill reinforcement and in providing increased opportunities for usage of the telescope. In the orientation with teachers and parents at the beginning of the school year, the teacher of students with visual impairments should describe the training program and the objectives in teaching the student to use a telescopic device. He or she should demonstrate the correct use of the device and state the expected norms for the student's usage. When the teacher of students who are visually impaired walks out the door, the classroom teacher will be the one reinforcing consistent usage. The teacher of students who are visually impaired—or the student with low vision—can demonstrate the correct use of the monocular telescope for the classroom teacher at the beginning of the school year. It is helpful to give the classroom teacher a sheet of "Tips for Teachers of Students Using Monocular Telescopes," similar to the one in Sidebar 5.6. Periodically, the teacher will monitor the student's application of skills by observing as he or she participates in activities with classmates. The teacher of students with visual impairments should augment observations with input from the classroom teacher regarding frequency, variety, and fluency of telescope usage. Some monocular telescope lessons should occur

---

Sidebar **5.5**

Goals and Objectives for Monocular Telescope Training

The following goals and objectives are purposely not written in measurable terms in order to enable the teacher of children who are visually impaired to customize them to individual students.

GOAL: *To demonstrate skills for monocular telescope maintenance*
OBJECTIVES: *The student will be able to:*

1. Hold the device properly.

2. Communicate the purpose of the device.

3. Clean the device appropriately.

4. Assume responsibility for the device.

5. Store the device in a convenient location for quick retrieval.

6. Initiate use of the device.

GOAL: *To demonstrate skills for the use of monocular telescopes*
OBJECTIVES: *The student will be able to:*

1. Position self for optimal viewing.

2. Scan the environment and locate stationary objects without the monocular telescope.

3. Locate stationary objects with the monocular telescope.

4. Focus on a stationary object.

5. Identify objects with the device.

6. Identify pictures with the device (e.g., line drawings, photos).

7. Scan on a horizontal plane, using landmarks to find stationary objects.

8. Adjust the focus for objects at varying distances.

9. Copy familiar symbols.

10. Scan with the device to locate signs/symbols/objects in a variety of planes.

11. Track movement at a consistent focal distance.

12. Develop a systematic scanning technique to locate a moving object by incorporating landmarks when available.

13. Incorporate focusing and track an object moving through a variety of focal planes.

---

during the regular classroom session, particularly during teacher demonstrations or assignments which necessitate the use of the monocular telescope.

Once the teacher of students who are visually impaired has covered care and handling of the monocular telescope, it is best for the student to have access to the prescribed optical devices at home, at school, and in other environments, so the devices should be readily available when needed. When the student demonstrates responsibility in using the telescope, he or she should then be allowed to transport the device from school to home. However, to avoid loss or breakage, it is best to obtain an additional device for extracurricular and home use, if possible. Some states and provinces provide low vision evaluations and will purchase prescribed devices for students.

Tips for Teachers of Students Using Monocular Telescopes

A monocular telescope is a small telescope which enables a student with a visual impairment to see print, pictures, diagrams, maps, faces, and demonstrations that occur at a distance. The following are some facts and adaptations which need to be considered if a monocular telescope is being used:

1. A monocular telescope severely restricts the visual field. The student will be taught by the teacher of students who are visually impaired or the O&M specialist to scan, thus enabling the student to pick up all visual information and to increase visual memory so he or she can copy more quickly and efficiently.

2. A monocular telescope is typically used for distance tasks only.

3. Copying while using a monocular telescope is laborious at first, and it will take the student longer to copy from the board and charts. You can help the student by modifying the length of the assignment until copying skills are mastered. Some ways of doing this include the following:

   a. Assign only the even or odd numbered problems.

   b. Have the student write only the answers to questions rather than recopy entire sentences, questions, and/or paragraphs.

Note: Decisions to modify assignments should be previously discussed with the teacher of students who are visually impaired and will require review as copying skills progress. Do not automatically assume that students with visual impairments should be required to do less work.

4. When a student who is visually impaired is using a monocular telescope, he or she should not have to walk up to the board or chart. The monocular telescope should allow the student to access information from the regularly assigned seat. Moving around the room hinders the student's speed, continuity of thought, and proficiency when reading or completing an assignment.

5. Ideal seating for a student using a monocular telescope should be facing the board or charts, thus permitting straight-on viewing. This position also enables the student to rest an elbow on the desk while looking through the monocular telescope to support the arm holding the device.

6. Once students are proficient at using the monocular telescope, most students prefer to sit with the group of their choice. A monocular telescope will enable the child to sit within the group. Singling out a visually impaired student's desk from the normal seating arrangement (to place him or her closer to the board) will probably not be necessary and may place the child at a disadvantage socially.

7. Monocular telescopes break easily and should be worn around the neck when in use and stored in a case otherwise. Please encourage students who are visually impaired to keep their monocular telescopes out of sight when the room is empty.

8. Do not allow other students to handle the monocular telescope.

9. Encourage the student to take the monocular telescope to school events (e.g., assemblies, film presentations, and field trips).

10. Check first with the teacher of students who are visually impaired before allowing the monocular telescope to be taken home (unless, of course, it is the student's own property).

TECHNIQUES FOR DEALING WITH TYPICAL PROBLEMS

From time to time, problems will arise within a monocular telescope training program. Typical problems include frequent breakage or loss of the monocular telescope, reluctance to use the monocular telescope, or the fact that the prescribed telescopic power no longer appears to be strong enough.

Breakage

Monocular telescopes are not indestructible. Before issuing a monocular telescope, devote time to familiarizing the student with the correct ways to handle and store it so that it does not get broken. Young children should be encouraged to wear the monocular telescope around their necks with the strap that is provided or to carry it in their pockets. If there is a concern about choking, attach a length of elastic or a break-away clasp (similar to the one found on cat collars) to the monocular telescope strap. Provide a felt bag or felt-lined box for storage in the student's desk or backpack. Breakage, however, is unavoidable. Theft is also a concern—teaching the student to safeguard equipment by keeping it out of sight is a safety measure that can prevent theft. In some situations, it may be necessary to store the device in the teacher's locked desk drawer. Allowing the other students to experiment with the monocular telescope will often satisfy curiosity and establish rules for the entire class. Since the emphasis is on frequent usage, avoid having to implement strict procedures that may ultimately discourage the student from using the device. Instead, be prepared to provide a backup monocular telescope. Developing a contract in which the student promises to store and handle the monocular telescope safely is sometimes useful.

Reluctance to Use the Monocular Telescope

Some children may be reluctant to use their monocular telescope because they feel self-conscious or singled out. The device may be too frustrating to use if they have not received a thorough training program, or if the device is not the correct power for the individual student. If monocular telescope training begins when children are as young as two years of age, many such problems can be circumvented by developing in the student a sense of self-confidence through self-advocacy. Children who are taught ways to access their environment tend to take a more active role in participating in visual experiences, and will ask for the visual conditions under which they have optimal viewing. However, it's not always possible to start with very young children, and occasionally problems

To Ranay Shepler
Moucler Alax

My name is Josh. My sister
is called Melodyn. Alax helps
my eyes. Alax helps me see the
words on the chalk bord and in
Loms, and on the bad
list. Every one wants
a secont glanse. I like one
part were it makes things look
little. And far away. My special
teacher Ranay helps me. I'm
glad the ways its turning out.

When children learn to use a monocular at a young age, they are less likely to feel self-conscious and more likely to develop positive feelings about its use, as did Josh who drew this picture of his monocular and wrote the accompanying story. It reads:

To Renae Shepler
Monocular Alex
My name is Josh. My sister is called Melody. Alex helps my eyes. Alex helps me see the words on the chalk board and in LOMS [a language arts program] and on the bad list. Everyone wants a second glance. I like one part where it makes things look little and far away. My special teacher Renae helps me. I'm glad the way it's turning out.

arise because a child will refuse to use the monocular telescope when the teacher of students who are visually impaired is not in the room. There are as many methods for dealing with these problems as there are personality characteristics of individual students. Some methods that work include the following:

1. Enlist support from the classroom teacher, parents, and O&M instructor to reinforce the student's monocular telescope use.

2. Develop a reward system or checklist which keeps track of the frequency of monocular telescope use. This checklist may be filled in by the other teachers, the student, and parents.

3. Take the student on an educational field trip to stimulate renewed interest in the monocular telescope.

4. Educate the student's classmates by demonstrating what low vision is like with and without low vision devices. Have the student, along with the teacher of students who are visually impaired as the "resident expert," present the information.

5. Make occasional visits to the classroom to see if the device is being used. Give credit when observing spontaneous usage.

Regardless of the teacher's efforts, some students will flatly refuse to use the device. Faced with this situation, the teacher can engage the student in a problem-solving approach, one that allows him or her to accomplish his or her distance activities. First, help the student make a chart which divides distance tasks into two categories: those which are crucial to academic success and those which are recreational. Establish the following nonnegotiable guidelines for the academic tasks. These guidelines might include the following:

◆ The work must be done.

◆ The student must not impose on others to complete the work.

◆ The student must be responsible for his or her own actions.

Following this discussion, the teacher and the student will examine each task on the list, such as reading the assignments from the board, and will brainstorm ways in which these tasks can be carried out. Pros and cons for each modification should be thoroughly discussed, and this discussion should address such issues as the following: "If I use this method, will I finish my work within a reasonable amount of time?" or "If I use this method, will I be imposing on others?" There are times the teacher will have to accept the student's decision, provided the work is ultimately completed on time. Frequently, students will decide that using a telescope and being able to sit anywhere in the class is more desirable than avoiding the telescope but having an assigned seat.

Need for a Stronger Prescription

During training or when the student is on a maintenance program for monocular telescope usage, use an eye chart periodically to check the power of the monocular telescope. If any differences in student performance are noticed, such as over- or underfocusing, an inability to read a previously achieved line on the chart, or complaints that the device is not strong enough, refer the student back to the eye specialist for a thorough exam. It is important not to allow the strength of the monocular telescope to mask a progressive eye condition. However, teachers should not encourage the student to obtain a stronger telescope before the student checks with an eye care specialist. As the student's needs change over time, a return visit to the low vision specialist will also be in order. A stronger monocular telescope or a variety of monoculars may be prescribed to meet the student's needs.

SUMMARY

Teaching monocular telescope use should be fun and enlightening for both teacher and student. While the activities listed in Appendix 5.A can make learning this new skill fun, the real motivation for the student will come when he or she perceives the difference the monocular telescope can make in independence and access to information. Using a monocular telescope can open up the world to a student with low vision—a world previously out of reach.

REFERENCES

Koenig, A. J., & Holbrook, M. C. (1995). *Learning media assessment of students with visual impairments* (2nd Ed.). Austin, TX: Texas School for the Blind and Visually Impaired.

Smith, A. J., & O'Donnell, L. M. (1992). *Beyond arm's reach: Enhancing distance vision.* Philadelphia: Pennsylvania College of Optometry Press.

Smith, M., & Levack, N. (1996). *Teaching students with visual and multiple impairments: A resource guide.* Austin, TX: Texas School for the Blind and Visually Impaired.

Activities for Monocular Telescopes

Activity	Positioning	Localizing	Scanning	Tracking	Focusing
Bird Watching: Cut out magazine pictures of birds that are found locally. Use the monocular telescope on a walk to find a bird. Attract birds to one spot by setting out a bird feeder. For older students, use a bird identification guide, and look up birds using a magnifier.	▲	●	▲	●	▲
I Spy: Hide toys/small objects and/or pictures around a room in several different planes (up high, on the floor, on uncluttered shelves). Ask a child to find them with a monocular telescope and describe them. This can also be done outside. For landmark clues, give hints—"I spy something red near the door."	▲	●	●	▲	●
Detective: Sit outside and watch people walking by or in the playground. Describe clothing/expressions, etc.	▲	▲	▲	●	▲

Chart Activities (copying): Prepare activities on 1 in. ruled chart tablets so you can carry them everywhere and cater to the interests of individual students. Use bright colorful markers, pictures cut from magazines, or your own drawings. Some activities include:
1. Copying poems, limericks, tongue twisters.
2. Copying sentences pertaining to an interesting topic.
3. Performing tasks which require the interpretation of the following formats:
   a. Fill in the blank.
   b. Matching 2 columns.
   c. Crossword puzzles.
   d. Reading recipes.
	▲	▲	▲	●	▲

(Place chart far enough away so child needs to use the monocular telescope.)

● = primary emphasis
▲ = skill reinforced

F. M. D'Andrea and C. Farrenkopf, Eds., *Looking to Learn,* New York: AFB Press, 2000. This form may be copied for educational use.

Activity	Positioning	Localizing	Scanning	Tracking	Focusing
Grocery Store Treasure Hunt: Use a monocular telescope to read aisle numbers and some items on each aisle. Activity cards can be made ahead of time by the teacher with aisle heading words that are to be found ("on what aisle would you find PET FOOD?"). In addition, cards for specific brands or items could be prepared ahead of time as prompts for finding these items using a monocular telescope ("Find Campbell's Tomato Soup").	●	●	●	●	●
Velcro Darts: Throw darts at dartboard, and use the monocular telescope to look at the dartboard and tally the score.		●			●
Drawing: Use the monocular telescope to look at a simple incomplete drawing, tell what's missing, and/or copy a picture and fill in the missing part.		●			●
Cardboard Tubes: Use cardboard tubes for initial training in localizing before giving the student a monocular telescope. The use of tubes can help the student understand the effects of field restrictions and movement when using a monocular telescope. Incorporate with "spy" games or pretend play.	●	●	▲		
"The Wall": When training a student to use horizontal scanning techniques, a special treat can be incorporated into the lesson. Place stickers on cracks between large bricks on a wall. The student can keep all the stickers he or she gets within a set time limit if they're in "order." The student should follow the lines between the bricks when scanning. Starting top left, the student should track from left to right, drop a row (more if small bricks), scan right to left, drop a row, etc.		▲	●		
Type a letter or words, which, if given in order, give the student a "secret" message. As the child progresses, numbers can be substituted for stickers. If the child follows the correct scanning pattern, the numbers should be in a specific order. Keep score.					
Riddles: Put riddle questions on a chart and answers on a separate chart. Set charts at varying distances so that the child needs to refocus to find answers to the riddles.	▲	▲	▲	▲	●
Kite Flying: (Must be sure sun is not behind the kite—it is better to do this on darker, cloudy days). Once the kite is in the air, the student can use the monocular telescope (scanning skills) to locate the kite, and then try to follow the kite.	●	▲	●	●	●
Students can also track airplanes and helicopters in the sky.					

(*continued*)

Activity	Positioning	Localizing	Scanning	Tracking	Focusing
Horn Honking Trucks: If a walkway can be found that goes over a major highway, this can be a great activity for tracking approaching objects. Stand above the highway and use the monocular telescope to watch for approaching semis. Track trucks and judge the distance so that when a truck is close enough for the driver to see you, the child can make the "blow your horn" sign (make fist and pulling motion, like pulling on a horn that is hung from a ceiling). Most truck drivers will respond by honking in return. This is great for younger children!	▲	●	●	●	
Secret Notes: Hide a note (written in 1-inch letters) in the room. Have the student use a monocular telescope and searching skills to find and read the note. Kids love getting personal notes!	▲	●	●	▲	▲
Mystery Puzzles: Write the child a message in "secret code." Have the key to the code presented at a distance on a chart. The child will need to use the monocular telescope continually to recheck with the key to solve the mystery code.		▲	●	●	▲
Picture Story: Tape pages of a picture book along a wall. Use the monocular telescope to view the pictures. For variety, mix the pictures up and ask the child to put them in order.			●		▲
Concerts/Plays/Movies: Encourage the use of the monocular telescope at rock concerts, plays, sports events, etc.	▲	●	▲	●	▲
Skeleton: Assemble two skeletons with movable limbs. When finished, move one skeleton across the room, and have the child use the monocular telescope to try to position his or her skeleton in the same position as the other.		▲			●
Menu Reading: Use the monocular telescope to read menus behind the counter at fast-food restaurants.		▲	●	●	▲
Facial Imitations: Move away from the child, and devise a game (keep score) to have the child use the monocular telescope to see your facial positions. Ask him or her to attempt to imitate them.		▲			●
Bubble Tracking: This is very difficult, but it is good for young advanced monocular telescope users. Take turns being the bubble blower, and try to track the bubbles with the monocular until they pop. Start by focusing on the blower's hand, which is holding the bubble wand, until the bubble is released; then track the bubble.			▲	●	●

Activity	Positioning	Localizing	Scanning	Tracking	Focusing
Sticker Mysteries: Purchase books with stickers attached in the back. These stickers are used within the text to complete the illustration to the story on each page. Detach the stickers ahead of time, and hide them around the room. Give landmark "clues" to help the child locate and identify the stickers with the monocular telescope. Place the stickers on the proper page.	▲	▲	●	▲	▲
Camera Focusing: With older students, transferring skills to a manual camera may not only enhance skills such as focusing, locating, and positioning, but they may also lead to the development of a great hobby. Explain that the mechanics for using a camera lens are basically the same as those for a monocular telescope.	●	●	▲	▲	●
Chalkboard Tracking I: Using a chalkboard, teach tracking patterns by writing personal messages or answers to riddles one letter at a time with connecting lines. If the student follows the lines and copies the letters in order, a secret message or riddle answer will emerge. Lines should mimic a typical reading pattern: moving from top-left, to top-right, down and back, left to right, down and back, etc. For the more advanced student, play "Beat the Clock" by doing this activity with the addition of a stopwatch.	▲	▲	●	●	▲
Chalkboard Tracking II: This is the same activity as in "Chalkboard Tracking I," but intentionally seat the student at an angle and use a broad enough expanse of the chalkboard to necessitate refocusing as the student moves in and out of visual planes.	▲	▲	▲	●	●
Nature Hikes: Nature hikes can often be a highly motivating way to move students to more advanced monocular skills. Use landmark cues for locating wildlife or plants that can only be viewed at a distance, or to identify plants in difficult-to-reach locations such as across a lake or chasm.	●	●	●	●	●
Star Gazing: Many students will see stars for the first time by using their monocular telescope. Watch for special events such as comets, and try to arrange nighttime viewing for students or their families.	▲	▲	▲		▲
ABC Game: This can be played indoors or outdoors. Have the student use the monocular telescope to locate letters of the alphabet, starting with A, then B, etc. Letters can be located on billboards, license plates, posters, etc.	▲	●	●	●	●

(continued)

Activity	Positioning	Localizing	Scanning	Tracking	Focusing
Simon Says Stickers: Stand at a distance from the student. Place a sticker on various parts of your body saying, "Simon says, 'put a sticker here.'" Play like the traditional Simon Says game, except the student needs to use the monocular telescope to locate the sticker. The student should have stickers that match those of the teacher. When the student visually locates the sticker on the teacher, the student puts a similar sticker on his or her corresponding body part (for example, a blue sticker on the knee, a gold star on the nose, etc.).	▲	●	●	▲	●
Treasure Hunt: Hide a "treasure" somewhere in the school. Use a hand-drawn map and clues to find the treasure. The student has to find the clues one by one. Be sure that finding the clues requires the use of the monocular telescope. Clues may be taped to the ceiling, above doors, or be hidden in a tree, etc.	●	●	●	▲	▲
Class Demonstrations: As students enter higher grades, you will want to include them in a short session with their class to explain their vision and use of adaptive devices. For older students studying the body or optics, the student who is visually impaired may want to present a special report on the optics of the monocular telescope, eyeglasses, and/or the eye. Explaining these concepts to someone else always increases self-understanding of the same concepts. Students may want to use some of the same techniques that were used to explain similar concepts to them when they were younger, such as the use of the overhead projector to explain "focus."	▲	▲	▲	▲	▲
Find the Teletubbies: Provide children with small figures of favorite characters (Teletubbies, Sesame Street, Barney, Power Rangers, Star Trek, Pokémon). Discuss distinguishing characteristics. Cut out (from coloring books) black-and-white pictures of characters that involve the same theme. Have students locate and identify matching characters. This can be as simple as having one picture of a Teletubby at a distance or as complicated as trying to locate several action figure pictures (or real figures) in several visual planes.	●	●	●	●	●

6 Activities and Games for Teaching Children to Use Magnifiers

CHRISSY COWAN AND RENAE SHEPLER

LTHOUGH MOST OF THE STUDENTS on the caseload of a teacher of students who are visually impaired typically require intervention for distance tasks, not all students will need magnification for near tasks. There are several reasons for this. Young children are usually able to hold print materials and objects closer to their eyes and focus for longer periods of time than older children because of better visual accommodation (see Chapter 4). Also, print size used for classroom materials is generally large—at least until the third or fourth grade—thereby making it easier for students with low vision to see the print. But if the teacher notices the student with a visual impairment straining and holding materials close to the face—so close that the child appears to be reading with his or her nose—it is time to consider assistive technology that will make the reading and viewing process less fatiguing. A visit to the low vision specialist is in order; here, the student can receive a clinical low vision evaluation

Some material in this chapter is from "Techniques for Teaching Young Children to Use Low Vision Devices," by C. Cowan & R. Shepler, 1990, *Journal of Visual Impairment & Blindness, 84,* pp. 419–421. Adapted with permission.

(see Chapter 3). The results of this assessment may lead to a magnification device being prescribed for the student (see Chapter 4).

The provision of large-type texts has been the traditional "quick fix" for students who appear to be struggling with seeing up close. However, this option is only part of a solution, and it can be problematic for several reasons:

- ◆ Large-print texts and reproduced enlargements of worksheets do not provide accessibility to countless other near tasks, which include nonprint activities such as inspecting insects in science class or identifying money.

- ◆ The overreliance on large-print books as the only available option can make students dependent on materials that other people prepare. A common scenario involves classroom teachers, assistants, and teachers of students who are visually impaired working to make sure everything is enlarged, thus creating a passive role for the student (and often a nightmare of organization for school staff). It is important for students to be as independent as possible, so they need to have as many options as possible available to them and they need to learn to choose which options work best in specific situations.

- ◆ Some students dislike "looking different" from their peers and would prefer to use regular print texts if they could be used comfortably.

- ◆ Some commercially marketed large-print products are large and bulky, and some have lower quality graphics and photographs than those in the original text. When graphs, charts and maps depend on color-coding but the large-print version of the text is only in black and white, the student does not receive all the information needed to understand the graphic.

Particularly in situations in which students with visual impairments receive services only infrequently, well-intentioned school personnel often order large-print texts with the assumption that with such texts the "problem" is fixed and that the student needs no further service. This may not be in the best interest of the child.

Commercial classroom materials are just a small part of a student's life experience. Creative teachers enrich their class environments with materials ranging from personal snapshots to current events stories from the newspaper. As soon as the student walks out the school door, countless additional opportunities for reading and exploration also present themselves. Examples of other printed materials that students need to read include menus, games, instructions and ingredients on packages, dosage directions on medicine bottles, warnings

Renae Shepler

With a handheld magnifier, children can explore
and learn about the world around them.

on product information manuals, maps, charts, graphs, legal documents, newspapers, personal letters, and bills. In addition, students need to engage in nonprint activities such as sewing on a button, cooking, enjoying photographs of the family vacation, removing a splinter, painting fingernails, applying mascara, operating dials and keypads on appliances, and examining interesting objects such as rocks, stamps, shells, flowers, feathers, and tadpoles, to name a few.

Magnification devices can assist students by increasing their access to print and nonprint classroom activities. The beauty of a magnifier is that it is inexpensive, small, portable, and easily obtainable. Training programs, which include exposure to magnifiers, give the student the opportunity to find the best way to access a variety of print and nonprint materials.

The most commonly used magnifiers for school-aged children include stand magnifiers and handheld magnifiers. Stand magnifiers rest on the viewing surface and come in many shapes, sizes, and powers. They are easier to work with than other magnifiers because the student does not have to hold the magnifier up off the page to focus it—the focal distance is always constant. One drawback to using a stand magnifier is that it works best when the surface to be magnified is flat. Reading a globe, pill bottle, or any other curved or tightly spaced surface (such as a card file) is tricky with a stand magnifier. Furthermore, stand magnifiers are too big to fit unobtrusively into a pocket. Handheld magnifiers are a variation of the old "Sherlock Holmes" model, with the magnifying lens at the end of a handle. Some variations of this type exist, such as a flashlight attachment with a lens at the end, folding "pocket" magnifiers that are very small, dome magnifiers that look like a glass paperweight and rest on the reading surface, and bar magnifiers that are shaped like a ruler and rest on an entire line of print. The handheld magnifier is harder to use than the stand magnifier because the student must be able to maintain a consistent focal distance when using the handheld magnifier. However, this style is much more versatile and inconspicuous, thus making it popular with students once they reach the middle school years and appearance becomes important.

LAYING THE GROUNDWORK

Introducing Magnifiers

Magnifiers are available from many sources, but they should first be prescribed by a qualified low vision specialist (see Chapters 3 and 4). The general education teacher may want to bring grandpa's magnifier from home to "help" the student with a visual impairment who appears to be struggling with small print. Before a trip to Wal-mart to buy what's marketed for the aging Baby Boomer generation, however, the teacher of students with visual impairments should refer the student to the low vision clinic for a thorough examination and recommendations for low vision devices. Once the devices have been purchased, the teacher will need to carefully plan a series of lessons which will be designed to familiarize the student with the many wonderful things he or she can see with the magnifier, as well as to provide a structured setting for learning and practicing the needed skills.

Prior to the visit to the low vision clinic, some teachers of students who are visually impaired may choose to set up a situation for the student that allows him or her to experiment with different types and strengths of magnification. The purpose of this activity is not to "prescribe" a device, insofar as this should be left to the low vision specialist who has both a vast array of optical devices and the knowledge of eye disorders and optics. However, the teacher can optimize the expertise of the low vision specialist by sharing information regarding the student's strengths, needs, and abilities with optical devices.

When first presented with an opportunity to use a magnifier, younger students seldom have the stamina and coordination to maintain a consistent focal distance with a handheld magnifier, and they will typically experience greater success with stand magnifiers. The teacher should demonstrate how to hold the magnifier. Then, using a near reading or symbol chart, the teacher can ask the student to identify the smallest symbols he or she can see comfortably. At this point the teacher is not instructing the student in correct magnifier usage but is rather gathering information for the low vision specialist. In addition, the student is gaining some exposure to magnification and some preparation for the visit to the low vision clinic.

Factors That Lead to Successful Magnifier Usage

Once the magnifier has been prescribed, the success of a magnifier training program depends on specific factors that should be in place before, during, and after training (see Sidebar 6.1). For example, the degree to which the student desires independence, the age at which he or she is initially exposed to the device, and the motivation level of the student to use a magnifier will all affect the rate at which the student will learn. When students are given the opportunity to explore their environment by using a magnifier at a young age (some

---

Sidebar 6.1

Factors That Lead to the Successful Use of a Magnifier

• Initial exposure to magnifiers at a young age.

• Desire for independence.

• Student motivation to complete the same activities as his or her peers.

• Positive attitude toward using a device.

• Support from family.

• Specific training which is inclusive of many environments.

• Availability of the device, including replacement devices.

• Coordination of efforts among the teacher of students who are visually impaired, family, and other professionals.

• The ability to maintain stability and motor coordination.

• Orientation for educators regarding appropriate situational usage.

• Orientation for peers to provide exposure to the device.

children have started as young as two years old), they are more likely to consider the magnifier an extension of their body, something that is needed to view the world with more clarity.

For older students, the teacher of students who are visually impaired can lay the groundwork to help the student and family to develop a positive attitude toward magnifier usage. Prior to the visit to the low vision specialist, the teacher may engage the family and student in a conversation relating to future academic and career goals, particularly as they relate to things the student would like to be able to see and read. For example, if the student is interested in music and would like to be able to read the lyrics on a compact disk insert, compare the opportunities available to a person who is able to use a magnifier to have access to desired materials to someone who is dependent on others. The motive in such a dialogue is to provide opportunities for the family and student to see the potential which exists both in and out of the school environment when one can use low vision devices.

Once magnifier training is underway, there are several additional factors that will contribute to increased acceptance of the device. Coordinating the training with family members, with support and related service personnel, and with other teachers will provide the student with many opportunities to practice using the magnifier throughout the day in natural settings. Before expecting others to participate in training, some initial demonstrations of how to use the device correctly will help others model proper usage for the student. In addition, an orientation to the device for the student's classmates will provide an opportunity to openly explore and discuss the purpose and properties of the device. When working with younger students, the teacher can set up a learning station in the corner of the classroom with a magnifier and a variety of interesting objects to inspect (perhaps a fish tank, mold spores, or a sand dollar). This effort will go a long way in helping the student with a visual impairment use his or her own personal device without feeling so different.

SKILLS AND TRAINING TECHNIQUES

Sidebar 6.2 lists the skills that students need to master in order to use the magnifier effectively. The skills are not listed in a strict order, however, because training sessions with the teacher of students who are visually impaired will incorporate many of the skills simultaneously, with some skills emerging more quickly than others. For example, when playing a game that requires the student to read print on game cards and on a playing board, several skills will be

---

Sidebar **6.2**

Skills for Using Magnifiers

- Appropriate positioning for optimal viewing

- Stabilizing reading material/object

- Stabilizing the hand using the magnifier

- Adjusting the head-to-lens distance

- Coordinating hand, head, and eye movements specific to the type of magnifier used

- Reading on a flat surface

- Reading a variety of print formats

- Tracking at a speed which allows for reading commensurate with reading level

- Developing stamina for the duration of an age/grade-appropriate assignment

- Selecting the appropriate magnifier for the task

- Using the magnifier for nonprint activities

- Developing skills to store and handle the magnifier in a responsible manner

- Communicating to others the uses and purposes of the magnifier

- Independently initiating the use of the magnifier in a variety of settings

---

utilized. The student must be positioned in a way that promotes optimal viewing. The reading material must be stabilized, as well as the hand holding the magnifiers. The head-to-lens distance must be adjusted to the various print surfaces, and changes of print format will necessitate additional skill development.

Some students, depending on their age, ability, and current needs, may only require minimal training. For example, some students may be able to access all print without using the magnifier, except for the fine print found on maps, charts, medicine bottles, and in telephone directories. Students whose needs are minimal will require specific skill training as determined by the student and educational team. If the student needs to use a magnifier only for short viewing periods, for example, increasing stamina may not be a goal.

Using enjoyable materials and activities that are age-appropriate will contribute to faster skill development. Appendix 6.A at the end of this chapter lists a variety of activities that can be used to teach the skills necessary for using magnifiers. For example, playing a Monopoly® game with an older student will promote several skills at once within a motivating context. Young students who are at a prereading level will most likely use the magnifier to explore pictures and the large print typically found in commercial picture books. However, these preschool-aged children should not be expected to read fluently with a magnifier until more advanced literacy skills are developed.

Positioning

Appropriate positioning for optimal viewing sets the stage for developing stamina later. Positioning involves both positioning of the actual material to be viewed and adjusting the posture, which will enhance comfort and increase the amount of time the student can maintain the activity. Slant boards (also called reading stands) that tilt the reading material toward the reader and provide a writing surface may reduce neck and back strain by making it possible to maintain a comfortable reading and writing position. Basic reading stands may be purchased at local office supply stores, while more elaborate ones, those designed specifically for readers who are visually impaired, may be purchased from the American Printing House for the Blind and from other specialty product suppliers (see the Resources section). Some students dislike traditional wooden stands because of their size and lack of portability. Smaller, more lightweight stands are easier to carry from class to class.

Other simple modifications for positioning materials include using either a three-ring binder turned horizontally or a clipboard. In addition to noticing

A three-ring binder angles the worksheet to a more comfortable position for this boy using his dome magnifier.

Renae Shepler

how the student positions the materials to be viewed, pay close attention to the furniture used by the student. The student's feet should be positioned flat on the floor, with a chair and desk that is the appropriate size for him or her. Consultation with an occupational therapist can be helpful in designing the ideal workspace for students with low vision.

Stabilizing the Material to be Viewed

Once the teacher has addressed positioning, stabilizing the reading material or object to be viewed falls into place rather easily. A flat, stable base (such as a table or desk) on which material can be rested is required. During training, the pages in a book can be made to lie flat by using large rubber bands and looping them around the outside edges of each half of the text. If a desk or table is not available (e.g., on a science field trip to a nature trail), the student can be taught techniques for holding the object to be viewed in a steady manner. While sitting, the student can stabilize the object to be viewed by resting the hand that is holding the object on a knee. While standing he or she can brace the arm against the body to help keep the object steady enough for inspection under the magnifier.

Stabilizing the Hand

In order to build reading speed and maintain tracking, the student will need to stabilize the hand using the magnifier. Stand magnifiers must rest on the material to be viewed and are thus most appropriate for flat surfaces. If, while looking through the stand magnifier, students say they see better by raising the stand magnifier up off of the flat surface, the power of the magnifier is probably not appropriate. Handheld magnifiers require more sophisticated coordination, because the hand holding the magnifier must maintain a consistent focal distance between the magnifier and the material to be viewed while tracking. The teacher of students who are visually impaired can teach each student how to stabilize the hand holding the magnifier by having him or her use the heel of the hand and/or the elbow as a brace. Then the student can practice maintaining a constant distance from the material. For training purposes, the teacher may prepare reading materials which are double-spaced to allow for ease of viewing.

Adjusting the Head-to-Lens Distance

Adjusting the head-to-lens distance pertains primarily to the use of the handheld magnifier. Students will need to experiment with the relationship between the distances of the head, magnifier, and viewing material. There are at least two ways to teach this concept. The first is to instruct the student to place the magnifier

This student has been taught to brace the hand holding the magnifier against the heel of his other hand to stabilize the magnifier while he examines the rock.

Renae Shepler

in front of the eye and then to bring the material to within a few inches of the magnifier. The student should slowly move the material away until clarity is achieved. Once this distance has been established, the teacher can check the student's position (posture) and the stability of the material to assist him or her in finding a comfortable combination for reading for an extended period of time. The second method involves having the student first place the magnifier directly on the material to be viewed and then slowly raise the magnifier toward the eye until the material comes into focus. With either method, the student should be aware of the greater field of view obtained by placing the head closer to the magnifying lens.

Coordinating Hand, Head, and Eye Movements

Once the skills of positioning, stabilizing, and adjusting the head and materials are learned, coordinating hand, head, and eye movements specific to the type of magnifier used will follow naturally, given time and practice. The process is easier when using a stand magnifier, thus making this a preferred first choice for students in the 2–8-year-old range or those with difficulties in motor coordination.

Reading on a Flat Surface

Reading print which is produced on a flat surface is a skill that is used frequently and is critical for developing literacy. Examples of flat surfaces include books, workbooks, worksheets, newspapers, notes, letters, compact disk covers, game cards, and boxes. This is a fun skill to teach because of the wide variety of motivating reading material that can be used to demonstrate to the student the capacity of the magnifier. Because they are flat, these materials make it easier to rest a stand magnifier on them. They also make it easier to rest the hand that is holding a handheld magnifier against the surface of the material, thus making it possible to maintain a constant focal distance. Flat surfaces are also better for building speed when practicing tracing a line of print (i.e., reading from left to right while staying on the line), and they should be introduced using a consistent scanning format. For example, the student should first scan the entire surface (that is, move the magnifier from left-to-right, and from top-to-bottom) to determine where information is placed on the page, and then use a consistent scanning pattern to access all the information. There are some reading materials, such as newspapers and paperback books, which do not lend themselves to early training programs because single spacing and very small print may be frustrating to beginning magnifier users.

Reading a Variety of Formats

Reading a variety of print formats involves multiple surfaces, print contrasts, and background graphics. Rounded print surfaces such as pill bottles, cans, globes, and thermometers require stabilizing skills that differ from those needed for flat surfaces. Furthermore, the magnifier that is used for flat surfaces may not be appropriate for smaller print and for rounded surfaces. Handheld magnifiers provide easy access to a wider variety of print surfaces and sizes, and efforts to include them in a training program as soon as possible are critical to enable the student to achieve greater flexibility. Maps are particularly challenging because they include multiple print sizes, contrasts, and background graphics. Using the unaided eye to determine the layout of the material is important before placing a magnifier in front of the eye to distinguish detail.

Many objects and books use a variety of print formats and background graphics to attract the viewer. Since textbooks written for children attempt to

This student can use her magnifier to read a variety of formats.

capture the child's interest in a variety of ways, they contain excellent examples of print sizes, colors, contrasts, and layouts. The teacher may collect an assortment of these materials by asking school personnel for out-of-adoption texts (older editions that are no longer used in classrooms) that are typically stored in the bookroom. Children's magazines with bright colors, diverse layouts, photographs, and interesting information are also a wonderful tool to motivate students, and they are readily available at bookstores or in the school's library. Depending on the age of the student, some favorites include *Ranger Rick, Contact Kids, Zillions, National Geographic World,* and *Nintendo Power.* The teacher could assemble a carry-all box with samples of a variety of print formats, such as the following: a stamp collection book and stamps, a thermometer, an empty pill bottle, a compact disk, magazines, a fortune cookie and fortune, an age-appropriate textbook, a map of the school or city, a menu, a local TV guide, schedules for area sporting events such as high school football games, comics from the paper, instructions to a computer game (followed by an opportunity to play the game), a Lego® instruction sheet (followed by an opportunity to assemble the Lego® toy), and a page from the telephone book or a student directory.

Tracking at Reading Speed

Tracking at a speed that allows for reading commensurate with reading level is a gradual process that requires much practice. Before tracking at a fast rate is possible, the student should have developed a reliable method for stabilizing the material. Furthermore, training on speed and stamina should not be implemented until students have acquired some fluency in reading. Tracking with the stand magnifier is easy because the student does not have to work to maintain the correct focal distance. If the student consistently loses the line of print, place a Post-It® note along the middle of the bottom of the stand magnifier. This creates a line marker, thereby making it easier for the student to keep on the line. Similarly, when the teacher of students who are visually impaired is introducing tracking with a handheld magnifier, an easy modification may be to use a line marker, such as a ruler, directly on the material being viewed. The student can keep a record of reading speed by noting his or her progress on an informal chart such as this one:

DATE	# OF WORDS READ IN 5 MINUTES	# OF MISTAKES
10/13/00	650	5
10/15/00	700	4

Periodically, the teacher should conduct an informal reading inventory to determine reading rates and types of miscues, especially if the classroom teacher has not already done this. Koenig and Holbrook's *Learning Media Assessment of Students with Visual Impairments* (2nd Ed.) (1995) is an excellent source of information about informal reading inventories for students who are blind or visually impaired.

Developing Stamina

Developing stamina for the duration of an assignment that is appropriate to the student's age and grade will come with practice and should not be expected at the beginning of a magnifier training program. Stamina will develop once the student has worked under controlled reading sessions which are monitored by the instructor. Short daily reading assignments are preferred over longer assignments until the student develops experience with the magnifier. Keeping track of the length of the material read and/or the amount of time spent reading helps the student see progress. Since the teacher of students who are visually impaired may not work with the student daily, he or she can schedule a 15–20 minute reading session, but the print materials—which are clear and double-spaced, if possible, as well as motivating—could be left at the school. The materials can also be assigned as homework for a minimum of four days of practice during a seven-day week for up to two months. The student, a teacher, a parent, family members, or caregiver can use a simple form that notes the date, title of reading material, number of lines read, and amount of time it took to read with the magnifier. Since reading speeds and stamina vary according to the reading ability and motivation of the student, it is difficult to state a specific goal. Ideally, students will be able to complete an assignment within the time allotted to the rest of the class.

Viewing Nonprint Materials

Using the magnifier for nonprint activities includes viewing objects such as bugs, coins, rocks, eyes, fingers, toes, teeth, and other objects too numerous to list. Using a magnifier with objects begins at a very early age and continues as needs and interests develop. Most children adore examining their world; thus, looking at objects is a good way to introduce the magnifier. Going on walks to collect "stuff" is a fun way to begin exploring the properties of a magnifier. Collecting and categorizing flowers, rocks, and bugs is a nice way to integrate using the magnifier with both the objects and the print and pictures in the field guides.

Selecting the Magnifier for the Task

Typically, the low vision specialist will prescribe a couple of different magnifiers of a particular power. For example, the specialist may suggest a "2.5× dome magnifier" and a "lighted 3× handheld magnifier." Once the student has been oriented to the different types of handheld and/or stand magnifiers prescribed and the tasks for which they can be used, learning to select the appropriate magnifier for the task will be necessary for the student to develop full independence with the devices. As they experiment with an array of tasks and magnifiers, students should keep a journal noting the preferred magnifier for the tasks they have tried. The student may use a spiral notebook to mark the date, the magnifier used, the material viewed, and whether or not it worked. For example:

> 7/13/00—Used a bar magnifier with the newspaper TV section and the back of a cereal box. It worked OK with the TV guide and I could read one whole line of shows on at 8:00, but it didn't work with the box.

The teacher of students with visual impairments and the student can review the journal entries together and make generalizations about how easy it was to use a particular magnifier. For example, if a handheld magnifier works better than a stand magnifier for viewing rocks and flowers, what conclusion can the student draw concerning the extended uses of this type of device? In addition to determining the type of device for the task, the student will need to develop a sense for when using a device is appropriate. For example, many students read well unaided, and they may require magnification only when print sizes are greatly reduced. Print on maps, in graphs, in charts, in picture captions, and in margin notes tends to be smaller than the print in the body of the text, thus necessitating spot viewing for these tasks only.

A timed sampling of reading speeds for reading regular print unaided, large print unaided, and regular print with a magnifier can assist educators and the student in choosing the most appropriate medium for classroom reading assignments. Depending on the situation, the student may read regular print unaided most of the time and require magnification only some of the time. Some students use braille as a primary reading medium, but they use a magnifier to view some print and pictures which accompany the reading material. Teaching the student a system for assessing and selecting the right method and materials for literacy develops a heightened sense of control and a positive self-concept in the student.

Using Games and Activities to Teach the Magnifier

The games and activities listed in Appendix 6.A are designed to be a motivating way to develop and maintain magnifier skills for a variety of ages. It is not necessary to cover all of the activities; rather, the teacher may pick and choose according to the age and interests of individual students.

Students above the third grade may initially benefit more from activities that are geared toward life skills reading, that is, reading required in the course of everyday activities. Beginning with the activities under the "Life Skills Reading with a Magnifier" section in Appendix 6.A, the teacher may assist the student in selecting activities that look interesting and then add other activities suggested by the student. For example, while taking a nature hike (refer to Appendix 6.A) a magnifier lesson can begin with an exploration of an interesting object, such as a fossil, then move to scanning a field guide to find a picture and description of the fossil, then end with a timed reading assignment about fossils in a library book or encyclopedia. The student can help expand this list of activities and games and then pass on the new ideas to another student to try.

INTEGRATING THE USE OF MAGNIFIERS

At the onset of a magnifier training program, the teacher should discuss with the student which visual tasks the student currently has difficulty completing to create a list of goals the student wishes to achieve. The teacher should also ask for input from the parents and other professionals to enlarge upon this list, thus creating a good starting point for programming.

Training should occur within the context of the student's individual and realistic needs, and it should include as many people and settings as possible to provide numerous opportunities for magnifier practice and usage. Once the student demonstrates responsibility in handling and storing the device, he or she should be encouraged to use the magnifier at home, trying out suggestions from the teacher about recreational and domestic tasks that can be made easier with a magnifier. Reading the notches on an oven dial or microwave setting enables the student to participate in a cooking activity. Reading such things as Pokémon or baseball cards, tags on Beanie Babies, and Monopoly board cards opens more options for social activity with peers. Applying fingernail polish and mascara increases independence in grooming. These tasks may require different types of magnifiers, which should be explored with the student.

Once the teacher of students with visual impairments has accumulated examples of near-vision tasks the student engages in regularly, the classroom teacher should be given a description of the magnifier training program, including the specific dates and times the teacher of students with visual impairments will need to work with the student either individually or within the framework of a class activity. The teacher of students who are visually impaired will need to explain that the ultimate goal for the student is the ability to read and view a variety of materials, including those made available to all students, to facilitate the transfer of skills to different situations, the teacher of students who are visually impaired may conduct some lessons on magnifier use in the classroom within the context of the classroom teacher's lesson.

The student's IEP should reflect goals and objectives similar to those listed in Sidebar 6.3, and the progress the student makes toward achieving the ultimate goal of using a magnifier to access a variety of materials should be noted regularly. Ideally, all teachers and the family will work together to provide multiple opportunities and expectations for the student as a way to encourage him or her to use the magnifier during the day.

When programming for students with multiple or cognitive disabilities, the teacher of students who are visually impaired should ask the student, school personnel, and family to report the student's schedule, identifying routines and tasks that are a part of the student's daily and weekly life. Examples of routines include getting ready for school, eating in a restaurant, watching TV with the family, playing a game during recreation time, working at school or in the community, or going to the mall. Within these routines are tasks or activities

Sidebar **6.3**

Goals and Objectives for Magnifier Training

The following goals and objectives are purposely not written in measurable terms in order to enable the teacher of students who are visually impaired to customize them to individual students.

GOAL: *To demonstrate skills for magnifier maintenance*
OBJECTIVES: *The student will be able to:*

1. Hold the magnifier properly.

2. Communicate the purpose of the magnifier.

3. Clean the magnifier appropriately.

4. Assume responsibility for the magnifier.

5. Store the magnifier in a convenient location for quick retrieval.

6. Initiate the use of the magnifier.

GOAL: *To demonstrate skills for magnifier usage*
OBJECTIVES: *The student will be able to:*

1. Position himself or herself for optimal viewing.

2. Stabilize the reading material/object.

3. Stabilize the hand using the magnifier.

4. Adjust the head-to-lens distance.

5. Coordinate the hand, head, and eye movements specific to the type of magnifier.

6. Use the magnifier to read on a flat surface.

7. Read a variety of print formats.

8. Track at a speed which allows for reading commensurate with reading level.

9. Develop stamina for the duration of an age- or grade-appropriate assignment.

10. Select the appropriate magnifier for the task.

11. Use the magnifier for nonprint activities.

that may involve magnification. For example, looking at a menu, finding a favorite show in the TV guide, looking closely at the game board spaces and cards, following instructions (print or picture symbols), or inspecting a clothing tag to find the price may all be accomplished with a magnifier. The teacher should observe the student as he or she participates in specific activities and then apply task analysis to determine the critical parts of the activity that require the use of a magnifier. If the task involves viewing a flat surface, a stand magnifier is preferable because it does not require focusing. A bar magnifier which is a ruler-shaped stand magnifier that enlarges an entire line of print, is even simpler because tracking is not needed; however, there is a trade-off for power and flexibility, because bar magnifiers are not particularly powerful and typically have a great deal of distortion. If appropriate, the occupational and physical therapists should be consulted to determine the best positioning to enhance magnifier usage.

Students with cognitive disabilities achieve a higher level of success when new concepts are taught within the context in which they will be applied (Goetz, Guess, & Stremel-Campbell, 1987). Teaching the use of a magnifier in the actual setting and with the actual materials that will be used will be important, because transference of learning from one setting to another is typically difficult for these students. For example, if the student wants to work as a library assistant shelving books, the student should read the numbers on the spines and place the books on the actual library shelf rather than practice in a classroom away from the library. Reading pricing information on products at the grocery store before they are placed in the shopping cart is more meaningful than practicing reading one product tag after another at school. The magnifier should be integrated into as many settings as possible, with the help of teachers and family members, in order to expand the opportunities for the student to learn how to use the magnifier. This team approach becomes particularly crucial as students transition into competitive employment. The ability to access more tasks and information through the use of magnification devices may make a difference in employability.

DEALING WITH TYPICAL PROBLEMS

Typical problems which may occur during magnifier training include breakage, loss, theft, reluctance to use the device, or the fact that the magnifiers chosen are no longer effective for the tasks required.

Breakage

Some stand magnifiers can be costly, and scratching and breakage is generally inevitable in the hands of a young child. From the moment the teacher of students who are visually impaired first introduces the device, the correct handling and storage should be modeled, including the use of a felt-lined box or fabric pouch to protect the magnifier. Young children tend to throw the magnifier in the same box with crayons, glue, and scissors. This is acceptable, provided that the magnifier is first stored in its protective box or pouch.

The student should have easy access to the magnifier at all times. Although storing the device in the teacher's desk may be necessary to discourage theft, this option is not ideal because it also places the teacher in the position of having to remember to retrieve the magnifier, thus limiting spontaneity for the student as well as diminishing the student's sense of responsibility. An orientation to magnifying devices for the entire class helps satisfy well-intentioned curiosity that peers may exhibit. This can be done by the teacher of students who are visually impaired—or, better yet, by the student. During this presentation, classmates can be asked to notify the student with a visual impairment or the teacher if they happen to see the device in the hands of another person, thereby discouraging misuse or theft. As students become older, they will be taught to take increasing responsibility for the device. However, additional devices should be available in the event that one is broken, lost, or stolen.

Reluctance to Use the Magnifier

Students may develop a reluctance to use a magnifier at different points in their lives. When exposure to magnifiers within the context of fun activities begins as early as the age of two, young children have a greater chance of developing positive attitudes toward the device. The magnifier becomes a necessary tool for daily existence. As students age and become more self-conscious, however, they may reject the device altogether.

Forcing the student to use the magnifier is impossible. Rewarding the desired completion of tasks is the goal. It helps to remember that the magnifier is a tool in an array of options that the teacher is helping the student to explore and develop. At this stage, it may help to return to the low vision specialist to preview and experiment with different designs of the same power magnifier, insofar as some can be more inconspicuous than others and therefore more acceptable to the student. Pocket magnifiers are particularly appealing for older students because they are small and can be slipped away quickly and easily.

The teacher of students who are visually impaired can also help the student understand the ability of the magnifier to help him or her complete tasks on his or her own, thus allowing him or her to demonstrate independence. In contrast, *not* using the magnifier would make the student dependent by forcing him or her to ask someone to copy material from the board, to enlarge books, or to read aloud. The desire for independence may help the student decide to use the magnifier.

Practicing in private locations and off-campus before integrating the device into the classroom can give the student exposure to the magnifier without the fear of being teased. Encouraging a student with low vision to meet a successful magnifier user and perhaps setting up a mentoring relationship can also help him or her get past the perceived stigma of "being different." Taking two students on a field trip in which each one will have to use his or her device is an enjoyable way to accomplish this goal. Some school districts hold an Olympic-like event at the end of the year in which students enter individual categories that involve using specific devices and that enable them to compete for prizes (Paul, 1992). Students work all year on perfecting skills and methods with their devices (for example, braille note takers, slates and styli, magnifiers, monoculars) and then meet on one big day to enter the events, eat lunch, and receive awards. These methods encourage students to use devices such as magnifiers; and these methods support the students' efforts.

Difficulty in Using the Magnifier

In cases in which the student states that he or she is having difficulty in using previously prescribed magnifiers or that he or she is experiencing difficulty with speed or accuracy, the teacher may talk to the parents and suggest that the student have a follow-up visit to the eye doctor to rule out a change in the student's eye condition. A return to the low vision specialist may also be in order, with questions pertaining to the current magnification used and the tasks with which the student is experiencing difficulty.

SUMMARY

The games and activities listed in Appendix 6.A are just an introduction to the ways in which learning to use a magnifier can be made interesting and enjoyable for students. When the teacher of students who are visually impaired has tried everything on the list, it is time for both teacher and student to look around and note the millions of natural activities people find interesting—and to note that using a magnifier will make it possible for the student to engage in these activities too. The magnifier is simply a tool that can help expand a person's capabilities to pursue those interests.

REFERENCES

Goetz, L., Guess, D., & Stremel-Campbell, K. (1987). *Innovative program design for individuals with dual sensory impairments.* Baltimore, MD: Paul H. Brookes Publishing Co.

Koenig, A. J., & Holbrook, M. C. (1995). *Learning media assessment of students with visual impairments* (2nd Ed.). Austin, TX: Texas School for the Blind and Visually Impaired.

Paul, B. (1992). High vision games net low vision gains. *Journal of Visual Impairment & Blindness, 86,* 63–65.

Activities for Teaching the Use of Magnifiers

Activity

Rock Hunt: Go for walks to pick up rocks. Use the magnifier to examine rocks and to find descriptions in a rock identification book. The end project could be a rock collection that is labeled and displayed.

Fingerprints: Use the magnifier to distinguish the fingerprints of a few people. Make thumbprint creatures with felt pens. Make a cartoon strip with fingerprint characters and captions.

Stamp Collections: Buy stamps at a post office according to the interest level of each child. Use the magnifier to identify the stamps and to describe the picture/print on the stamp. For foreign stamps, locate the country on a globe or map using the magnifier.

Picture Game: Cut out small pictures from magazines or old workbooks, etc., and paste them onto construction paper to make cards. Do not laminate to avoid excess glare on the surface of the pictures. Use a game board approach, one in which the child rolls the dice, draws a card, and identifies the picture with a magnifier. If it is identified correctly, the player moves forward. If not, he or she loses a turn.

Cards: Use a regular deck of cards to play games such as "Go Fish" using a magnifier to identify cards.

Hidden Pictures: Using hidden pictures similar to ones printed in the magazine *Highlights for Children,* ask child to develop a system of scanning with a magnifier to find hidden objects. A clear piece of acetate may be placed over the page at first with a scanning plan mapped out to help the child. Reinforce left-to-right progression and top-to-bottom.

Life Skills Reading with a Magnifier: Examples:

cooking	warranties	CD/album covers	recipes in books and on
school menu	newspaper	cans	cans & boxes of food
radio dials	instructions on cosmetics	maps/charts	oven temperature settings
bills/receipts	medicine bottles	bank statements	

Board Games: Use the magnifier with board games which require reading cards with fine print (e.g., Monopoly® or Trivial Pursuit®).

Lego Assembly: Try to construct Legos® by following the instructions. Use a stand magnifier for instructions and a handheld magnifier for checking the Lego® assembly to see if it matches the directions.

Look-It: Hold a magnifier close to a mirror while the child looks through the magnifier into the mirror. This is a good conversation starter for the structure of the eye, which can lead to further discussion of the student's eye conditions.

Yearbook: Yearbooks can provide a great source of small, detailed group pictures. Many elementary schools have yearbooks, so this activity can be highly motivating for all ages. Use the magnifier to locate familiar faces in group pictures, to access the index in the back, to read picture captions, and to identify details in pictures.

Calorie Counting: This activity is often of high interest to teenage students. Use a magnifier to read calorie content (or other information). A quick trip to the grocery store (or access to a supply of typical teenage foodstuffs including soda cans, candy bars, chip bags, etc.) will provide a wider variety of formats and challenges for magnifier users.

Collections: Almost any child will have a "collection" of something (Beanie Babies, Matchbox Cars, McDonald's toys, Barbie dolls, rocks, baseball cards, fossils). If a student doesn't already have a collection that he or she is aware of, a quick trip to the library or book store will provide them with a wealth of guides that will usually either inspire them to start a collection or make them realize that the pile of fast-food restaurant toys at home is already a collection. Collection guides provide a wide array of print formats (charts, diagrams, and detailed pictures) on which to practice.

Nature Hikes: Pack several reference guides (fossils, rocks, flowers, birds, bugs, etc.) in a backpack and go on a nature hike with students. Use the magnifiers to examine objects and to access information in the nature guides related to the objects.

Field Trip Planning: Make an agreement to take your student on a field trip if the student gathers all the information for the field trip. Typical skills required may include using a phone book to call restaurants to see what time they open for lunch, reading bus schedules, and using city maps to plan routes.

CD Packages: Play a CD and ask the child to locate a song on the CD package.

Treasure Hunt: Have a treasure hunt with clues presented on a variety of materials which require differing magnifier techniques and possibly even different magnifiers. Clues may be presented on curved surfaces, hidden among a variety of visual information so that the student will need to search for it systematically, written on specific pages of reference books so that the student needs to use guide words, etc. This is an easy activity to modify for any age level.

Secret Messages: Write secret messages one letter at a time with the letters connected by lines to imitate a typical reading and/or tracking and scanning pattern. Move from top left to top right, down and back, left to right and so on.

Riddles: Hide riddle answers by writing the answer one letter at a time on a surface. The letters should be written so that a left-to-right, down-and-back, left-to-right tracking pattern is used. This way, the student will come across the letters in the correct order. Letters may be hidden in this manner on a pictorial background to add a challenge.

Activities and Games for Teaching Children to Use a CCTV

FRANCES MARY D'ANDREA

WHAT IF STUDENTS with low vision had a magic box that could instantly enlarge any book placed under it to the exact size needed? Not only could a student change the size of the print, but he or she could also change the contrast, the brightness of the image, and even whether the text could show up as white print on a black background instead of the usual black print on white. Such a "magic box" does exist: It is a closed-circuit television system, or CCTV. A CCTV is simply a video camera that projects an image onto a monitor or television screen; hence, such devices are sometimes also called video magnifiers. This electronic device can be a valuable tool in the classroom, home, and workplace, one that increases access to print by enlarging and enhancing books and other printed materials. While CCTVs are widely found in schools, very little research exists about their use in teaching children with low vision to read and write. Therefore, much of this chapter is written based on experience and anecdotal evidence from the point of view of a teacher.

All CCTVs require a camera, a light source, and a monitor on which to see the image, but this simple description encompasses a great deal of variety in styles. For example, some models come with a color camera, some with black and white. In some cases, the monitor is part of the system; in others, a standard

Carol Farrenkopf

This student is using a stand-alone CCTV with a fixed camera to read her French workbook. The monitor is "in line," or on top of the camera unit.

TV set, computer monitor, or LCD display can be used. Most CCTVs include various knobs for other features, such as focus, brightness control, contrast, and the ability to reverse polarity (to change from a black image on a white background, to a white image on a black background). Some types of systems contain a tray or movable table on which to place the printed materials. This tray can move horizontally and vertically and is often referred to as an "X-Y table." Other models have handheld cameras that the user moves along the text he or she wants to read. The many variations in styles and features add to the versatility of these machines. These features will be discussed in more detail later in this chapter.

PROS AND CONS OF USING A CCTV SYSTEM

CCTVs can be beneficial reading and writing tools for students with low vision. Such devices can instantly enlarge text placed under the camera, and the image can be customized to fit the student's own specific requirements (such as the size, color, or contrast of the image). Students can view print at a comfortable reading distance rather than bring the book close to their eyes or stoop over to bring their eyes close to the page. Thus, a CCTV can reduce the physical fatigue some students experience while reading. Students can learn to write under the camera and watch the monitor to make sure their writing is legible. Depending on the complexity of features built into the machine, students can adjust several controls to find the image that allows them the best combination of image size, color, contrast, and brightness—in other words, the image that suits their individual needs. Children can also use a CCTV to enlarge pictures, graphics, and even small objects (such as coins, plants, insects, and other things with very small details), thus further adding to their enjoyment and understanding of books, maps, and items in their environment.

For all their benefits, CCTVs also have their disadvantages. Although new designs are making some models more portable than ever before, they are still not as easy to carry as handheld optical devices (such as magnifiers) or large-print materials. Models not specifically designed to be portable can be fairly heavy (about 35 pounds or more). All CCTVs require some sort of power source, so they either must be plugged in or run off a battery. They also require a certain amount of care. Because the main components are a camera and light source, they are breakable and may not survive a lot of jostling. When they require maintenance and repair, it may not be possible to locate a local repair shop, so they must be shipped to the manufacturer or vendor to be serviced or to replace parts. CCTVs can also be expensive. Simple models with few features can cost under $1,000. More elaborate models could be in the range of several thousand dollars. Generally, the more features the CCTV has, the more expensive it will be. More built-in features also mean that more training may be required to learn to use the machine independently. Because of the expense and the trade-offs of using a CCTV system, it makes sense to evaluate carefully how useful it would be to a student before it is purchased.

Before the school system considers a CCTV purchase, the student must have both a functional low vision evaluation and a complete clinical low vision evaluation (see Chapters 2 and 3, respectively). The clinical low vision specialist can discuss with the teacher, the student, and the parents, family, or caregivers all the options available that can be used to help the student access printed materials, including the use of a CCTV. A functional vision assessment (FVA) may indicate to the teacher that additional options are needed by the student to enable him or her to function best in school and other environments. Remember that a CCTV is just one choice from an entire array of high- and low-tech options that may assist the student, such as large print, prescribed optical devices, the use of dark-lined paper with a black marker, braille, and recorded materials. The job of the teacher of children with visual impairments is to make the student as independent and efficient as possible, to increase the number of alternatives

> **Sidebar 7.1**
>
> ## Factors That Indicate a Student May Benefit from a CCTV
>
> • The student has variable or fluctuating eyesight that results in varying needs for magnification.
>
> • The student uses a variety of reading materials not practically available in large print.
>
> • The student's print textbooks use a variety of type sizes and styles that may not be large enough for him or her to read in large print or with handheld magnification devices.
>
> • The student has difficulty reading handwriting—his or her own or others'—or creating legible handwriting.

the student is comfortable using, and to determine which tool allows the greatest amount of success in completing specific tasks. Sidebar 7.1 lists factors that may indicate that the use of a CCTV is appropriate for a particular student.

CHOOSING A CCTV

Deciding whether a student could benefit from a CCTV and then on which model to buy can be a complex decision. There are many styles and options available, and the student may not need all the available features. In those cases in which a CCTV is to be shared among several students (such as in a resource room), the teacher should also think of the versatility of a particular machine and if it will meet the various needs of several students. Before choosing a system that will be used in a school, several factors should be considered: the type of model, what features are needed, and where the machine will be used. These factors are interrelated. A careful comparison of features—keeping the needs of the student in mind—can help the teacher choose one model over another. Each of the factors will be examined in more detail.

Models Available

Three basic types of CCTVs are often found in schools: a stand-alone model, a model without a built-in screen that requires a hookup to a monitor or television set, or one with a handheld camera. A head-mounted model also exists; in this model, the camera is mounted at eye level and the monitor is built into the head gear, but such a system is less commonly used. This may change in the near future, however, as these systems become smaller and easier to use. Also becoming more common are CCTV systems that are designed to be used with computers (see Sidebar 7.2).

Sidebar **7.2**

Computer-Compatible Video Magnifiers

Another CCTV option that teachers can consider is a video magnification system designed to be used with a computer. This system shares the computer's monitor so there is no need for a separate CCTV monitor. Images from both sources (the computer and CCTV) can appear on the screen. Particularly useful to computer users, these video magnifiers are compatible with any screen magnification software on the market. With a computer-compatible video magnifier, it is possible to conveniently switch between the magnified computer screen image and the magnified CCTV screen image. The user can even split the screen so that two images are seen at once, with the computer image appearing on one half of the screen and the CCTV image on the other. Thus, the image from the CCTV's video camera of a textbook or worksheet shares the screen with the computer's screen image—such as the computer's operating system or the software application in use. This allows a student to view his or her science textbook comfortably, for example, while at the same time using the computer to write up a lab report.

Computer-compatible video magnifiers are expensive items. A simple system with a black-and-white camera will still cost well over $1,000, and more sophisticated systems with a color camera will cost much more than that. The systems do not come with a monitor as other CCTVs do, because the manufacturer assumes that the computer's monitor will be used. The monitor can be placed with the video magnifier on a platform above the camera to provide in-line viewing, or it can be positioned with the computer and next to the video magnifier. A foot pedal often comes with a computer-compatible video magnifier to provide the user with hands-free switching between the computer and the video magnifier.

There is considerable variety among the various computer-compatible video magnifiers on the market today. The teacher or school system considering the purchase of one of these systems will need to carefully consider all the options available on specific systems. For example, one system offers on-screen features such as a clock, calendar, and calculator that are controlled from an external keypad. Another system allows users to save magnified images on the computer. One low-cost system allows for toggling between the computer and the video magnifier but does not offer a split-screen capability. As with any technology purchase, the needs of the user, the flexibility of the system, and the benefits and costs of a particular option must be weighed.

—*Mark Uslan*
Manager, Technical Evaluation Services,
National Technology Program, American
Foundation for the Blind

Stand-Alone CCTVs

The stand-alone type of CCTV has a fixed or "mounted" camera, an X-Y table, and a monitor that can be either on top of the camera or placed off to the side. (This configuration will be discussed later in more detail in the section on setting up a workstation.) To use this type of device, the student turns on the machine and places the material on the X-Y table; the image is then shown on the attached monitor. The X-Y table can be moved from side to side and toward and away from the user so that the student can view the entire page of the material. The benefit of the stand-alone model is that it is a complete unit. It does not need any further hookups to make it work; it can simply be plugged in

Mark Wilkinson

Video magnifiers are CCTVs that connect to a computer and allow the student to switch between using the computer monitor to view the image on the CCTV or the computer screen.

and used immediately. Its relative simplicity is one reason that it is the most common type of CCTV used in schools. However, stand-alone models are heavy; they are generally used in one fixed spot, and they are not likely to be moved from place to place within the school. Some of the stand-mounted models now are "foldable" so that the stand holding the monitor collapses flat to increase their portability somewhat.

CCTVs with Separate Monitors

Some models combine the convenience of the stand-mounted camera with the flexibility of a separate monitor. Often, a standard television set can be used in place of the monitor. CCTVs that can hook up to a TV are more portable; an individual can use the model anywhere there is a monitor or TV to plug into (e.g., in different classrooms, at home, on vacation, or at grandma's house). These models tend to be less expensive than the stand-alone types, but they require the user to find a compatible monitor on which to view the enlarged image. In addition, the quality of the image is also dependent upon the quality of the TV set. This is an important consideration, since a poor viewing image will result in visual fatigue, and the student will not be able to work as long or as accurately. For educational use, the best option is to purchase a high-quality monitor for the CCTV.

CCTVs with Handheld Cameras

If size and portability are concerns, another option is a CCTV with a handheld camera. The camera is not fixed in position as with the other models, but it is built into a small plastic case about the size of a pack of cards. The user must roll the camera across the surface of the text and then read from the image displayed on the TV or monitor. (Some of these models come with a monitor, but many do not.) Since the camera is moved along the surface of the reading material, it can be used to read print from items that are not flat, such as soup cans and medicine bottles. Some handheld models come with very small monitors that enable the CCTV to be carried in a backpack. This would allow an older student to bring the CCTV into stores and other places previously out of the reach of the old stand-mounted models. These models cannot easily be used for writing unless some sort of stand to hold the camera in place is also offered as an option; with such a stand the paper can be in focus while the individual writes. In addition, handheld cameras are generally difficult for very young children and students with physical disabilities to use because good motor control is required to track lines of print.

Head-Mounted Systems

Head-mounted systems have become more common in recent years. Some of these systems are not available through catalogs but must be purchased from specific low vision clinics. However, a few vendors now sell them directly to consumers. The beauty of the head-mounted system is its hands-free nature. With the camera mounted at eye level and the monitor built into the head gear, both hands are free to work on typing or other tasks. Another type of head-mounted system uses a handheld camera (see the accompanying photo), and some head-mounted systems have an auto focusing feature that will bring distant objects into focus as the wearer turns his or her head. The head-mounted systems are not often found in schools because of their price, the weight, and their relative rarity. They also have an unconventional look that may make some students self-conscious. However, the new head-mounted systems that are being designed are smaller, lighter, and less obtrusive than ever before. This is an area to watch because of the rapid development of new technology.

Coleen Lou/Wendy Mans/Mans International

This young girl is using a head-mounted CCTV to read a book. This system uses a handheld camera.

Features

Sidebar 7.3 lists some of the features commonly found in CCTV systems. Deciding what features may be useful for a particular student depends to some extent on the types of materials that need to be enhanced. For example, a student who primarily uses a CCTV for higher mathematics because of the small print size of complex equations may not particularly need the option for color. Students who will use the CCTV to view color-coded maps, photographs, art work, and other materials that depend on discerning colors will benefit from the color feature. Students who have motor impairments that would inhibit the ability to move the X-Y table may benefit from a motorized tray.

Budgetary considerations also affect what model is purchased. As mentioned earlier, the more features a unit has, the more expensive it is likely to be. The teacher will have to carefully weigh the benefits of each feature and the needs of the particular student. The questionnaire in Sidebar 7.4 can help the teacher prioritize these features and make a decision on what model to purchase.

Sidebar **7.3**

Features Commonly Found in CCTVs

Different features may be useful for different students, not only because of the materials they need to view and the uses to which the systems will be put but also because of the nature of the students' visual impairments. Because environmental factors such as illumination, brightness, contrast, and color affect each individual's vision differently, students will vary in their need to adjust each of these variables. The following CCTV features are commonly available.

• Black-and-white vs. color
Black-and-white may be quite adequate if the student just uses the CCTV to read text and can use optical devices (or no adaptation) for color photos and maps. Color systems are beneficial for students who often use books (especially in content areas such as science and social studies) that have color photographs, who do workbook activities and other activities that require color vision, and who read color-coded maps. Black-and-white models are generally less expensive than color models.

• Other color options
Some CCTVs enable the user to vary text and background color, so the student can find a combination that is easy to read (for example, purple words on a pale yellow background).

• Focus options
Variable-focus machines allow students to focus according to their personal needs and can accommodate various sizes of text. *Fixed-focus* machines are less expensive, but their image size depends on the size of the monitor the image is displayed on. *Auto-focus* machines keep the image in focus even while the size of image is being changed. Auto-focus CCTVs are generally more expensive.

• Magnification
CCTVs generally have a large range of magnification; some can magnify up to 60 times (Uslan, Shen, & Shagrai, 1996). For students who have fluctuating vision or use a variety of textbooks with different print sizes, the ability to vary the size of the image is a helpful feature.

• Contrast
Another useful feature is the ability to vary the contrast between the background and the text. Some students favor a higher contrast image, others prefer low contrast.

• Variable brightness
For students who are light sensitive (photophobic), having the ability to darken the screen somewhat is important in order to avoid eye strain.

• Positive/negative image (also called reverse polarity)
Some students prefer to read white print on a black background rather than black print on a white background. Reverse polarity allows the student to do this at the flick of a switch. The student may have to readjust the brightness and contrast after changing polarity.

• Tray (also called X-Y table)
The standard X-Y table generally comes with both friction brakes to limit the vertical movement of the image and margin stops to limit the horizontal movement. Learning to use these features effectively will be an important skill. Some models come with a motorized tray that moves automatically at a preset speed. This feature may be good for students who have physical disabilities, but it is fairly complex to set.

• Line features
Most CCTV models allow the user to display only part of the screen at a time. This feature, called screen blocking, can be used to isolate either one line of text at a time or as much of the screen as desired. This feature is useful for students who find it difficult to attend to a full screen of enlarged text
(continued)

Sidebar **7.3** (continued)

and frequently lose their place. Knobs on the machine control how much of the top and bottom of the screen is black, leaving a space in the middle where the text is displayed. Blocking a portion of the viewing area is also a useful strategy for students who have light sensitivity (photophobia) and prefer to read from a screen with a reduced amount of light (Lund & Watson, 1997).

A related feature allows a dark horizontal line to appear on the screen that underlines the text the student is reading. This can help the student keep his or her place when reading long passages of text.

• Split screen
This feature allows the screen to be split into two images, such as one on the student's textbook and the second on the blackboard. These systems have two cameras and need to be adjusted properly to focus on each area. Other models with a split screen have only one camera and are designed to work with a computer. In that case, the screen can be split to enlarge the image on the computer and also enlarge what is on the X-Y table.

• Monitor size
The purchaser may have the option to pay more for a larger monitor (for example, a 21 in., rather than a 17-inch, monitor). Larger monitors do take up a lot more room, however, and may not fit easily onto a table or desk. The monitor may be so big that it is unwieldy for young children to use. Smaller, portable monitors are now available with LCD displays.

• Other special features
Some split screen systems are available with a foot switch that allows the user to alternate between screens. Another model has a keypad for clock, calendar, and calculator options. CCTVs are now available that allow the built-in camera to swivel so it can focus on distant objects and then on the material on the student's desk. In this way, the student can use the CCTV to observe a science experiment or read the blackboard, and then swivel the camera to focus on the science book on his or her desk.

Making the Purchase

Some models of CCTVs are available from specialty catalogs (see the Resources section), but it is generally advisable to actually try out various models first before purchasing one. If it is at all possible to try out a particular machine with the student, the teacher should take advantage of that option. Because of the range of models and features, it is only by hands-on testing of several types that a clear picture of the pros and cons for each student can be seen.

The American Foundation for the Blind's (AFB) National Technology Program regularly reviews and evaluates all types of new technology devices designed for people who are blind or visually impaired, including CCTVs. These reviews are published regularly in the *Journal of Visual Impairment & Blindness* and in *AccessWorld* (see, for example, Shen & Uslan, 1996a; 1996b; 1997; Uslan & Chan, 2000; Uslan & Lin 1997; Uslan & Shen,1996), but they can also be received directly from the National Technology Program or on the AFB's Web site.

Sidebar 7.4

CCTV Features Questionnaire

Student Name: _____   Date: _____

Grade: _____

1. The student often uses material that contains important information in color.

                yes   possibly   no

2. The student will be taking the machine from place to place.

                yes   possibly   no

3. The student will be using the device to enlarge his or her handwriting.

                yes   possibly   no

4. The student has fine or gross motor involvement which will limit his or her ability to move the tray.

                yes   possibly   no

5. The student must often work from the classroom chalkboard at the same time as from books.

                yes   possibly   no

6. The student already uses screen magnification or speech on a computer.

                yes   possibly   no

7. Other students will be sharing this CCTV and have similar needs.

                yes   possibly   no

8. There is minimal classroom space where this machine will be placed.

                yes   possibly   no

Many of the major manufacturers of CCTVs have local or regional vendors from whom teachers can get up-to-date information and try out the machines first-hand. Teachers can also see the latest models at state, provincial, and national conferences of professional organizations such as AER (the Association for Education and Rehabilitation for the Blind and Visually Impaired) or at technology conferences (such as Closing the Gap). A list of manufacturers appears in the Resources section.

SETTING UP A CCTV IN SCHOOL

WHERE TO PUT THE CCTV

If a nonportable system is chosen, the first question is where in the school the CCTV should be placed. For an elementary school child, the classroom in which the child is doing the majority of reading and writing is an obvious place. For older students who change classes frequently, the library, resource room for students with visual impairments, English or Language Arts classroom, or other academic classroom may be the first choice. The placement may be based either on where the student will be doing the most sustained reading or on the class in which the printed texts most need the flexible enlargement a CCTV can give (for example, the math textbook may have a wider variety of very small symbols that are difficult for the student to see). If the student is using school library resources for a number of classes (for example, doing research for a history project, reading a variety of poems for an English class paper, and reading current science and news magazines for a science project), then the library may be a good central location. A central location will probably be necessary if more than one student will be sharing a CCTV. In that case, the resource room for students who have visual impairments may be a logical place, although the library or other location used by the students could also work well.

In cases in which the CCTV is placed in a central location rather than in the room with the student, it is advisable to set some guidelines with the student, parents, and teachers on when the student is allowed to leave class to use the machine. For example, a system may be developed in which a student may be excused during class to go to the library or resource room to take a math test, as long as staff is available to proctor the student. (Allowing the student to occasionally leave class to use the CCTV is also a good opportunity to teach students responsibility and time management skills!) In some cases, security of the system may become an issue if it is not under the watchful eye of a knowledgeable teacher. Curious students may damage the CCTV if they do not know what it is used for. The teacher of students who are visually impaired should ensure that there is adequate supervision wherever the machine is placed.

In some cases, CCTVs have been placed on wheeled carts so that they can be moved from class to class with the student. This approach is not recommended, however, for several reasons. It increases the possibility that the machine could fall off the cart and possibly be damaged—or worse, it could injure a student. Rolling a heavy machine—especially through the kind of crowded hallways found in most junior high and high schools—could be dangerous if it collides with other students. In schools in which there are steps to maneuver, rolling the CCTV from class to class is impractical, if not impossible. If at all possible, setting the CCTV in a central location is preferable to moving a large stand-mounted system from room to room; if portability is a major concern, then the pros and cons of a system specifically designed to be carried from place to place should be investigated.

Setting Up a Workstation

Once the issue of where the CCTV is needed has been addressed, a workstation that is suitable for the student's needs can be designed. Stand-mounted systems especially require ample space for the machine—as well as for the student's books and other materials. Setting up a workstation in the classroom is an important consideration, and it should be based on correct ergonomics—that is, the workstation should be physically adapted to the human body, and in particular to the physical characteristics of the student (for example, size, height, right- or left-handedness, etc.). Models in which the monitor is placed directly above the camera are often referred to as "in-line" models as opposed to "free-standing" where the monitor can be placed off to the side of the X-Y table. In-line CCTVs require less room, but for very young children the monitor can be

Carol Farrenkopf

This student has designed a CCTV workstation that is comfortable and efficient for her needs, with the monitor on top of the camera.

up so high that the child must crane his or her neck to see the image clearly, or he or she is limited to looking only at the bottom of the monitor. When the monitor is placed off to the side, the image may be at a better height, but reaching the control knobs and manipulating the X-Y table can be a problem. Teachers of younger children will have to experiment a bit to find the most comfortable and workable setup for the CCTV. The low vision specialist and the occupational therapist may also be able to offer valuable feedback. Poorly designed workstations will cause the student to fatigue more easily and could cause neck and shoulder muscles to become sore and stiff. The more comfortable the student is at the workstation, the more work he or she will be able to complete.

The workstation should be situated so that the student will still be able to interact with the class. A computer cart or table can be a good place to put the CCTV. If the cart has wheels, the system can be moved short distances around the room easily and safely. These tables often have built-in shelves that hold books and other materials, and they are usually designed to be the correct height for older students who are seated, thus enabling them to see the monitor clearly (or else they are designed to have adjustable shelves). The CCTV should be placed away from the windows to prevent glare, which can make the screen hard to read. Because these systems are breakable, they should be placed away from the main line of traffic so that a student doesn't accidentally bump into it and knock it over—or trip over the power cord.

PRACTICE MAKES PERFECT

Learning to use the CCTV requires practice like any other skill. Some students may be comfortable with basic features within a week or two, while it may take others months to master the use of the CCTV. Students must learn to move the tray smoothly, to read without skipping lines, to use the different features for various effects (for example, enlarging text, brightening image), and to use all the features independently. It is important that teachers offer training in the use of CCTVs and not assume that the student will "just naturally" pick it up (LaGrow, 1981).

There is no research that suggests at what age to start teaching a child to read using a CCTV. However, as with any other tool, the teacher can certainly introduce the child to it at a very young age (such as kindergarten), starting with such activities as looking at very small objects and examining photographs and pictures in books. The student may not need a CCTV for reading tasks until third or fourth grade, when students typically start to use reference books (for example, encyclopedias) not generally found in large print; some books may use such small print that the student's optical devices may not be adequate to enlarge the image sufficiently. However, it is a good idea to familiarize the student with the CCTV *before* he or she needs to use it regularly for reading tasks.

Students should realize that when viewing objects under the CCTV, the higher the magnification, the larger the image, so less can fit on the screen at one time (i.e., there is a smaller field of view). The more on the screen at one time (i.e., lower magnification), the less manipulation of the X-Y table is needed to view everything on the tray. Therefore, students will probably not wish to have the CCTV on the highest magnification settings for all tasks. While it may be fun for the student to create the largest images possible with a CCTV—and there may be times that the highest level of magnification is preferred (such as when examining very small items in science class, etc.)—it is generally not the most efficient way to do all reading tasks. The goal is to provide sufficient magnification of the image while maximizing the amount of material on the screen.

The skills needed for using the CCTV for reading and writing are listed in Sidebar 7.5. The teacher of students who are visually impaired will need to assess the student's capabilities on each item and then choose activities that will teach and reinforce each skill. The appendixes at the end of this chapter suggest some games and activities that teachers can use with students learning to read and write with a CCTV system. The suggested activities can be individualized

---

Sidebar **7.5**

SKILLS FOR READING WITH THE CCTV

1. The concept of "in focus" and how to focus the image.

2. How to change the image size and then focus.

3. How to spot or locate an image on the page and then focus.

4. How to move the tray systematically:

   A. Tracking left to right.

   B. Moving the tray away from oneself to move down the page.

5. Following a line of text.

6. Following multiple uses of text.

7. Using various features, such as a line marker.

8. For students with learning difficulties, use perceptual cues, such as color coding, to indicate the beginning and end of lines or dotted lines to separate lines of text. Then gradually fade out cues.

SKILLS FOR WRITING WITH THE CCTV

1. Getting accustomed to writing while looking at the monitor.

2. Drawing simple shapes.

3. Drawing lines.

4. Writing words.

to fit the student's interests and needs. Use of age-appropriate materials is also important. For example, a high school boy learning to use a CCTV may be more motivated to read and examine photographs in a skateboarding magazine than in a primary grade storybook.

Learning to Read with the CCTV
Familiarization

The teacher should allow plenty of time for the student to become familiarized with the features of the CCTV. The child can experiment a bit with the features, such as color, size, and brightness, while looking at a photograph or small, interesting object. Discuss with the student the uses of the CCTV and how it can be used for a variety of school tasks.

Focusing

Discuss with the child the concepts of "in focus" and "out of focus"; also talk about the fact that images in focus are easier to recognize and identify. Use several fun and motivating images to get the student to practice this skill until the student is proficient and can quickly focus the machine.

Enlarging an Image

The teacher can present letters and pictures at various magnifications to evaluate at which size the student best recognizes the image. After the teacher presents this skill and familiarizes the child with the knob used to change the image size, the student should then be allowed to experiment with the size and focus knobs to learn to use these two features together. The teacher should manipulate the X-Y table at this point so that the student can concentrate on locating, enlarging, and focusing the images.

Learning to Use the X-Y Table to View One Row

The use of the movable X-Y table is one of the trickiest things for a student to learn. Since the table moves in four directions to allow the user to view an entire page, it takes some practice to learn to move the table horizontally to read one line of text and then back to the left to the beginning of the next line. It is not unusual for a beginner to skip lines while reading or to experience confusion while trying to search for a particular section of the text.

CCTVs with attached X-Y tables have "friction brakes" built into them that inhibit table movement toward and away from the user (that is, movement that shows the top and bottom of a page). Margin stops are a feature that limit horizontal movement (similar to those on a typewriter). At first, the teacher should control the movement of the table with both the brake and margin stops. Then the teacher can set the table brake so that the tray can only move horizontally. This makes it less likely that the child will "slip off" the row he or she is viewing. The activities listed in Appendix 7.A suggest some strategies teachers can use to develop this skill in children.

Learning to View More Than One Row

Once the student can locate the pictures or words in one row, he or she needs to learn to move the tray back to the left to find the beginning of the next row. (The table brake will have to be loosened to allow some vertical movement.) The teacher can use perceptual cues to indicate the beginning and end of a row. Perceptual cues are added reminders to help a child with a particular activity. For example, a green dot can be placed at the beginning of the row, which would cue the child that this is the "starting place" for the row. A red dot can be placed at the end of a row to mean "stop." If the student has a black-and-white CCTV, the teacher can use the words *go* and *stop* or a smiley face and a hand (like a policeman's hand for "stop") as cues for the student on where to start and stop on a line before moving on to the next line.

If the student is still having difficulty finding the next line of text, the teacher can put a perceptual cue, such as dotted lines, between lines of text. The student can then learn to track back along the dotted line and then down to find the beginning of the next line. Dotted lines can also be drawn from the end of one line diagonally to the beginning of the next line.

When the student can locate the beginning of the second line of text and move the tray, a third line can be added. Additional lines of text or pictures can be put on the page until the student can easily move the tray to track from left-to-right and from the top-to-bottom of the page. Again, the use of motivational text (such as jokes, quotations, song lyrics, etc.) is helpful. The teacher can also number the lines of text both at the beginning and at the end of each line to assist the reader to find the beginning and end of each line (Lund & Watson, 1997).

If the student continually skips lines while reading, comprehension will suffer. The teacher should encourage and reinforce the use of context cues while reading and also ask the student to stop and ask, "Does this make sense?"

Learning to Use Screen Blocking and the Line Marker

For students who find it difficult to attend to a full screen of enlarged text and who lose their place frequently, as well as students who have light sensitivity (photophobia), the option of screen blocking can help. However, since the amount of space needed to view a line of text is dependent upon the size of the magnification needed, students must first review their initial CCTV skills so that they are able to set the size and focus of the image before turning on the blocking feature.

The line marker feature produces a thin black line that can be used as a reference point on the screen. The teacher can also use this feature as a perceptual cue, as described in the section on reading more than one line.

Learning to Scan a Page

One of the last skills a student will probably develop is the ability to quickly skim a page to locate particular words and phrases. But before the skill of scanning for words is introduced, the child can practice skimming the page in a number of games (see Appendix 7.A).

Students also need to learn to skim down columns and then go to the top of the next column. This will be an important skill for math class. Teachers should also remind the student to look for clues such as the operation sign (that is, the plus sign or the minus sign) so that he or she will know when to go to the top of the next column of numbers.

Students also need to learn that some textbooks put in special typography (such as italics, underscoring, or bold) or special symbols (e.g., asterisks, bullets, and arrows) to draw attention to key words and important ideas. These cues can help the student skim for new vocabulary, preread questions, and use other study aids. By middle school, the student should be able to scan a page quickly for particular text, such as words that appear in bold or italics (Lund & Watson, 1997).

It is not uncommon for reading speed and efficiency to suffer when the student first begins using the CCTV—that is, until the student becomes proficient. In providing initial reading training, the teacher should use materials at the student's independent reading level—materials that the child is familiar with and has no difficulty decoding. In this way, the student is learning the new skills of the CCTV and does not also have to concentrate on new content at the same time. Gradually, reading speed and efficiency will increase. Again, there is no recent research that has been done on children who are visually impaired, but in a study conducted in 1981 (LaGrow, 1981), students who had received training in the use of a CCTV were able to increase their reading speed; one student tripled his original reading rate. The balance between magnification level and reading speed needs to be closely monitored by the teacher of students with visual impairments. The teacher should keep ongoing records of the student's reading speed as he or she learns to use the CCTV. The record should include information about the type of material read, as well as the student's reading speed (in words per minute), miscues, and comprehension.

Teaching Writing with a CCTV

Writing with a CCTV can be especially difficult because students must learn to watch the screen as they write rather than watch their hand. The teacher of students with visual impairments can make this a fun skill to practice by varying the materials and methods used and by allowing sufficient practice in learning the skills needed to successfully master the CCTV. The activities in Appendix 7.B provide some suggestions. Again, the teacher should start with easy activities first rather than with something that has to be handed in to be graded.

Familiarization

The teacher should start by letting the child just "scribble" and play with a marker on paper while watching the screen. This activity can also be introduced with the teacher putting his or her hand over the student's writing hand to guide it. The paper may be taped to the tray at first to keep it from moving while the student is scribbling. At this stage, the friction brake should be set to allow only limited horizontal movement of the tray.

Drawing Shapes

On unlined paper, the student can go from scribbling to drawing simple shapes such as circles, squares, and triangles. The teacher should remind the student to watch the monitor, not his or her hand, while drawing.

Drawing Long Lines

Once the student has learned to draw a variety of shapes using the CCTV, he or she will progress to the skill of drawing long lines that necessitate moving the X-Y table. This skill can be taught by using activities similar to those used for learning to track an individual line when reading (see Appendix 7.B).

Handwriting Skills

When teaching the student to write under a CCTV, the teacher may choose to use dark-lined paper at first (available from various mail order catalogs listed in the Resources section). As students gain proficiency, phase out the use of dark-lined paper; begin to use thinner-lined paper, and eventually graduate to regular loose-leaf paper.

The teacher can also add perceptual cues both to remind the student to go back to the left side of the paper and to discourage skipping lines. One cue is to put a strip of brightly colored paper along the left margin. The student can learn after finishing on one line to go back to the "red strip" (or whatever color the student likes) all the way on the left side of the paper.

Again, be sure to allow the student to practice first on things that don't have to be turned in for a grade. Writing skills with a CCTV generally take some time to develop.

SUMMARY

While a CCTV may be a more costly option than some other magnifying devices, it can also be a good investment. The versatility of a CCTV, with its various features for size, color, contrast, and clarity of image, make it a useful tool for increasing literacy skills in students with low vision. Future trends making CCTVs smaller, lighter, more versatile, and more affordable will only make CCTVs easier to use and more obtainable. The CCTV remains a valuable tool, and learning to use one efficiently can add to the options available for individuals with low vision, thus enabling them to increase literacy, employability, and access to information.

REFERENCES

AFB National Technology Center. (1999). Closed-circuit television systems. Fact sheet. New York: American Foundation for the Blind.

Hanford, M. (1989). *Great Waldo search.* Boston: Little, Brown.

LaGrow, S. J. (1981). Effects of training on CCTV reading rates of visually impaired students. *Journal of Visual Impairment & Blindness, 75,* 368–373.

Lund, R., & Watson, G. R. (1997). *The CCTV book: Habilitation and rehabilitation with closed circuit television systems.* Synsforum ans. Frolund: Norway.

Miller-Wood, D. J., Efron, M., & Wood, T. A. (1990). Use of a closed-circuit television with a severely visually impaired young child. *Journal of Visual Impairment & Blindness, 84,* 559–565.

Presley, I. (1999). Personal communication.

Shen, R., & Uslan, M. M. (1996a). A review of two low-cost television systems: The Big Picture and the Magni-Cam. *Journal of Visual Impairment & Blindness,* News Service, *90,* pp. 6–10.

Shen, R., & Uslan, M. M. (1996b). A review of two portable closed-circuit television systems: The Max-Eye and the Passport. *Journal of Visual Impairment & Blindness,* News Service, *90,* pp. 10–14.

Shen, R., & Uslan, M. M. (1997). A review of Acrontech's Elite series of closed-cirucit television systems. *Journal of Visual Impairment & Blindness,* News Service, *91,* pp. 16–21.

Steiner, J. (1998). *Look-Alikes.* Boston: Little, Brown.

Uslan, M. M., & Chan, G. (2000). Optelec's Clear View 700 video magnifier for use with computers. *AccessWorld, 1,* 14–22.

Uslan, M. M., & Lin, M. (1997). A review of Xerox's Outlook closed-circuit television system. *Journal of Visual Impairment & Blindness,* News Service, *91*(2).

Uslan, M. M., & Shen, R. (1996). A review of three low-cost stand-mounted closed-circuit television systems. *Journal of Visual Impairment & Blindness,* News Service, *90*(3), 1–7.

Uslan, M. M., Shen, R., & Shagrai, Y. (1996). The evolution of video magnification technology. *Journal of Visual Impairment & Blindness, 90,* 465–478.

Wick, W., & Marzollo, J. (1992). *I Spy: A book of picture riddles.* New York: Scholastic.

Activities for Teaching the Use of the CCTV for Reading

Familiarization

What Did I Change? After viewing an image of a picture with the CCTV, the student will close his or her eyes (or look away) while the teacher changes one of the settings (e.g., makes the image slightly larger, changes the polarity or color, moves a line marker, etc.). The child gets points for identifying which knob was used to change the image and extra points for changing it back! Next it's the student's turn to stump the teacher.

Focusing

◆ **What Is This?** Using a familiar picture or letter of the alphabet, the teacher can present a large image (such as a drawing of a familiar object) out of focus. First, the teacher can ask the student to guess what image is shown on the monitor; then the teacher can have the student turn the focusing knob until the image is clear to see if he or she guessed correctly.

◆ **Match the image:** The teacher can present two large pictures (or words written in large print) and ask the student which one he or she thinks will match the blurred image on the CCTV. The student must then focus the image to see if the guess was correct.

Enlarging an Image

◆ **Family Tree:** Examine family photos with a CCTV. This can be especially fun with a color CCTV. If the teacher can obtain photos of the student over a period of years, the student can put the photos in chronological order using details included in the picture (e.g., hair length, missing front teeth, clothing worn).

◆ **A Face in the Crowd:** Faces in group photographs are generally quite small. Can the student find himself or herself in class pictures? How many classmates can be identified in the class picture? Older students may want to peruse the high school yearbook to find friends in group pictures.

Learning to Use the X-Y Table to View One Row

◆ **Over the River and Through the Woods:** The teacher can make worksheets that show a picture on the left with a dotted line "path" that leads to another picture. The student can locate the first picture and then move the tray to follow the line to locate the second picture. (The teacher can set the margin stops to limit the horizontal movement of the tray at first, if necessary.) The pictures might be a rabbit with a path leading to a carrot, a dog to a bone, putting the car in a garage, etc. Pictures of favorite objects such as toys, cartoon characters, trucks, celebrities, etc., can also be cut from magazines. Sometimes, inexpensive workbooks with these "follow the path"-types of activities can be found at teacher supply stores. The pictures of these ready-made worksheets may need to be reduced on a photocopier if they are very large (Ike Presley, 1999, personal communication).

◆ **Stepping Stones:** Use small stickers or small pictures cut from magazines of personal interest to the student (e.g., dinosaurs, trucks, animals, etc.), and stick them in one row on a sheet of paper. The teacher can have the student practice moving the tray systematically from left to right to locate all the pictures in the row.

◆ **Reading Letters and Numbers:** The teacher can write letters of the alphabet in a row for the student to read aloud while moving the tray to the left. Older students may prefer to practice with numbers, such as the phone numbers of friends and local pizza delivery companies.

◆ **Read the Message:** When the student is comfortable reading letters, simple sentences presented on one line at the student's independent reading level can be used. Tongue twisters, silly sentences, and popular phrases can be used.

Learning to View More Than One Row

◆ **Riddles:** The teacher can put a simple riddle on one line of text for the student to read aloud. To find the answer to the riddle, the student must move the tray to display the next line of text.

◆ **Use Motivational Text,** such as jokes, quotations, song lyrics.

◆ **Use Easy Books:** Books such as those from Rigby Education (see the Resources section) and others can be used to practice reading more than one line of text since these books have simple pictures and limited print on each page. Uncluttered pages with a large amount of white space (wide margins, few lines of text, and extra space between the lines) are easier to read for CCTV beginners. High interest, low vocabulary books can be substituted for older students.

◆ **Visual Tracking Materials:** Ann Arbor Publications (see the Resources section) produces a set of materials developed for visual tracking and visual discrimination skills. This set of books includes exercises such as visually tracking lines of text to find alphabet letters in order, tracking lines of words to find a target sentence, and skimming over lines of words to find certain letters. Exercises such as these can be effective practice materials for using the CCTV to build speed and accuracy in reading. These exercises can be timed, and the results can be graphed. The student can then try to beat his or her previous time to increase speed in moving from line to line.

Learning to Use Screen Blocking and the Line Marker

◆ **Line Marker as Reference Point:** This can give the student opportunities to practice using the line marker for real-life activities such as "summarizing figures in a column" (Lund & Watson, 1997, p. 107).

Learning to Scan a Page

◆ **Scavenger Hunt:** The student can go on a "scavenger hunt" by searching for particular pictures scattered throughout a page. For example, the teacher can use stickers or pictures cut out from magazines and then ask the student to find the members of a certain category (such as, "The animals have escaped from the zoo and are hiding in this garden. See if you can find all the animals from among the pictures of flowers.").

◆ **Use Commercial Picture Books:** The *I Spy* series of picture riddle books (such as Wick & Marzollo, 1992), the *Where's Waldo?* books (for example, Hanford, 1989) or the *Look-Alike* books (such as Steiner, 1998) have interesting and detailed photos and drawings that are fun to look at. The teacher can have students look for the requested items.

◆ **Word Search:** Words can be used for scanning activities instead of pictures. The teacher can use commercially available word search puzzles or create some using vocabulary words, names of the student's friends and family, or the student's own name. The teacher can ask the student to find the numbers 1 through 10 in order scattered around the sheet. These games can be timed with a stopwatch, and the student can keep track of progress on graph paper.

(continued)

◆ **CCTV for Activities of Daily Living:** Students will want to use the CCTV to read newspaper want ads, to read the small print in advertisements and on bills, to follow directions on the back of food packages to look up a telephone number in a directory, and so on.

◆ **CCTV for Recreation and Leisure:** The student can use the CCTV to read cards for games such as Monopoly®, Trivial Pursuit®, etc. He or she may also find a CCTV useful when reading the TV guide and the newspaper for sports scores, movie times, and the daily comics.

Activities for Teaching
Use of the CCTV for Writing

Familiarization

◆ The teacher should start by letting the child just "scribble" and play with a marker on paper while watching the screen. This can also be introduced with the teacher putting his or her hand over the student's writing hand to guide it. The paper may be taped to the tray at first to keep it from moving while the student is scribbling. At this stage, the friction brake should be set to allow only limited horizontal movement.

Simple Shapes

◆ **Simple Shapes:** On unlined paper, the student can go from scribbling to drawing simple shapes such as circles, squares, and triangles. The teacher should remind the student to watch the monitor, not his or her hand, while drawing.

◆ **Copying from a Model:** The student can practice copying a shape from a model. Again, start with simple shapes (circles, smiley faces, etc.), and then gradually move to more complex designs. The model should be on the screen at the same time the child is copying it.

◆ **Marking Answers:** Practice such tasks as making a mark or circling a letter (as on a multiple-choice activity) rather than writing out the entire answer. Commerical materials, such as the Ann Arbor tracking materials mentioned in the reading activities in Appendix 7.A, can be used for writing practice, too. Ask the child to circle or mark the letters and words as he or she finds them.

◆ **Create a Picture:** The student draws a shape on the paper under the CCTV, and the teacher adds something to that shape. The student adds another detail to the picture, and then it's the teacher's turn again. The student and teacher take turns adding features to create a unique design or an amusing picture (monsters, funny faces, strange machines, etc.).

Drawing Lines

◆ **Follow the Path:** Similar to the activities for tracking a line listed in the reading activities, the teacher can also create worksheets for writing practice. On these worksheets, the student must draw a line from a dog to a bone, a car to a garage, and so on. At first, the student can trace a dotted line from picture to picture; the dotted line can be faded out until the child is drawing the line without tracing.

◆ **Don't Hit the Wall:** Simple worksheets can be made on which the student must draw. He or she must stay within the lines—that is, keep "within the path." The child can be asked to draw a line to "stay on the sidewalk" or to "keep car on the road." Simple mazes (either commercially made or teacher-made) can also be used to practice this skill

◆ **CCTV for Activities of Daily Living:** Students will also want to practice using the CCTV to fill out job applications, to write out checks and fill in the check register, to pay bills, to edit their own work, to keep a pocket-sized address book, etc.

◆ **CCTV for Recreation and Leisure:** Students can enjoy using the CCTV to fill out a crossword puzzle, to write out invitations to a party, to learn calligraphy, to write and illustrate a children's story for a younger sibling, etc.

Resources

TEACHERS OF CHILDREN who are visually impaired need access to a wide variety of resources and information. The listings in this section, although not exhaustive, attempt to meet this need by supplying information about sources of information, products, and services mentioned throughout this book that will help teachers and their students with low vision. More complete information and listings can be found in the *AFB Directory of Services for Blind and Visually Impaired Persons Living in the United States and Canada,* published by the American Foundation for the Blind (AFB). Because technology changes rapidly, readers are advised to contact the sources for particular products, as well as AFB's National Technology Center at (212) 502-7642 or techctr@afb.net for up-to-date information.

NATIONAL ORGANIZATIONS

The organizations listed in this section generally provide information and referrals, hold conferences for professionals, publish books and journals, and serve as advocates for people who are visually impaired.

American Foundation for the Blind
11 Penn Plaza, Suite 300
New York, NY 10001
(212) 502-7600; (212) 502-7662
(TTY/TDD); (800) AFB-LINE
FAX: (212) 502-7777
E-mail: afbinfo@afb.net
http://www.afb.org
Provides services to and acts as an information clearinghouse for people who are visually impaired and their families, professionals, organizations, schools, and corporations. Operates the National Technology Center and the Career and Technology Information Bank; stimulates research and mounts program initiatives to improve services to visually impaired persons, including the National Literacy Program and the National Technology Program, and the American Foundation for the Blind (AFB) Textbook and Instructional Materials Solutions

Forum. Advocates for services and legislation; maintains the M. C. Migel Library and Information Center. Produces videos; and publishes books, pamphlets, the *Directory of Services for Blind and Visually Impaired Persons Living in the United States and Canada,* the *Journal of Visual Impairment & Blindness,* and *AccessWorld.*

AFB Midwest
401 N. Michigan Avenue, Suite 308
Chicago, IL 60611
(312) 245-9961
FAX: (312) 245-9965
E-mail: chicago@afb.net

AFB Southeast/National Literacy Center
100 Peachtree Street, Suite 620
Atlanta, GA 30303
(404) 525-2303
FAX: (404) 659-6957
E-mail: atlanta@afb.net; literacy@afb.net

AFB Southwest
260 Treadway Plaza
Exchange Park
Dallas, TX 75235
(214) 352-7222
FAX: (214) 352-3214
E-mail: afbdallas@afb.net

AFB West
111 Pine Street, Suite 725
San Francisco, CA 94111
(415) 392-0383
FAX: (415) 392-0383
E-mail: sanfran@afb.net

Governmental Relations Group
1615 M Street, N.W., Suite 250
Washington, D.C. 20036
(202) 457-1487
FAX: (202) 457-1492
E-mail: afbgov@afb.net

Canadian National Institute for the Blind
1929 Bayview Avenue
Toronto, ON, M4G 3E8
Canada

(416) 486-2500
FAX: (416) 480-7677
http://www.cnib.ca
Provides services to people who are blind or visually impaired through a network of divisional offices throughout Canada.

Closing the Gap
P.O. Box 68
Henderson, MN 56044
(507) 248-3294
FAX: (507) 248-3810
E-mail: info@closingthegap.com
http://www.closingthegap.com
Holds conferences and workshops on technology for people with disabilities. Publishes a bimonthly newsletter, *Closing the Gap.*

Council of Citizens with Low Vision International
1155 15th Street N.W., Suite 1004
Washington, D.C. 20005
(800) 733-2258
http://www.cclvi.org
Serves as an advocacy group and provides information on low vision concerns. It publishes a quarterly newsletter with topics related to low vision adaptive aids and devices.

Lighthouse International
111 East 59th Street
New York, NY 10022
(212) 821-9200; (800) 829-0500; (212) 821-9713 (TTY)
http://www.lighthouse.org
Provides information on low vision examination with children. It is a national clearinghouse for educational products, large print materials, talking products, and a variety of adaptive devices that are sold through catalog.

National Association for Parents of Children with Visual Impairments (NAPVI)
P.O. Box 317
Watertown, MA 02471-0317
(800) 562-6265

FAX: (617) 972-7444
E-mail: napvi@perkins.pvt.k12.ma.us
http://www.spedex.com/napvi

**National Association for Visually
Handicapped (NAVH)**
22 West 21st Street
New York, NY 10010
(212) 889-3141
FAX: (212) 727-2931
E-mail: staff@navh.org
http://www.navh.org
Acts as an information clearinghouse and referral center regarding resources available to persons who are visually impaired. A low vision aids store, a support and discussion group, and quarterly newsletters are available online.

**National Library Service for the
Blind and Physically Handicapped**
Library of Congress
1291 Taylor Street, N.W.
Washington, D.C. 20542
(202) 707-5100; (800) 424-8567
FAX: (202) 707-0712
E-mail: nls@loc.gov
http://www.loc.gov/nls
Conducts a national program to distribute free braille and recorded materials of a general nature to individuals who are visually impaired. Provides reference information on all aspects of visual impairment and other physical disabilities that affect reading.

PROFESSIONAL ORGANIZATIONS

The organizations listed here provide professional membership opportunities in addition to serving as sources of information and referral.

American Academy of Ophthalmology
P.O. Box 7424
San Francisco, CA 94120-7424
(415) 561-8500
http://www.eyenet.org
Provides general information brochures on low vision and eye conditions.

American Academy of Optometry
6110 Executive Boulevard, Suite 506
Rockville, MD 20852
(301) 984-1441
FAX: (301) 984-4737
E-mail: aaoptom@aol.com
http://www.aaopt.org
Promotes excellence in standards of optometric practice. Fosters research and publishes *Optometry and Vision Sciences.*

American Optometric Association
243 North Lindbergh Boulevard
St. Louis, MO 63141
(314) 991-4100

FAX: (314) 991-4101
http://www.aoanet.org
Strives to improve the quality of vision care through promoting high standards, continuing education, information dissemination, and professional involvement. The website includes information on refractive errors, common eye problems, contact lenses, description of tools and techniques used in a typical low vision exam by an optometrist, and resources for parents and teachers of students who are visually impaired.

**Association for Education
and Rehabilitation of the Blind
and Visually Impaired**
4600 Duke Street, Suite 430
P.O. Box 22397
Alexandria, VA 22304
(703) 823-9690
FAX: (703) 823-9695
E-mail: aer@aerbvi.org
http://www.aerbvi.org

Serves as the membership organization for professionals interested in the promotion, development and improvement of all phases of education and rehabilitation of blind and visually impaired children and adults. Promotes all phases of education and work for people of all ages who are blind and visually impaired, strives to expand their opportunities to take a contributory place in society, and disseminates information. Subgroups include Division 7, Low Vision. Publishes *RE:view, AER Report, Job Exchange Monthly,* and *RT News,* a quarterly newsletter.

Council for Exceptional Children Division on Visual Impairment

1920 Association Drive
Reston, VA 20191-1589
(703) 620-3660; (888) CEC-SPED
(703) 264-9446 (TTY)
FAX: (703) 264-9494
http://www.cec.sped.org
The largest international professional organization for individuals serving children with disabilities and children who are gifted. Primary activities include advocating for appropriate government policies; setting professional standards; providing continuing professional development; and assisting professionals to obtain conditions and resources necessary for effective professional practice. Publishes numerous related materials, journals, and newsletters.

BOOKS, JOURNALS, AND OTHER MATERIALS

Journals

AccessWorld: Journal of Technology for Consumers with Visual Impairments
American Foundation for the Blind
11 Penn Plaza, Suite 300
New York, NY 10001
(717) 632-3535, (888) 522-0220
FAX: (717) 633-8920
http://www.afb.org

Journal of Visual Impairment & Blindness
American Foundation for the Blind
11 Penn Plaza, Suite 300
New York, NY 10001
(717) 632-3535, (888) 522-0220
FAX: (717) 633-8920
http://www.afb.org

RE:view
Heldref Publications
Helen Dwight Reed Educational Foundation
1319 18th Street, N.W.
Washington, D.C. 20036-1802
(202) 296-6267; (800) 365-9753
FAX: (202) 296-5149
http://www.heldref.org

Books

AFB Directory of Services for Blind and Visually Impaired Persons Living in the United States and Canada
AFB Press
11 Penn Plaza, Suite 300
New York, NY 10001
(800) 525-3044
http://www.afb.org

Beyond Arm's Reach: Enhancing Distance Vision
Pennsylvania College of Optometry Press
8360 Old York Rd.
Elkins Park, PA 19027
(215) 780-1361

The CCTV Book
Lighthouse International
Professional Products Division
938-K Andreasen Dr.
Escondido, CA 92029
(800) 826-4200
FAX: (800) 368-4111
http://www.lighthouse.org

Dictionary of Eye Terminology
(3rd edition)
Triad Publishing Company
P.O. Box 13355
Gainesville, FL 32604
(800) 525-6902; (352) 373-5800
FAX: (352) 373-1488
http://www.triadpublishing.com

Developmental Test of Visual Motor Integration
Modern Curriculum Press
4350 Equity Drive
P.O. Box 2649
Columbus, OH 43216-2649
(800) 526-9907
FAX: (614) 771-7361
http://pearsonlearning.com

Functional Vision and Media Assessment for Students who are Pre-Academic or Academic and Visually Impaired in Grades K through 12 and Functional Vision and Media Assessment Report
Consultants for the Visually Impaired
P.O. Box 8594
Hermitage, TN 37076
(615) 885-0764

Learning Media Assessment of Students with Visual Impairments: A Resource Guide for Teachers (2nd edition)
Texas School for the Blind and Visually Impaired
1100 West 45th Street
Austin, TX 78756-3494
(512) 206-9240
http:/www.tsbvi.edu

Manual of Ocular Diagnosis and Therapy (4th edition)
Little, Brown and Company
3 Center Plaza
Boston, MA 02108-2084
(617) 227-0730
http://www.littlebrown.com

Motor-Free Visual Perception Test
Western Psychological Services
12031 Wilshire Boulevard
Los Angeles, CA 90025
(310) 478-2061; (800) 648-8857
FAX: (310) 478-7838
http://www.wpspublish.com

Oregon Project for Visually Impaired and Blind Preschool Children
Jackson Education Service
101 North Grape Streeet
Medford, OR 97501
(503) 776-8550

A Resource Manual for the Development and Evaluation of Special Programs for Exceptional Students, Volume V-E: Project IVEY: Increasing Visual Efficiency
Florida Department of Education
Education Product Distribution Center
325 West Gaines Street, Room 644
Tallahassee, FL 32399-0400
(850) 487-0186

Test of Visual-Perceptual Skills (nonmotor)-Revised; Motor-Free Visual Perception Tests: Revised and Vertical; and *Slosson Visual-Motor Performance Test*
The Speech Bin
1965 25th Avenue
Vero, FL 32960
(800) 477-3324

Vision for Doing: Assessing Functional Vision of Learners who are Multiply Disabled
Moray House Publications
Holyrood Road, Edinburgh EH8 8AQ
Scotland
also aviailable from the
Royal National Institute for the Blind (RNIB)
Books Sales Service, Garrow House
190 Kensal Road
London, England W10 5BT
020-8968-8600
FAX: 020-8960-3593
E-mail: djohnson@mib.org.uk

Online Resources

ATRC (Adaptive Technology Resource Centre)
http://www.utoronto.ca/atrc/
Contains issues related to accessibility and technology for individuals who are disabled.

LOVNET: The Low Vision Network
http://vision.psych.umn.edu/www/lovnet/lovnet.html
Contains general information and resources for researchers, clinicians and others interested in low vision. It has links to support and discussion groups, and resources for persons with low vision.

Low Vision Gateway
http://www.lowvision.org
Contains resources specifically for those interested in low vision. It includes definitions of optical terms, purposes and processes in low vision evaluation, an up-to-date list of optical devices and explanations of optical and non-optical devices and treatments for various eye conditions. It also includes links to sites and pages concerned specifically with children and educational issues.

Low Vision Information Center
http://www.lowvisioninfo.org
A nonprofit organization that provides information about low vision, low vision devices, and a variety of resources. Also publishes a newsletter.

National Eye Institute
http://www.nei.nih.gov/
Contains basic, simply explained information for consumers about vision-related concerns. A glossary of vision terms related to the low vision evaluation can be found at this site. It also has a clinical studies database, funding and grant information, a variety of publications, and a National Eye Health Education Program with materials for teachers.

Texas School for the Blind and Visually Impaired
http://www.tsbvi.edu
This website contains numerous ideas, strategies, lesson plans, and resource information for teachers of students who are visually impaired. Links to other related websites are also available.

V.I. Guide
http://www.viguide.com
This website is a guide to resources on the Internet for parents and teachers of children who are visually impaired. Resources available on this site include information on technology, low vision aids, and a variety of eye conditions.

World Friends
http://hale.ssd.k12.wa.us/friends/wf_home.htm
Contains a listing of magazines available on the Internet, directed at students with disabilities.

Sources of Catalogs and Mail Order Distribution

The organizations listed in this section specialize in distributing a wide variety of adapted products for people who are blind or visually impaired. Products can usually be ordered through catalogs available from the individual companies or from web sites. Some of the companies also sell or distribute the low vision optical devices, such as magnifiers and telescopes, discussed in this book. As emphasized throughout this book, however, optical devices should be prescribed only by a low vision specialist.

American Printing House for the Blind (APH)
1839 Frankfort Avenue
P.O. Box 6085
Louisville, KY 40206-0085
(502) 895-2405; (800) 223-1839
FAX: (502) 895-1509
E-mail: info@aph.org
http://www.aph.org
Functional vision assessment materials such as the *Diagnostic Assessment Procedure (DAP), Visual Efficiency Scale,* and *ISAVE* can be purchased through APH.

Ann Morris Enterprises
890 Fams Court
East Meadow, NY 11554
(516) 292-9232; (800) 454-3175
FAX: (516) 292-2522
http://www.annmorris.com

Exceptional Teaching Aids
20102 Woodbine Avenue
Castro Valley, CA 94546
(510) 582-4859; (800) 549-6999
FAX: (510) 582-5911

Lighthouse Low Vision Products
36-20 Northern Boulevard
Long Island City, NY 11101
(800) 829-0500; (800) 334-5497;
(800) 453-4923
FAX: (718) 786-5620

LS&S Group
P.O. Box 673
Northbrook, IL 60065
(708) 498-9777; (800) 468-4789
FAX: (847) 498-1482
http://www.lssgroup.com

Maxi-Aids
42 Executive Boulevard
P.O. Box 3290
Farmingdale, NY 11735
(516) 752-0521; (800) 522-6294

FAX: (516) 752-0689
http://www.maxiaids.com

Sources of Closed-Circuit Televisions and Video Magnifiers

In addition to the sources for CCTVs listed here, they can also be purchased through many of the mail-order houses in the previous section. For additional information about CCTV systems, readers can contact the AFB National Technology Center at (212) 502-7642 or techctr@afb.net

Enhanced Vision Systems
2130 Main Street, Suite 250
Huntington Beach, CA 92648
(714) 374-1829; (800) 440-9476
FAX: (714) 374-1821
E-mail: info@enhancedvision.com
http://www.enhancedvision.com

Eschenbach Optik of America
904 Ethan Allen Highway
Ridgefield, CT 06877
(203) 438-7471
FAX: (888) 799-9200
E-mail: eschen@ntplx.net

Innoventions
5921 S. Middlefield Road, Suite 102
Littleton, CO 80123-2877
(303) 979-6554; (800) 854-6554
FAX: (303) 727-4940
E-mail: magnicam@magnicam.com
http://www.magnicam.com

Magnisight
3360 Adobe Court
Colorado Springs, CO 80907
(800) 753-4767
FAX: (719) 578-9887
E-mail: sales@magnisight.com
http://www.magnisight.com

OVAC
67-555 E. Palm Canyon Dr. Unit C-103
Cathedral City, CA 92234
(800) 325-4488
FAX: (760) 321-9711
E-mail: info@ovac.com
http://www.ovac.com

Optelec USA
4 Liberty Way
P.O. Box 729
Westford, MA 01886
(978) 392-0707; (800) 828-1056
E-mail: optelec@optelec.com
http://www.optelec.com

PulseData International
351 Thornton Road, Suite 119
Lithia Springs, GA 30122-1589
(888) 734-8439
FAX: (770) 941-7722
E-mail:pdi_inc@mindspring.com

Tagarno of America
615 Otis Drive
Dover, DE 19901
(302) 734-9630; (800) 441-8439
FAX: (302) 764-8654
E-mail: info@tagarno.com
http://www.tagarno.com

TeleSensory Corp.
520 Almanor Avenue
Sunnyvale, CA 94086
(408) 616-8700; (800) 227-8418
FAX: (408) 616-8720
E-mail: info@telesensory.com
http://www.telesensory.com

Vision Technology
8501 Delport Drive
St. Louis, MO 63114
(314) 890-8300; (800) 560-7226
FAX: (314) 890-8383
E-mail: vti@visiontechinc.com
http://www.freedom-machines.com

Sources of Other Products and Materials

This section lists sources of specific assessment tools, teaching materials, and other products listed in this book.

Ann Arbor Publishers
Division of Academic Therapy Publishers
20 Commercial Blvd.
Novato, CA 94949
(415) 883-3314; (800) 422-7249
FAX: (415) 883-3720
E-mail: atpub@aol.com
http://www.atpub.com/
Publishes a set of materials for visual tracking and visual discrimination skills.

Carolina Biological Supply Company
2700 York Road
Burlington, NC 27215
(800) 334-5551
FAX: (800) 222-7112
http://www.carolina.com
Distributes penlights, Snellen acuity distance charts, and color vision tests.

DAAS Consulting
P.O. Box 93545
Nelson Park PO
Vancouver, BC V6E 4L7
Canada
(604) 669-8529
Distributes a vision simulation kit.

Lighthouse Low Vision Products
36-20 Northern Boulevard
Long Island City, NY 11101
(800) 829-0500; (800) 334-5497; (800) 453-4923
FAX: (718) 786-5620
Supplies Lighthouse and Lea visual acuity testing charts among other low vision products.

Rigby Education
500 Coventry Lane

Crystal Lake, IL 60014
(800) 822-8661
FAX: (815) 477-3990
http://www.rigby.com
Publishes the Rigby Literacy line of easy books with simple pictures and limited print on each page.

Stoelting Company
620 Wheat Lane
Wood Dale, IL 60191
(630) 860-9700
FAX: (630) 860-9775
http://www.stoeltingco.com
Publishes a functional vision inventory for children who are multiply and severely handicapped.

Vision Associates
7512 Dr. Phillip Boulevard, #50-316
Orlando, FL 32819
(407) 352-1200
Supplies color vision tests, a cone adaptation test, contrast sensitivity charts and materials, functional vision assessment kits and materials, visual field tests, depth perception tests, Lea visual acuity tests (near and distance), Precision Vision Cone Adaptation Test, and a nonmotor test of visual perception skills.

George Zimmerman Vision Simulation Kit
1923 Woodside Road
Glenshaw, PA 15116-2113
(412) 487-2818
Distributes a vision simulation kit.

GLOSSARY

Absorptive lenses Eyeglasses with lenses tinted to absorb much of the sun's light and prevent it from entering the eye; sunglasses.

Academic literacy Conventional school-based reading and writing skills.

Accommodation The ability of the eye to maintain a clear focus as objects are moved closer to it by changing the shape of the lens.

Achromatopsia A congenital defect in or absence of cones, resulting in an inability to see color and in reduced clear central vision.

Acquired/Adventitious Occurring or appearing later in life.

Alternate cover test *See* cross-cover test.

Aniridia A congenital malformation (usually incomplete) of the iris, accompanied by nystagmus, photophobia, reduced visual acuity, and often glaucoma.

Anisometropia Different refractive errors of at least one diopter in the two eyes.

Anterior chamber The space between the iris and cornea inside the eye, filled with aqueous fluid.

Astigmatism A refractive error caused by a spherocylindrical curvature of the cornea; corrected with a cylindrical lens.

Binocular vision Vision that uses both eyes to form a fused image in the brain and results in three-dimensional vision.

Biomicroscope (slit lamp) A microscope of different magnifying powers that projects a beam of light whose size, shape, and focus can be altered, which is used to examine in detail the structures of the eye.

Bioptic telescope A miniature telescope mounted into a person's regular eyeglasses, positioned above or below the direct line of sight when facing forward, which is used for distance viewing.

Blind spot *See* Scotoma.

Blink reflex *See* Defensive blink response.

Cataracts A clouding of the lens, which may be congenital, traumatic, secondary to another visual impairment, or age related. When a cataract is surgically removed, an intraocular lens implant, contact lens or spectacle correction is necessary to provide the refractive function of the absent lens.

Central visual field The central portion of the visual field that is perceived by the macula portion of the retina.

Choroid The vascular layer of the eye, between the sclera and retina, that nourishes the retina; part of the uveal tract.

Clinical low vision evaluation A clinical evaluation to determine whether a person with low vision can benefit from optical devices, nonoptical devices, or adaptive techniques to enhance visual function.

Clinical low vision specialist An ophthalmologist or optometrist who specializes in low vision care.

Closed-circuit television system (CCTV) A device that provides electronic magnification by means of a video camera that projects the image onto a monitor.

Coloboma Congenital cleft in some portion of the eye, caused by the improper fusion of tissue during gestation; may affect the optic nerve, ciliary body, choroid, iris, lens, or eyelid.

Color vision The perception of color as a result of the stimulation of specialized cone receptors in the retina.

Concave lens A lens that spreads out light rays and is used to correct for myopia. Also called Minus lens.

Cones Specialized photoreceptor cells in the retina, primarily concentrated in the macular area, that are responsible for sharp vision and color perception.

Confrontation visual field testing A method for making a rough assessment of peripheral vision, which may suggest the need for more precise visual field testing.

Congenital Present at birth.

Conjunctiva A thin membrane lining the inner surface of the eyelid and part of the outer surface of the eyeball (not including the cornea).

Contact lens A small plastic disc containing an optical correction that is worn directly on the cornea as a substitute for eyeglasses.

Contrast sensitivity The ability to detect differences in grayness and background.

Convergence The movement, as an object approaches, of both eyes toward each other in an effort to maintain fusion of separate images.

Convex lens A lens that bends light rays inward and is used to correct for hyperopia. Also called Plus lens.

Cornea The transparent tissue at the front of the eye that is curved to provide most of the eye's refractive power.

Corneal reflection test *See* Hirschberg test.

Cortical visual impairment (CVI) Visual impairment resulting from a disturbance of the visual pathways to the brain and/or the occipital lobes of the brain, the area that monitors visual sensations. The rest of the visual system may remain intact.

Counting fingers A functional assessment of the alignment of the eyes that involves establishing the individual's fixation on a visual target, covering one eye, and observing any corrective movement of the uncovered eye.

Cross-uncover test An assessment of the alignment of the eyes that involves establishing the individual's fixation on a visual target, covering one eye, and observing any corrective movement of the uncovered eye.

Cross-cover test or Alternate cover test An assessment of phorias and ocular muscle imbalance involving fixating on an object while an assessor alternately covers each eye with an occluder and observes any corrective eye movements as each eye is uncovered and resumes fixation.

Cylindrical lenses A lens whose shape is a segment of a cylinder, used to correct the refractive error in astigmatism.

Defensive blink response A contraction of the eyelid muscles to close the lids that occurs spontaneously when there are sudden loud noises, bright lights, sneezing, or a perceived visual threat.

Depth perception The overlapping of two slightly dissimilar images from the two eyes to give three-dimensional vision.

Diabetic retinopathy The range of retinal changes associated with long-standing diabetes.

Diopter The unit of measurement for the refractive power of a lens.

Diplopia Double vision resulting from the lack of fusion of the two images received by the two eyes.

Divergence The movement of the two eyes outward (away from each other) to maintain binocular vision.

Doll's eye response or Vestibular ocular reflex An involuntary association of head and eye movement usually found in infants in which the eyes do not move as quickly and independently as the head does, so that the eyes appear to move in the direction opposite to the direction in which the head is turning.

Eccentric viewing The use of a portion of the retina that is not specialized for sharp vision when a portion of or the entire fovea has become nonfunctional. This usually results in a head tilt or repositioning of the eyes.

Electronic magnification systems Machines that produce enlarged images, including closed-circuit televisions, computer systems, and low vision enhancement devices.

Emergent literacy The earliest phase in literacy learning, in which young children are actively engaged in experimenting with reading and writing and in gaining meaning from these activities.

Enucleation Surgical removal of the eye.

Environmental adaptations-modifications Changes in the environment to maximize the use of vision.

Environmental manipulation Changing lighting, contrast, color, distance, and the size of objects in the environment to enhance visual functioning.

Electroretinogram (ERG) An electrophysiological test of retinal function; the wave forms show the function of rods, cones, and bipolar cells.

Esophoria The tendency for the eye to deviate inward.

Esotropia A form of strabismus in which one or both eyes deviate inward.

Exophoria The tendency for the eye to deviate outward.

Exotropia A form of strabismus in which one or both eyes deviate outward.

Farnsworth panel D15 test A diagnostic test to determine type of color deficiency.

Field *See* Visual field.

Field expansion systems A variety of optical devices for individuals with reduced visual fields, including prism lenses, mirror magnifiers, and reverse telescopes.

Figure-ground perception The ability to distinguish an object from its background.

Fixation Coordinated eye movements to enable an image to focus on the fovea.

Focal distance The distance between a lens and the point at which parallel light rays are brought to a focus.

Focus The bending of light by a lens.

Forced preferential looking A means of testing the vision of nonverbal or preverbal children in which both plain and patterned stimuli are presented to the right and then the left; the movement of the individual's eyes, which indicates preference for the pattern, is noted.

Fresnel prisms A series of plastic prisms applied to regular eyeglass lenses that are used to correct eye deviations or to displace peripheral information onto areas of the retina.

Functional literacy The ability to apply reading and writing skills to practical tasks in everyday life.

Functional vision The ability to use vision in planning and performing a task.

Functional vision assessment (FVA) An assessment of an individual's use of vision in a variety of tasks and settings, including measures of near and distance vision; visual fields; eye movements; and responses to specific environmental characteristics, such as light and color. The assessment report includes recommendations for instructional procedures, modifications, adaptations, and additional tests.

Glare An annoying sensation produced by too much light in the visual field that can cause both discomfort and a reduction in visual acuity.

Glaucoma A condition characterized by an increase in intraocular pressure, visually associated with a buildup of aqueous fluid, which may cause damage to the nerves of the retina and the optic nerve; may result in visual field defects if left untreated.

Hemianopsia A defect in either half of the visual field. Also called Hemianopia.

Hirschberg test or Corneal reflection test A test used to assess tropias by observing the position of reflection of a light in the corneas of both eyes.

Hyperopia (farsightedness) A refractive error caused by an eyeball that is too short; corrected with a plus (convex) lens.

Hypertropia The upward deviation of one eye; hyperphoria is the tendency of one eye to turn upward.

Hypotropia The downward deviation of one eye; the least common of the eye deviations classified as strabismus.

Individualized Education Program (IEP) A written plan of instruction by a transdisciplinary educational team for a child who receives special education services that include the student's present levels of educational performance, annual goals, short-term objectives, specific services needed, duration of services, evaluation, and related information. Under the Individuals with Disabilities Education Act (IDEA), each student receiving special services must have such a plan.

Iris The colored portion of the eye that expands or contracts to control the amount of light entering the eye.

Ishihara color plates A series of patterns of colored dots used to identify color perception difficulties. The individual must distinguish colors to see numbers or trace a pathway.

Jaeger system A test of near vision using graded sizes of letters or numbers.

Keratometer An instrument for measuring the curvature of the cornea that is used to measure astigmatism.

Lea Symbols Acuity tests depicting symbols (circle, house, apple, and square) that are used for testing a child's visual acuity.

Learning media assessment (LMA) A structured procedure that measures an individual's primary learning channel or channels, the best literacy medium, and the efficiency of that literacy medium.

Legal blindness Visual impairment in which distance visual acuity is 20/200 or worse in the better eye after best correction with conventional lenses or visual field restriction is 20 degrees or less, often used as a criterion for determining eligibility for benefits or services in the United States and Canada.

Lens The transparent, biconvex structure within the eye that allows it to refract light rays, enabling them to focus on the retina; also, any transparent substance that can refract light in a predictable manner.

Leukokoria A condition characterized by the appearance of a whitish mass in the pupillary area in back of the lens.

Light-absorptive lenses *See* Absorptive lenses.

Light-dark adaptation The ability of the eye to adjust to lighting conditions in a variety of situations.

Lighthouse Distance Visual Acuity Chart A chart used to measure distance visual acuity at either 2 or 4 meters.

Light perception The ability to discern the presence or absence of light, but not its source or direction.

Light projection The ability to discern the source or direction of light, but not enough vision to identify objects, people, shapes, or movements.

Literacy medium The form of the printed word (print or braille) that an individual uses to read and write.

Loupe A convex lens for magnifying that can be used in monocular or binocular forms, mounted in front of the eye, for viewing small objects at a very close distance.

Low vision A visual impairment after correction, but with the potential for use of available vision, with or without optical or nonoptical compensatory visual strategies, devices, and environmental modifications, to plan and perform daily tasks.

Macula A small portion of the retina, with a concentration of cones for sharp central vision, that surrounds the fovea.

Macular degeneration Deterioration of central vision caused by a degeneration of the central retina.

Magnifier A device to increase the size of an image through the use of lenses or lens systems; may be fixed focus (stand types, bar varieties) or variable focus (handheld).

Minus lens *See* Concave lens.

Monocular Involving or affecting a single eye.

Monocular telescope A telescope that can be used by the preferred eye.

Monocularity The loss of vision in one eye due to injury or enucleation.

Motility, ocular Eye movement controlled by the extraocular muscles.

Multidisciplinary team Professionals from various disciplines who conduct separate assessments and provide individual services.

Myopia (nearsightedness) A refractive error resulting from an eyeball that is too long; corrected with a concave (minus) lens.

No light perception (NLP) The total absence of vision.

Nonoptical devices Devices or modifications that do not involve optics, used to make visual information more accessible to individuals with low vision, such as book stands, trays, positioning-seating, modifications of illumination, and large print when indicated.

Nystagmus An involuntary oscillation of the eyes, usually rhythmical and faster in one direction; may be side to side or up and down.

Occipital lobe The posterior part of the brain that is responsible for vision and visual perception; it includes the visual cortex, which is the cerebral end of the visual pathway.

Occluder A device used to cover an eye, as when testing the visual acuity or visual fields of each eye.

Ophthalmologist A physician who specializes in the medical and surgical care of the eyes and is qualified to prescribe ocular medications and to perform surgery on the eyes. May also perform refractive and low vision work, including eye examinations and other vision services.

Ophthalmoscope An instrument containing a series of lenses used to examine the interior of the eye.

Optical device Any system of lenses that enhances visual function. Also called Low vision device.

Optic disk The point at which the nerve fibers from the inner layer of the retina becomes the optic nerve and exits the eye; the "blind spot" of the eye.

Optic nerve The sensory nerve of the eye that carries electrical impulses from the eye to the brain.

Optometrist A health care provider who specializes in refractive errors, prescribes eyeglasses or contact lenses, and diagnoses and manages conditions of the eye as regulated by state/provincial law.

Orientation and mobility (O&M) instructor A professional who specializes in teaching travel skills to visually impaired persons, including the use of a cane, dog guide, or sophisticated electronic travel aids, as well as the sighted guide technique.

Peripheral visual field The side portion of the visual field which is perceived by parts of the retina outside the macula.

Phoria The tendency of the eyes to deviate, which is controlled by the brain's efforts to achieve binocular vision.

Phoropter A device used by eye care specialists to analyze the refractive error in persons with intact central vision using various lenses to determine which provide the best correction.

Photophobia Light sensitivity to an uncomfortable degree; usually symptomatic of other ocular disorders or diseases.

Photoreceptor cells Retinal cells (rods and cones) that convert light to electrical impulses that can be transmitted to the brain.

Plus lens *See* Convex lens.

Presbyopia A decrease in accommodative power (focusing at near distance) caused by the increasing inelasticity of the lens-ciliary muscle mechanism that occurs approximately anytime after age 40.

Prism lenses Special triangle-shaped lenses that are incorporated into regular eyeglasses to redirect the rays of light entering the eye, resulting in a realignment of the eyes or, in some cases, a shifting of images to permit binocular vision.

Projection magnification Increasing the size of an image to be viewed by the process of projection, such as by projecting the image of text onto a monitor.

Prosthesis An artificial eye (or other body part).

Ptosis A drooping of the eyelid caused by paralysis or weak eyelid muscles; it may be congenital. Ptosis requires surgical correction if the droop interferes with vision.

Pupil The hole in the center of the iris through which light rays enter the back of the eye.

Pupillary response A reflexive constriction of the pupil when light stimuli are presented. Also called Pupillary responses.

Refraction The bending of light rays as they pass through a substance. Also, the determination of the refractive errors of the eye and their correction with eyeglasses or contact lenses.

Refractive errors Conditions such as myopia, hyperopia, and astigmatism in which parallel rays of light are not brought to a focus on the retina because of a defect in the shape of the eyeball or the refractive media of the eye.

Relative-distance magnification Increasing the size of an image on the retina by bringing the object to be viewed closer to the eyes.

Relative-size magnification Increasing the size of an image on the retina by increasing the size of an object to be viewed, such as with large print.

Retina The inner sensory nerve layer next to the choroid that lines the posterior two-thirds of the eyeball. The retina reacts to light and transmits impulses to the brain.

Retinal detachment The separation of the retina from the underlying choroid, nearly always caused by a retinal tear. It usually requires surgical intervention to prevent loss of vision.

Retinitis pigmentosa (RP) A group of progressive, often hereditary, retinal degenerative diseases that are characterized by decreasing peripheral vision; some progress to tunnel vision, whereas others result in total blindness if the macula also becomes involved.

Retinoscope A handheld device used to project a light onto the pupil to measure the eye's refractive error by evaluating the behavior of the light reflected back from the retina.

Retinopathy of prematurity (ROP) A series of retinal changes (formerly called retrolental fibroplasia), from mild to total retinal detachment, seen primarily in premature infants, that may be arrested at any stage. Believed to be connected to the immature blood vessels in the eye and their reaction to oxygen, but may be primarily the result of prematurity with very low birthweight. Functional vision can range from near normal to total blindness.

Rods Specialized retinal photoreceptor cells that are located primarily in the peripheral retina, responsible for seeing form, shape, and movement and that function best in low levels of illumination.

Scanning Repetitive fixations that are required to look from one object to another.

Sclera The tough, white, opaque outer covering of the eye that protects the inner contents from most injuries.

Scotoma A gap or blind spot in the visual field that may be caused by damage to the retina or visual pathways. Each eye contains one normal scotoma, corresponding to the location of the optic nerve disk, which contains no photoreceptors.

Snellen chart The traditional eye chart whose top line consists of the letter *E* and which is used in routine eye examinations.

Stereoscopic Characterized by seeing objects in three dimensions.

Strabismus An extrinsic muscle imbalance that causes misalignment of the eyes; includes exotropia, esotropia, hypertropia, and hypotropia.

Sty An external infection of an eyelash follicle at the eyelid margin.

Teacher of students who are visually impaired A specially trained and certified teacher who is qualified to teach special skills to students with visual impairments.

Telemicroscope A lens system in which an adaptation called a reading cap is used on a telescope to provide additional plus lens power to an existing system, transforming the telescope into a viewing device for intermediate distances.

Telescope A lens system that makes small objects appear closer and larger.

Tonometry Measurement of intraocular pressure (pressure within the eye).

Tracing Visually following single or multiple stationary lines in the environment, such as hedge lines, roof lines, or baseboards.

Tracking Visually following a moving object.

Tropia Marked deviations in the alignment of the eyes that cannot be controlled.

Typoscope A device consisting of a piece of cardboard with a slit in it, used to minimize visual distraction and help keep one's place when reading printed material.

Vestibular ocular reflex *See* Doll's-eye response

Visual acuity The sharpness of vision with respect to the ability to distinguish detail, often measured as the eye's ability to distinguish the details and shapes of objects at a designated distance; involves central (macular) vision.

Visual clutter A combination of images and backgrounds that provides distracting details for some individuals who are unable to select a single object from its background (figure-ground difficulties).

Visual efficiency The extent to which available vision is used effectively.

Visual field The area that can be seen when looking straight ahead, measured in degrees from the fixation point. Also called Field of vision.

Visual impairment Any degree of vision loss that affects an individual's ability to perform the tasks of daily life, caused by a visual system that is not working properly or not formed correctly.

Visual stimulation An instructional program that provides a rich and stimulating environment, thus encouraging the visual system to react, and reinforcing visual functioning.

Visual skills training A systematic program of instruction, using direct and planned reinforcement procedures, that teaches a set of specific visual skills that would otherwise be acquired incidently. Specific skills include visual attending (fixating), visual examining, and visually guided motor behaviors, to name a few.

Vitrectomy The surgical removal of the vitreous and its replacement with a saline solution.

Vitreous A transparent, clear, jelly-like substance that fills the back portion of the eye between the lens and the retina and that maintains the shape of the eyeball.

Work Environment Visual Demands (WEVD) Protocol An instrument that is sometimes used to analyze the visual demands of a job or work environment.

Working distance The distance between the eye and an object being viewed, such as a page being read.

Index